The Eisenhower Presidency, 1953–1961

SEMINAR STUDIES IN HISTORY

The Eisenhower Presidency, 1953–1961

RICHARD V. DAMMS

An imprint of Pearson Education

London · New York · Toronto · Sydney · Tokyo · Singapore · Hong Kong · Cape Town
New Delhi · Madrid · Paris · Amsterdam · Munich · Milan · Stockholm

PEARSON EDUCATION LIMITED

Head Office:
Edinburgh Gate
Harlow
Essex CM20 2JE
Tel: +44 (0)1279 623623
Fax +44 (0)1279 431059

London Office:
128 Long Acre
London WC2E 9AN
Tel: +44 (0)20 7447 2000
Fax: +44 (0)20 7240 5771
Website: www.history-minds.com

First published in Great Britain in 2002

The right of Richard V. Damms to be identified as author
of this work has been asserted by him in accordance
with the Copyright, Designs and Patents Act 1988.

ISBN 0 582 36818 9

British Library Cataloguing in Publication Data
A CIP catalogue record for this book can be obtained from the British Library

Library of Congress Cataloging in Publication Data
A CIP catalog record for this book can be obtained from the Library of Congress

10 9 8 7 6 5 4 3 2 1

Typeset by 7 in 10/12 Sabon Roman
Produced by Pearson Education Asia Pte Ltd.,
Printed in Malaysia, LSP

The Publishers' policy is to use paper manufactured from sustainable forests.

CONTENTS

INTRODUCTION TO THE SERIES

Such is the pace of historical enquiry in the modern world that there is an ever-widening gap between the specialist article or monograph, incorporating the results of current research, and general surveys, which inevitably become out of date. *Seminar Studies in History* is designed to bridge this gap. The series was founded by Patrick Richardson in 1966 and his aim was to cover major themes in British, European and world history. Between 1980 and 1996 Roger Lockyer continued his work, before handing the editorship over to Clive Emsley and Gordon Martel. Clive Emsley is Professor of History at the Open University, while Gordon Martel is Professor of International History at the University of Northern British Columbia, Canada, and Senior Research Fellow at De Montfort University.

All the books are written by experts in their field who are not only familiar with the latest research but have often contributed to it. They are frequently revised, in order to take account of new information and interpretations. They provide a selection of documents to illustrate major themes and provoke discussion, and also a guide to further reading. The aim of *Seminar Studies in History* is to clarify complex issues without over-simplifying them, and to stimulate readers into deepening their knowledge and understanding of major themes and topics.

PREFACE

This study is intended as an introductory overview of the major themes of the Eisenhower presidency. Given the veritable cottage industry of 'Eisenhower revisionism' over the last three decades, the progressive declassification of United States government documents from the 1950s, and the increasing availability of information from European and Asian archives for the era, an attempt to produce a balanced synthesis on the Eisenhower presidency would seem to be particularly timely. Works such as this must necessarily rely heavily on the labours of others. Owing to the vagaries of the publishing world, however, only direct quotations are fully attributed in the text. The guide to further reading provides a more comprehensive listing of the works that were particularly useful for this study. As will become readily apparent, the pioneering works of Stephen Ambrose, Robert Divine, Richard Immerman, Iwan Morgan, and Elmo Richardson and Chester Pach, Jr are indispensable.

In the course of completing this monograph, I have accumulated numerous debts of gratitude. The staff at the Eisenhower Presidential Library was always gracious and efficient, and Dr Jim Leyerzapf and Kathy Struss greatly facilitated my research over the course of several visits. The Department of History at Mississippi State University, under the leadership of Charles Lowery and then Godfrey Uzoigwe, provided financial and technical support at several crucial stages in the manuscript's development. Student workers Jeffrey Lucas, Gwen Humphreys, and Mandy Crocker assisted with transcribing the documents and Peggy Bonner provided numerous invaluable services. Gordon Martel was a model editor: patient, generous and with a keen eye for detail that resulted in a substantially better manuscript. Michael J. Hogan, my former adviser and now Dean of Humanities at the Ohio State University, served as a role model and friend, and his stimulating seminars provided the setting in which many of the themes here were first explored. Most importantly, I would like to thank my wife, Jennifer, and our children, Rachael, Colin and Kelsey, whose love and support made everything possible. This book is dedicated to them.

ACKNOWLEDGEMENTS

We are grateful to the following for permission to reproduce copyright material:

The John Hopkins University Press for the letters: from Eisenhower to Bradford Grethen Chynoweth of 13th July 1954 published in *The Papers of Dwight David Eisenhower* vol.15 and from Eisenhower to Winston Churchill of 18th February 1955 published in vol.16, ed. Louis P Galambos et al; and University Press of Kansas for the letter: from Eisenhower to Swede Hazlett of 21st July 1953 published in *Ike's Letters to a Friend 1941–1958* ed. by Robert Griffith.

CHRONOLOGY

1890

        Dwight D. Eisenhower born.

1911–15

        Eisenhower attends US Military Academy, West Point.

1928

        Eisenhower graduates from Army War College.

1933–39

        Eisenhower serves as personal assistant to Army Chief of Staff Douglas MacArthur.

1941

August	Eisenhower named Chief of Staff, Third Army.
7 December	Japan attacks Pearl Harbor.

1942

14 February	Eisenhower made Chief of the War Plans Division, War Department, Washington, DC.
June	Eisenhower assumes command of US forces, European Theatre of Operations.
6 August	Eisenhower named head of the Allied Expeditionary Force for the North African landings.

1943

July	Allied invasion of Sicily.
September	Allied invasion of Italian mainland; Italy surrenders.
December	Eisenhower assumes command of Allied invasion of France.

1944

6 June	D-Day invasion of France.
December	Eisenhower promoted to five-star general.

1945

May	Eisenhower accepts German surrender.
August	Japan sues for peace; Eisenhower visits Moscow.
19 November	Eisenhower named Army Chief of Staff.

1947

March	Truman Doctrine commits United States to a global policy of containment of communism.
June	Marshall Plan of economic aid to Western Europe.
July	National Security Act provides greater unification of the armed forces.

1948

February	Eisenhower resigns from Army to assume presidency of Columbia University.

1949

April	North Atlantic Treaty Organization (NATO) created.
29 August	Soviet Union explodes an atomic device.
October	People's Republic of China established.

1950

25 June	Korean War begins.
September	President Harry Truman approves NSC–68.
December	Eisenhower named Supreme Allied Commander, Europe.

1951

February	Eisenhower assumes NATO duties in Paris.

1952

30 March	President Truman announces he will not seek re-election.
12 April	Eisenhower declares his intention to resign his NATO command and seek the Republican presidential nomination.
1 June	Eisenhower returns to the United States and begins campaigning.
11 July	Eisenhower secures the Republican presidential nomination.
24 October	Eisenhower declares he will 'go to Korea' if elected.
4 November	Eisenhower elected president.
30 November	Eisenhower departs to review the situation in Korea.

1953

20 January	Eisenhower inaugurated as president.
11 February	Eisenhower refuses clemency for the Rosenbergs.
5 March	Josef Stalin dies.
16 April	Eisenhower's 'Chance for Peace' speech.
27 July	Korean Armistice signed.
12 August	Soviet thermonuclear test.
August	Iranian Prime Minister Mohammed Mossadeq overthrown.
30 October	Eisenhower approves NSC–162/2, the 'New Look'.
8 December	Eisenhower's 'Atoms for Peace' proposal outlined.

1954

1 March	American BRAVO thermonuclear test in the Pacific.
13 March	French garrison at Dien Bien Phu besieged by Viet Minh.
29 March	Dulles seeks 'United Action' to contain communism in Indochina.
7 April	Eisenhower explains the 'domino theory'.
April–June	Army–McCarthy televised hearings.
7 May	French garrison at Dien Bien Phu surrenders.
8 May	Geneva Conference on Indochina opens.
13 May	St Lawrence Seaway bill signed into law.
17 May	Supreme Court issues *Brown vs. Board of Education* ruling.
16–18 June	Guatemala 'invaded' and Arbenz overthrown.
2 August	Omnibus Housing Act becomes law.
30 August	French National Assembly rejects the European Defence Commnity Treaty.
3 September	People's Republic of China bombards Quemoy islands.
8 September	SEATO created.
19 October	Anglo-Egyptian Treaty obligates Britain to abandon Suez military base by June 1956.
23 October	Paris Accords on West German rearmament.
2 November	Midterm elections return Democratic majorities in Congress.
2 December	McCarthy censured by US Senate; Taiwan Mutual Defense Treaty signed.

1955

29 January	Formosa (Taiwan) Resolution authorizes use of US forces to defend Taiwan and 'related areas'.
28 February	Israeli raid on Egyptians in Gaza.
16 March	Eisenhower announces intention to use nuclear weapons in event of war with China.

9 May	Federal Republic of Germany regains sovereignty and joins NATO.
15 May	Austrian Peace Treaty signed.
31 May	*Brown II* ruling by US Supreme Court.
11 July	Eisenhower cancels Dixon-Yates contract.
18–24 July	Geneva Summit and 'Open Skies' proposal.
24 September	Eisenhower suffers heart attack.
26 October	Ngo Dinh Diem proclaims an independent Republic of Vietnam.

1956

25 February	Khrushchev's 'secret' speech to Twentieth Party Congress.
29 February	Eisenhower announces re-election bid.
12 March	Southern Manifesto pledges 77 southern congressmen and 11 senators to resist school desegregation.
9 April	Administration unveils civil rights legislation.
16 April	Eisenhower vetoes omnibus farm bill.
28 May	Revised Agricultural Act signed into law.
29 June	Federal Aid Highway Act becomes law.
19 July	Secretary of State John Foster Dulles withdraws offer of US aid to build Aswan Dam.
23 July	Civil rights bill passes the House of Representatives but dies in the Senate.
26 July	Egyptian President Gamal Abdel Nasser nationalizes the Suez Canal.
23 October	Anti-Soviet uprising in Budapest.
29 October	Israeli invasion of Egypt.
30 October	Anglo-French 'ultimatum' to Egypt and Israel.
31 October	Anglo-French aircraft bomb Egypt.
4 November	Soviet forces crush Hungarian uprising.
5 November	Anglo-French paratroopers land in Port Said.
6 November	Eisenhower re-elected; main Anglo-French landings in Suez Canal Zone.
December	Anglo-French forces withdraw from Egypt.

1957

16 January	Treasury Secretary George Humphrey predicts a depression unless federal spending is cut.
7 March	Congress approves Eisenhower Doctrine for the Middle East.
14 July	Iraqi monarchy overthrown in pro-Nasser coup.
13 August	Syria expels several US diplomats implicated in attempted coup.
21 August	Soviets test intercontinental ballistic missile.

9 September	Civil Rights Act signed into law.
14 September	Eisenhower meets with Arkansas Governor Orval Faubus to resolve Little Rock school desegregation crisis.
24 September	Eisenhower orders federal troops to Little Rock.
4 October	Soviets launch Sputnik.
3 November	Soviets launch Sputnik II.
25 November	Eisenhower suffers minor stroke.
December	Eisenhower attends NATO meetings in Paris and offers US missiles to allies.

1958

31 January	First US satellite, Explorer I, launched.
February	Harold Stassen eased out as special assistant for disarmament.
31 March	Soviets announce unilateral nuclear test suspension.
15 April	Eisenhower vetoes Rivers and Harbors bill.
28 April	Eisenhower offers Soviets talks on the technical feasibility of monitoring a nuclear test ban.
13 May	Nixon party mobbed in Caracas, Venezuela.
1 July	Geneva Conference of Experts convenes to examine means of monitoring a nuclear test ban.
15 July	US marines land in Lebanon.
29 July	NASA created.
6 August	Defense Reorganization Act signed into law.
22 August	Eisenhower offers nuclear test ban talks and a twelve-month test moratorium to Khrushchev.
23 August	China initiates second offshore islands crisis.
2 September	National Defence Education Act signed into law.
22 September	Chief of Staff Sherman Adams resigns amid allegations of influence-peddling.
4 November	Democrats increase congressional majorities in midterm elections.
10 November	Khrushchev announces intention to sign a separate peace with German Democratic Republic.
27 November	Khrushchev establishes six-month deadline for a satisfactory settlement on Berlin.

1959

1 January	Fidel Castro comes to power in Cuba.
March	Khrushchev accepts foreign ministers' conference on Berlin and Germany.
13 April	Eisenhower proposes atmospheric nuclear test ban.

15 April	Castro visits United States; Secretary Dulles resigns.
18 April	Christian Herter named secretary of state.
24 May	John Foster Dulles dies.
27 May	Dulles's funeral; Soviet ultimatum on Berlin expires without incident.
19 June	Senate rejects nomination of Lewis Strauss for secretary of commerce.
26 August	Eisenhower vetoes omnibus public works bill.
10 September	Congress overrides Eisenhower's public works bill veto, his first such defeat.
14 September	Landrum–Griffin Act becomes law.
15 September	Khrushchev visits the United States.
31 October	Moratorium on nuclear tests expires but Eisenhower seeks no new tests.

1960

13 February	Soviet–Cuban trade and aid agreement.
17 March	Eisenhower approves covert action against Castro.
1 May	U-2 shot down over Soviet Union.
6 May	Civil Rights Act signed into law.
13 May	Eisenhower vetoes depressed areas bill.
16 May	Paris Summit meeting ends after one session.
27 July	Nixon secures Republican presidential nomination.
24 August	Eisenhower fails to recall following any of Nixon's advice.
8 November	Kennedy elected president.

1961

3 January	Eisenhower breaks diplomatic relations with Cuba.
17 January	Eisenhower's farewell address.
17 April	Bay of Pigs operation fails to topple Castro.

1969

28 March	Eisenhower dies.

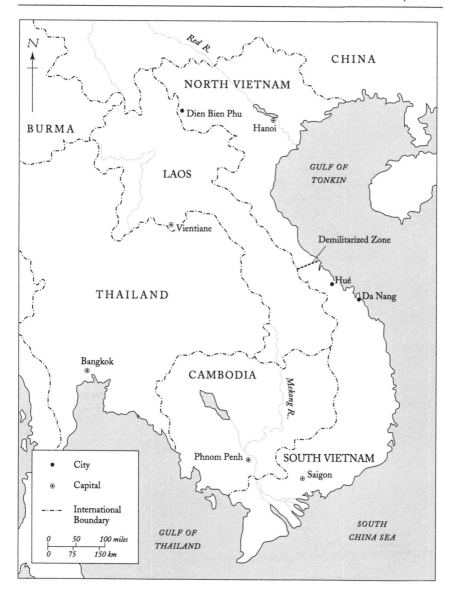

Map 1   Indochina, 1954

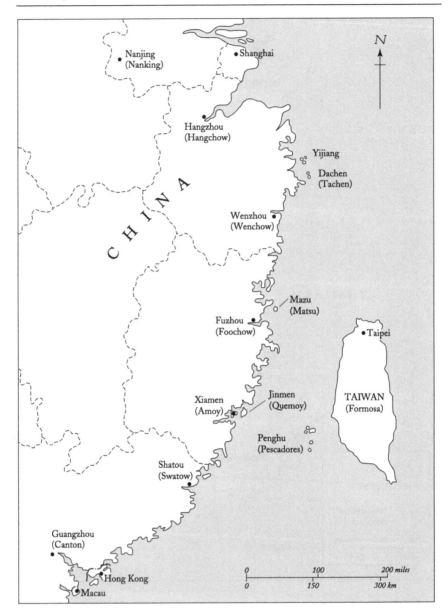

Map 2   Taiwan and the Offshore Islands

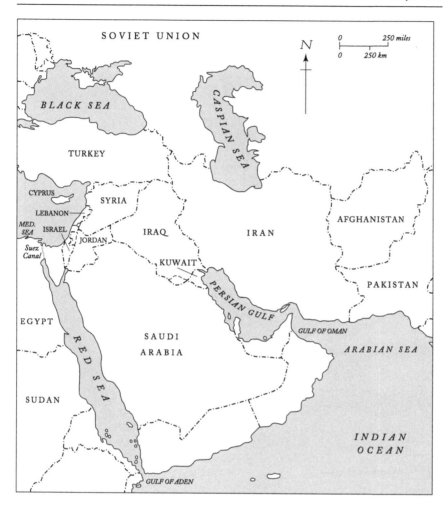

Map 3 The Middle East

Map 4   NATO and the Warsaw Pact, 1955

CHAPTER ONE

INTRODUCTION

No American president has undergone such a thoroughgoing re-examination by historians in the last generation, nor experienced such an improvement in reputation, as Dwight David Eisenhower. Shortly after the thirty-fourth president left office, the conventional wisdom held that Eisenhower was a personable, decent, honest man who nevertheless had led the nation unimaginatively throughout the decade of the 1950s and had failed to capitalize on his unquestioned personal popularity to rally the American people behind any noble cause. Worse, he had delegated primary responsibility for his administration's major domestic and foreign policies to outspoken, influential aides, such as the unpopular White House Chief of Staff, Sherman Adams, and the inveterately anti-communist Secretary of State, John Foster Dulles. Political observers in the late 1950s and early 1960s generally lamented the 'great postponement' under Eisenhower, a period when nothing had been done to address such pressing social problems as poverty and racism (Shannon, 1958). A 1962 poll of American historians seemed to confirm such judgements, ranking Eisenhower a lowly twenty-second among all American presidents, only one place higher than Andrew Johnson, at that time the only president to have been impeached (Schlesinger, 1962; DeSantis, 1976; Burk, 1988; Broadwater, 1991).

The 1962 historians' poll marked the nadir of Eisenhower's reputation among intellectuals. As Eisenhower's successors grappled unsuccessfully with an unpopular war in Vietnam, urban uprisings, social protest movements, budget deficits, spiralling inflation and economic stagnation, Americans began to look back upon the relative calm and prosperity of the Eisenhower years with a sense of nostalgia. As early as 1967, journalist Murray Kempton suggested that contemporaries had grossly underestimated Eisenhower's achievements. Compared with the flawed activism of John F. Kennedy and Lyndon B. Johnson, Eisenhower's deliberately restrained leadership had carefully avoided partisan rancour, kept the nation on a sound economic footing, initiated work on the modern interstate highway system, built the St Lawrence Seaway, and, most importantly, kept the peace (Kempton, 1967). Garry Wills went even further, characterizing Eisenhower as a 'political genius' whose awkward public statements and apparent delegation of responsibility were a shrewd act to disguise his true involvement in his administration's policies, convey the impression of a national leader above party, and generate public confidence (Wills, 1969).

The journalistic reassessments of Eisenhower in the late 1960s and early 1970s represented the first ripples of a tide of Eisenhower revisionism that would engulf the historical profession over the next decade. Not only did Eisenhower's reputation benefit from an increasingly favourable comparison with his successors, but also the gradual opening of the holdings of the Dwight D. Eisenhower Presidential Library after Eisenhower's death in 1969 enabled scholars to document the president's central role in meetings with the National Security Council, the Cabinet, personal aides and congressional leaders. The Eisenhower diaries, in particular, provided remarkable insight into Eisenhower's thinking on contemporary issues. The newly-available archival evidence effectively laid to rest the notion that Eisenhower was diffident, uninformed and not thoroughly involved in directing his administration's major policies. By the mid-1970s, detailed works by Herbert Parmet, Peter Lyon and Charles C. Alexander began to present a more favourable portrait of the thirty-fourth president. Parmet argued that Eisenhower's restrained, middle-of-the-road presidency was exactly what most Americans wanted in the affluent, comfortable 1950s (Parmet, 1972). Lyon criticized Eisenhower's bellicose anti-communist foreign policy, particularly his interventionism in the Third World, but conceded that his calm leadership managed to keep the peace in the face of numerous crises (Lyon, 1974). Similarly, while unsympathetic to Eisenhower's conservative views, Alexander recognized that the president had nonetheless succeeded in 'holding the line' against any further expansion of the welfare state, demands for more vigorous prosecution of the Cold War and pressure to expand the military (Alexander, 1975).

The high tide of Eisenhower revisionism arrived in the early 1980s, with important studies by political scientist Fred I. Greenstein and historians Robert Divine and Stephen Ambrose. Greenstein built on Wills's earlier observations to identify a carefully-crafted 'hidden-hand' leadership style. Eisenhower, he argued, skilfully worked behind the scenes to promote his policies while delegating responsibility for articulating them to subordinates who would then have to bear the brunt of public scrutiny and criticism. Contrary to earlier critics who condemned Eisenhower for refusing to stand up to Senator Joseph McCarthy's anti-communist witch-hunting, Greenstein suggested that it was actually Eisenhower who quietly masterminded the downfall of the junior senator from Wisconsin (Greenstein, 1982). Divine's generally sympathetic overview of Eisenhower's major foreign policies praised the president for steering the nation through several difficult crises and avoiding war. While unable to achieve his larger goals of reducing Cold War tensions and halting the nuclear arms race, Eisenhower nevertheless provided a 'model of presidential restraint' that his successors would have been well-advised to emulate (Divine, 1981: 155). Finally, in a richly-detailed biographical study, Ambrose painted a picture of a president very much in control of the policy-making process. Although Eisenhower failed to end the Cold War and seize the moral high ground in the case of African-American civil rights, he 'almost single-handedly' held down defence spending, supported economic policies that produced a decade of prosperity, and excelled at crisis management. In sum, it was a 'magnificent performance' (Ambrose, 1984: 626). A new poll of presidential historians in the early 1980s reflected the influence of these more positive appraisals. Eisenhower now ranked ninth, achieving the status of a 'nearly great' president.

In the course of the last decade, the ending of the Cold War, the disintegration of the Soviet Union, the opening of additional archival holdings in the United States and Europe, and the increasing availability of carefully-researched, archival-based monographs providing in-depth analyses of various aspects of the Eisenhower years have made possible a more balanced and sophisticated understanding of the Eisenhower presidency. Most scholars now largely accept the basic tenets of Eisenhower revision- ism, most notably that Eisenhower was an informed, thoughtful, hands-on policy-maker, but recent analyses place more emphasis on the substance and efficacy of his policies. The purpose of this study is to provide a general introduction and critical overview of the Eisenhower presidency and synthesize much of the current scholarship. As will become readily apparent, this introduction to the Eisenhower era relies heavily on the monographic literature that preceded it. The basic thesis here is that the Eisenhower administration was neither as reactionary as the early critics claimed nor as unerringly successful as the later revisionists suggested.

Eisenhower's storybook rise from humble origins as the third son of a mid-western family of modest means to Supreme Commander of the Allied Expeditionary Forces in Europe during World War II and mastermind of the successful D-Day invasion of France made him an ideal presidential candidate in the eyes of many. As a professional military man, Eisenhower frequently expressed disdain for politics and politicians and believed that soldiers should confine themselves to purely military matters, but as early as 1943 journalists suggested that his leadership qualities well-suited him for the nation's highest office. By that time, under the guidance of his mentor, Army Chief of Staff George C. Marshall, Eisenhower had risen from being a relatively obscure lieutenant colonel in the Third Army to commander of the successful Anglo-American invasions of North Africa in 1942 and Sicily and Italy in 1943. Preoccupied with winning the war and maintaining Allied unity, Eisenhower had little patience for speculation about a political candidacy. Nevertheless, throughout his military career, he repeatedly demonstrated remarkable political and diplomatic skills. He rose through the ranks of the interwar army, an intensely political organization in its own right, survived a stint as mercurial General Douglas MacArthur's aide in the 1930s, and exhibited the tact and shrewdness to forge a working wartime coalition among such inflated egos as British Prime Minister Winston Churchill, Field Marshal Bernard Law Montgomery, General George S. Patton and Free French leader Charles de Gaulle. Following his acceptance of the German defeat in the west and promotion to five-star general, many Americans viewed Eisenhower as the nation's greatest military hero. Thus, despite repeated protestations that he harboured no political ambitions, both Democratic and Republican leaders continued to bandy the name of Eisenhower as a potential presidential candidate with mass appeal. During the July 1945 Potsdam Conference, even President Harry S. Truman offered to assist Eisenhower in securing the Democratic nomination for president in the 1948 election, which the general politely declined.

Eisenhower's political education continued in the postwar years. He inherited Marshall's position as Army Chief of Staff in 1945, presided over Columbia University from 1948 to 1950, and eventually became the first Supreme Commander for the newly-created North Atlantic Treaty Organization (NATO) in 1951. In each of these positions, Eisenhower remained intimately involved in the discussion and implementation of national security policy, but he grew increasingly uneasy with the direction in which the nation was heading. As Army Chief of Staff, Eisenhower supervised the rapid demobilization demanded by the American public, but he quickly became frustrated with the intensely political atmosphere in Washington. More ominously, as relations between the West and the Soviet Union deteriorated into a state of Cold War, he worried about the lack of a coherent strategy for maximizing the nation's limited resources to contain the communist threat. In the name of efficiency, he supported a system of universal military training and greater unification of the armed forces. Congress never approved the former, but Eisenhower helped to shape the controversial 1947 National Security Act that subordinated the individual services to a National Military Establishment, later called the Department of Defense. He supported President Truman's request for aid to Greece and Turkey and generally endorsed the policy of containment, but worried about the administration's piecemeal approach to defence strategy and his fellow officers' failure to appreciate that true national security required a sound economy and spiritual strength in addition to military might. Without a clear strategic concept and recognition of the need to balance means and ends, Eisenhower feared that the nation courted disaster. Such concerns became even more urgent when the Cold War took a dramatic turn for the worse. The explosion of a Soviet nuclear device in 1949 and the outbreak of the Korean War the following year persuaded Eisenhower to accept Truman's request to return to active duty as NATO Supreme Commander. As expected, Eisenhower's appointment bolstered European confidence in the twelve-nation collective security system and helped to sell the idea of a long-term American military commitment to Western European defence to the American public. The bloody stalemate in Korea and the Truman administration's adoption of the alarmist National Security Council Paper 68, which forecast impending war with the communist world and advocated a massive, permanent military build-up, however, were important factors in Eisenhower's decision to accept his friends' entreaties and run for the presidency in 1952 as a Republican.

A second set of factors in Eisenhower's decision to seek the presidency were his concerns for the future of the Republican Party and the nation's apparent drift towards socialism under Democratic presidents Franklin D. Roosevelt and Truman. At Columbia University, Eisenhower cultivated friendships and associations with some of the nation's wealthiest business leaders, most of whom were moderate, internationalist Republicans. He found that he shared their anti-statist views, particularly the notion that high taxes, rising government expenditures and an expanding federal bureaucracy would ultimately undermine the nation's economic health and erode individual freedoms. Having failed to win the presidency since the Great Depression, Republicans desperately sought a candidate with broad popular appeal who could wrest back control of the federal government before it was too late. In 1948, Eisenhower expected that his friend, New York Governor Thomas E. Dewey, would be that candidate and so turned aside both Republican and Democratic efforts to recruit him. When Dewey unexpectedly lost to Truman, however, Eisenhower began a quiet campaign to position himself to accept a 'draft' in 1952 should no suitable alternative Republican be available. The emergence of Senate Minority Leader Robert A. Taft of Ohio as the frontrunner among Republican candidates added urgency to the covert manoeuvres by Eisenhower's internationalist friends. Taft had opposed NATO and the Marshall Plan, preferred an Asia-first foreign policy, and had little knowledge of foreign affairs generally. Taft's candidacy convinced Eisenhower to enter the race for the Republican presidential nomination, both to safeguard the collective security system that he deemed vital to winning the Cold War and to prevent yet another Republican defeat in the general election. The unpopular Truman's decision not to seek re-election made Eisenhower's entry into the presidential race somewhat easier as he would not now have to run against his commander-in-chief. After resigning his NATO post, Eisenhower returned to the United

States in mid-1952 and, at a bitterly-contested Republican convention in Chicago, won the nomination on the first ballot (Pickett, 2000).

During the 1952 general election, Eisenhower performed a delicate balancing act. As the candidate of the minority party, he had to secure not only the traditional base of Republican voters but also a substantial number of independents and disaffected Democrats. Eisenhower and his campaign manager and friend, Senator Henry Cabot Lodge of Massachusetts, shrewdly papered over significant differences between Republican internationalists and isolationists, Atlanticists and Asia-firsters, by downplaying his role in NATO and emphasizing Truman's loss of China to the Communists. They also delegated the drafting of the party's foreign policy platform to Republican stalwart John Foster Dulles. Capitalizing on his image as a war hero and statesman who would remain above politics, Eisenhower turned to surrogates to deliver the more shrill partisan attacks on the Democrats and their record. His young running-mate, Senator Richard M. Nixon of California, and Wisconsin Senator Joseph R. McCarthy hammered home the campaign themes of 'Korea, communism and corruption' with alacrity. Eisenhower remained largely above the fray and never referred to his opponent, Illinois Governor Adlai Stevenson, by name. On the most pressing issue of the day, the ongoing war in Korea, Eisenhower made no specific policy proposals. Instead, he simply stated: 'I shall go to Korea.' It was enough. On election day, Eisenhower comprehensively defeated Stevenson by more than six million popular votes and carried all but nine states. He was the first Republican in a generation to capture the traditionally Democratic southern states of Tennessee, Texas, Florida and Virginia. His personal popularity enabled the Republicans to win both houses of Congress by a narrow majority: 221 to 214 in the House of Representatives, and 49 to 47 in the Senate. Faced with such little margin for error and significant divisions among fellow Republicans, however, Eisenhower recognized that he would need to steer a moderate, bipartisan course in order to govern effectively.

CHAPTER TWO

THE MIDDLE WAY

Dwight D. Eisenhower entitled the first volume of his presidential memoirs 'mandate for change', but the narrow margin of the Republican victory belied such a claim. While certainly underscoring Eisenhower's tremendous personal popularity, the election results also seemed to confirm the American public's preference for a government that would cater to what one scholar has termed 'the vital centre'. Indeed, even had Eisenhower not been dependent on a degree of Democratic support to govern, he was philosophically sympathetic to the notion of a middle-of-the-road administration that would seek bipartisan consensus. In domestic affairs, Eisenhower's priority was to lay the foundation for a healthy economy by bringing the budget into balance, lifting wartime economic controls and taxes, and arresting the trend towards statism. Some of Eisenhower's fellow Republicans, particularly the so-called Old Guard, wanted to go much further, however, and envisioned sweeping tax cuts and a roll back of the New Deal and Fair Deal welfare state programmes of the 1930s and 1940s. Eisenhower worked to moderate their views, but with mixed success. In fact, some of Eisenhower's most troublesome political problems during his first administration would come from within the Republican Party.

EISENHOWER'S POLITICAL PHILOSOPHY

Dwight D. Eisenhower came to the presidency with a set of deeply-held convictions about the proper role of the federal government in the modern age and the ideal society. As a professional military man, he had developed a yen for efficient organization, a strong dislike for politics and politicians, a suspicion of popular democracy and a deep commitment to duty and disinterested public service. His philosophy has been described by one historian as the 'corporate commonwealth'. He sought to resolve the contradictions of modern capitalism by fostering a harmonious society free of class conflict, selfish acquisitiveness and divisive party politics. Like the social thought of the last Republican president, Herbert Hoover,

Eisenhower stressed the mutual interdependence of classes and economic interests. He once wrote to a friend 'that agriculture, labor, management and capital frequently speak of themselves as if each were a separate and self-sufficient enterprise or community. Yet the simple fact is that each is helpless without the others; only as an effective member of an integrated team can any one of them prosper' (Griffith, 1984: 91). Like Hoover, Eisenhower envisioned a mutually cooperative society where interest groups would voluntarily work together for the common good to achieve order, stability and progress.

The key to achieving this corporate commonwealth, Eisenhower believed, was to seek balance, a 'middle way' in his words, between labour and capital, liberalism and conservatism, and the federal government and the private sector [*Doc. 1*]. Like many of the Old Guard conservative members of his Republican Party, Eisenhower wanted to check what he viewed as the dangerous New Deal/Fair Deal drift towards statism. Unlike them, however, he envisioned a positive, if limited, role for the state in the nation's political economy. He recognized that it would be politically impossible to dismantle popular New Deal programmes, such as Social Security, that now had built-in constituencies. In some areas, moreover, he believed that the state had a responsibility to 'prevent or correct abuses springing from the unregulated practice of a private economy' (Griffith, 1984: 92). The government could also function to bring competing interests and groups together to foster social harmony and blend the individual and the public good. On several occasions, Eisenhower repeated the dictum attributed to Abraham Lincoln: 'The legitimate object of government is to do for a community of people whatever they need to have done but cannot do at all or cannot do so well. In all that the people can individually do ... for themselves Government ought not to interfere' (PPP, 1953: 395).

Eisenhower frequently expressed his distaste for politics, by which he meant the narrowly selfish actions of particular interest groups and classes. He believed that his Democratic predecessor had pandered to uneducated public opinion for political gain at the expense of the common good. Eisenhower instead resolved to govern in the national interest, and sought like-minded public-spirited leaders from the private sector who could exercise disinterested judgement on the pressing issues of the day. Harkening back to a theme of turn-of-the-century progressivism, Eisenhower exhibited great faith in elite leadership by enlightened expert administrators who could stand above narrow self-interest and partisan politics.

Eisenhower's vision of a corporate commonwealth was shared by many progressive-minded business leaders. During the 1930s, so-called corporate liberals in the business community had endorsed certain New Deal reforms aimed at promoting economic stability, but had remained wary of any move towards state socialism. During World War II, thousands of corporate managers had participated in a highly productive and mutually beneficial business–government partnership to mobilize the nation's resources for war. The war had also witnessed the emergence of new, progressive business groups, such as the Council for Economic Development (CED) and the Advertising Council. These organizations promoted continued cooperation between business and government in order to moderate economic conflict, regulate markets, promote international trade, and foster economic growth. At the same time, they also urged on the federal government responsible fiscal and monetary policies conducive to private enterprise. In Eisenhower, these corporate liberals saw a means of wresting political power back from the New Dealers and securing the kind of positive, but limited, state intervention in the economy that they favoured. Indeed, business leaders such as Paul G. Hoffman of the Studebaker Corporation, Thomas J. Watson of International Business Machines, Philip D. Reid of General Electric, financiers Clifford Roberts and John Hay Whitney, and publishers Helen Rogers Reid and Henry Luce were crucial to Eisenhower's election. They reinforced his own conviction that it was his duty to run, backed him financially and editorially, and bolstered his views on political economy. Not surprisingly, as president, Eisenhower turned to some of these same corporate leaders to provide the expert leadership he preferred.

ECONOMIC POLICY

Eisenhower's 'middle way' philosophy was most evident in his administration's major economic policies. While he pleased conservatives by eliminating Truman's Korean War price control mechanisms, moving towards a balanced budget, and reforming the New Deal system of agricultural price supports, he nevertheless oversaw a modest expansion of the welfare state in other areas.

Eisenhower came to office determined to reduce federal spending, balance the budget, cut taxes, and restore the proper balance between the public and private sectors. Like most Republicans, he was appalled that Democratic presidents Roosevelt and Truman had only been able to achieve three balanced budgets during their twenty years in power. Such profligacy seemed to court economic disaster by fuelling inflation, cheapening the value of the dollar, and undermining private initiative. Between 1940 and 1952, partly as a result of military requirements, the value of the dollar had fallen 50 per cent and the national debt had more than tripled. Total local, state and federal government spending had risen from 12 per cent of national income in 1929 to 33 per cent by 1953, with the federal government's share rising from one-quarter to three-quarters of that amount. Restoring fiscal integrity, Eisenhower believed, was vital to creating the conditions most conducive to long-term economic growth and prosperity (Saulnier, 1991).

Eisenhower's key economic advisers reinforced his fiscal views. Secretary of the Treasury George M. Humphrey, former head of the Mark A. Hanna Company, a Cleveland-based industrial holding company, frequently reminded Eisenhower and his Cabinet colleagues of the need for economy in government, balanced budgets, a sound dollar and corporate tax relief to promote business confidence. Although Humphrey developed a close personal friendship with the president, his economic advice was perhaps less influential than that of Arthur F. Burns, the Columbia University economist who became Eisenhower's first chairman of the Council of Economic Advisers (CEA). Created by the 1946 Employment Act to advise the president on economic matters, the CEA under Truman had fallen into disrepute with many Republicans for its partisan advocacy of administration programmes. Eisenhower, however, revamped the three-member panel and appointed Burns, an expert on the business cycle, as his personal economic adviser. Under Burns, the CEA became Eisenhower's economics research staff. Like Eisenhower, Burns worried that constant deficit spending would lead to persistent, creeping inflation that would devalue the currency, erode business confidence, and cause a serious economic downturn. Despite his emphasis on price stability, however, Burns was flexible enough to contemplate compensatory budget deficits during periods of recession. Indeed, under his influence, the administration began to move towards the notion of a stabilizing budget, an idea championed by the Committee for Economic Development. The stabilizing budget entailed compensatory deficits during periods of economic downturn, when government revenues declined and unemployment payments increased, which would be offset by surpluses during more prosperous times. Rather than balancing the budget every year, the stabilizing budget would achieve balance between revenues and outlays over the course of the business cycle.

Eisenhower intended a reduction in federal spending to be his administration's first order of business. He inherited from Truman a Fiscal Year 1954 (July 1953–June 1954) budget proposing $78.6 billion in expenditures and projecting a deficit of almost $10 billion. Eisenhower quickly recognized that Republican election promises of tax cuts in 1953 and a balanced budget by 1954 were out of the question. He submitted a revised budget to Congress in April with estimated expenditures of $74.1 billion and a deficit of $5.6 billion, provided that temporary Korean War taxes scheduled to expire in mid-1953 were extended until the end of the year. Almost all of the savings came from national security programmes, where Eisenhower cut projected force levels and reduced mutual security funding for America's allies. Even with these reductions, federal expenditures were barely a billion dollars less than Truman had spent in 1953.

The revised budget represented an early test of Eisenhower's 'middle way' philosophy and leadership of his own party. The new estimates immediately ran into resistance from more conservative congressional Republicans, particularly Senate Majority Leader Robert Taft and New York Representative Daniel A. Reed, chairman of the House's tax-writing committee. Both favoured bigger cuts in order to eliminate the deficit. They also wanted to fulfil the party's campaign promise of tax reductions and feared the political consequences for Republicans in 1954 if they failed to deliver. But Eisenhower remained adamant that further economies in national security expenditures could only be accomplished after hostilities in Korea ended. Working through loyal Republicans in the House, the administration successfully employed parliamentary manoeuvres to prevent Reed's bill for immediate tax relief from coming to a vote and by-passed his committee to enact a temporary extension of the Korean War taxes. Congress, in effect, endorsed the administration's position that deficit reduction should take priority over tax reduction.

While Congress moved to restore fiscal integrity and curb inflation by cutting spending, Eisenhower's Treasury Department also attempted to secure long-term financial stability by lengthening the average maturity of the outstanding federal debt. The fact that much of the national debt came due in a short time greatly complicated the task of stabilizing federal finances. When the Treasury borrowed on a short-term basis, moreover, the funds often came from the commercial banking system, which tended to increase the money supply and raise inflationary pressures. In June, the Treasury offered $1 billion in bonds of thirty years maturity bearing an interest rate of 3.25 per cent. The issue attracted long-term investors and was quickly oversubscribed, but an unintended consequence was to draw funds out of the mortgage market, raising the cost of borrowing for home buyers and suppressing housing starts.

Eisenhower's economic views soon faced their first real challenge. The combined impact of further military retrenchment after the Korean armistice in July, the Federal Reserve's tight money policy to offset anticipated postwar inflation, the Treasury's stabilization plan, falling farm prices and a natural downturn in the business cycle pushed the economy into recession by late 1953. In the course of the 1953–54 downturn, the gross national product shrank by 3 per cent and unemployment edged up from 2.5 to 6.1 per cent. Throughout the slump, Eisenhower demonstrated his commitment to a conservative variant of Keynesian economics. While reassuring the nation that the economy was fundamentally sound, he worked behind the scenes to stimulate recovery. Although he continued to pare overall federal spending, he authorized accelerated outlays for government projects already funded. In order to accelerate private home construction, the administration liberalized the terms for federally-insured home mortgages, and Eisenhower privately urged bankers to lower interest rates. Significantly, the administration modified its position on taxes, now endorsing tax cuts before achieving a balanced budget. In April 1954, Eisenhower signed a Republican-backed bill to reduce Korean War excise taxes and later won congressional support for an administration measure to stimulate investment by reducing taxes on corporate dividends and increasing business depreciation allowances. These modest counter-cyclical measures, along with increased unemployment insurance payments and a loosening of monetary policy by the Federal Reserve, helped to bring about recovery by September 1954.

Despite the economic downturn, Eisenhower continued to make progress towards a balanced budget. His 1955 budget was the first to benefit from the end of hostilities in Korea and the adoption of a new strategic concept (discussed in detail in the next chapter), which reduced military expenditures by $8.1 billion over 1954 levels. The administration held down overall expenditures to $64.6 billion. Although the 1953–54 recession and tax cuts reduced revenues, Eisenhower's savings kept the budget deficit at a modest $4.2 billion. The following year, expenditures crept back up to $66.5 billion, but a booming economy brought in larger than expected receipts of $68.1 billion, resulting in a small surplus on the eve of the presidential election. Eisenhower could justifiably claim that his fiscal and monetary policies had put the nation's financial affairs back on a sound footing.

While generally seeking to hold down the federal budget and reduce the tax burden, a combination of political and philosophical factors led Eisenhower to maintain the New Deal's modest social welfare programmes. When his older brother, Edgar, took up the call of those more conservative Republicans who complained about the administration's timidity in rolling back the welfare state, he pointedly replied: 'Should any political party attempt to abolish Social Security, unemployment insurance, and eliminate labor laws and farm programs, you would not hear of that party again in our political history' (Chandler and Galambos, 1996: 15.1386). Indeed, in such areas as public housing, social security and health insurance, Eisenhower pursued his 'middle way' philosophy to establish a 'floor that covers the pit of disaster' for American workers (Griffith, 1982: 102). The major difference between Eisenhower's approach and that of his Democratic predecessors was a new emphasis on private initiative.

Eisenhower enjoyed mixed success in expanding social welfare benefits. His first State of the Union message in 1953 called for greater 'safeguards against the privations that too often come with unemployment, old age, illness and accident' (PPP, 1953: 32). The following year, Congress acted on the president's recommendations and expanded Social Security coverage to 10.5 million additional workers and raised monthly benefits. Eisenhower's health care proposals fared less well. Like most Republicans, he opposed the vaguely-defined but unquestioned evil of 'socialized medicine', but he hoped to find a way to extend private health insurance to the 63 million

Americans without any coverage. The administration proposed a health reinsurance plan, consisting of a federal fund to underwrite the risks of private health insurance carriers who extended coverage to high-risk consumers, mostly the poor, elderly, and rural dwellers. Liberal Democrats in Congress condemned the plan as a massive subsidy to insurance carriers. Instead, they supported compulsory national health insurance to be administered through the Social Security system. The American Medical Association and many insurance companies, meanwhile, adamantly opposed any move whatsoever towards a national system of 'socialized medicine'. The ideological divide proved to be unbridgeable. The reinsurance plan died in committee in 1954 and never resurfaced.

Eisenhower's housing proposals encountered strong resistance from many congressional Republicans. The 1949 Housing Act had sought to alleviate the postwar, low-cost housing shortage by providing for federal construction of 810,000 public housing units over the next six years, but the Korean War had intervened to limit construction to about a quarter of that total. In September 1953, Eisenhower appointed a twenty-member Advisory Commission on Government Housing Policies and Programmes to recommend a comprehensive approach to the continuing shortage. Democratic critics charged, with good reason, that the commission was heavily weighted in favour of banking, real estate and construction interests hostile to the whole concept of public housing. The following January, based on the commission's suggestions, Eisenhower requested legislation to assure construction of a million housing units during 1954. The plan emphasized private initiative, providing for expanded federal mortgage insurance for old and new homes, grants and loans for renovation of older homes, slum clearance and urban renewal, and lower down-payment requirements on federally-insured loans for low-income housing. To the dismay of conservatives, it also included a scaled-down public housing component, calling for federal construction of 140,000 new units over four years. Eisenhower successfully fended off a House Republican effort to eliminate all new public housing construction, but he eventually accepted a compromise that limited the number of new units to be built in any given year to the number of units demolished through urban renewal programmes. The net result of the 1954 Omnibus Housing Act was that by the end of the decade more poor people had been displaced through urban renewal than had been housed in new public housing.

Eisenhower was determined to reduce the role of the federal government in agriculture, which had become the nation's most expensive domestic programme by the early 1950s. He wanted to replace the Depression-era system of farm subsidies with a new programme that would 'minimize governmental interference in the farmer's affairs, ... permit desirable shifts in production, and ... encourage farmers themselves to use initiative in meeting changing economic conditions' (PPP, 1953: 27). Central to the old programme was an arcane system of rigid price supports for six basic commodities (wheat, corn, cotton, rice, tobacco and peanuts) at 90 per cent of 'parity', defined as the price of the commodity in relation to operating costs equivalent to the relationship between prices and costs in the period 1910–14. In return for these supports, farmers limited production by restricting the acreage for each commodity and had the right to store some or all of their crop with the Commodity Credit Corporation (CCC) and receive a loan of up to 90 per cent of the commodity's parity price. In favourable market conditions, farmers could sell the crop and repay the loan, but if prices remained low farmers could sign over the crop to the CCC as full payment for the loan. Eisenhower claimed that the whole system was fundamentally flawed. Improved farming methods often undermined acreage restrictions, resulting in continued surpluses, falling commodity prices and huge amounts of crops in federal storage, which in turn perpetuated overproduction and low prices.

Secretary of Agriculture Ezra Taft Benson, a staunch advocate of the free market, led the administration's drive to rationalize the farm programme. In 1954, over the objections of some Republicans from farm states, Congress enacted a system of flexible price supports ranging from 82.5 to 90 per cent of parity. The sliding scale supposedly restored market forces and helped to eliminate surpluses by allowing the secretary to adjust price supports in accordance with market conditions. In fact, flexible price supports had little immediate effect on the problem of surpluses and declining farm incomes. By mid-1956, commodity stocks in CCC storage had more than doubled, prompting the administration to pursue further reforms. Eisenhower proposed a Soil Bank, whereby farmers would be subsidized for taking land out of production. The Democratic-controlled Congress, looking to make political hay out of an agricultural bill in a presidential election year, tied the Soil Bank to a restoration of rigid price supports at 90 per cent parity. An angry Eisenhower vetoed the 'jumbled-up, election-year monstrosity' (Eisenhower, 1963: 557). A few weeks later, Congress relented and established the Soil Bank. Even so, the technical complexities and intricate politics that constituted the 'farm problem' seemed to be intractable, and Eisenhower would be forced to revisit it during his second term.

The president had rather more success in reducing the federal role in natural resource development. He advocated 'a partnership of state and local communities, private citizens, and the Federal Government, all working together', but the administration's policies generally favoured private enterprise and local initiative (PPP, 1953: 26). In 1953, for example, the administration pushed through a measure that ceded ownership and mineral rights in submerged offshore lands to the adjacent states, many of which then granted development rights to private corporations. Similarly, the 1954 Atomic Energy Act promoted private development of nuclear power by requiring the Atomic Energy Commission (AEC) to license private corporations to produce and market nuclear electric power and restricting AEC power production to experimental purposes. In the same vein, Eisenhower encouraged Secretary of the Interior Douglas McKay to reverse a Truman-era decision to build a high concrete dam and federally-operated power facilities at Hells Canyon in Idaho in favour of three privately-constructed low dams on the Snake River. Even the St Lawrence Seaway project, connecting the Atlantic Ocean with the Great Lakes through the St Lawrence River, only received the administration's support after the original provisions for federal construction of hydroelectric facilities had been excised. In all these cases, Eisenhower demonstrated his preference for private and local resource development over any expansion of federal authority.

For most conservatives, the Tennessee Valley Authority (TVA) represented the most controversial resource development project. Created in 1933 to provide flood control and electrical power to a seven-state region, opponents charged that the TVA was a prime example of government paternalism. Eisenhower personally opposed any further expansion of the TVA, publicly referring to it as an example of 'creeping socialism' that had to be turned back. His remarks provoked such an outcry that he felt compelled to reassure TVA supporters that he had no intention of selling it off to private interests, as advocated by some Republicans. Nevertheless, Eisenhower made clear that he considered the TVA an unwarranted example of sectional favouritism that unfairly competed with private enterprise. He appointed a new TVA director who shared his views and attempted to move the agency towards a self-sustaining basis. In his determination to halt any further TVA expansion, Eisenhower ordered the AEC to contract with a private company, Dixon-Yates, rather than the TVA, to provide power to its facility in Paducah, Kentucky. The decision not only angered public power advocates but also caused a minor conflict-of-interest scandal when it was revealed that a government consultant had simultaneously been advising Dixon-Yates. Eisenhower managed to sidestep the controversy when the city of Memphis decided to build its own municipal power plant, which freed up power from existing TVA facilities for the AEC and allowed the administration to cancel the Dixon-Yates contract.

The domestic programme that epitomized Eisenhower's public–private partnership approach, and its inherent flaws, was the 1954 Federal Aid Highway Act. Eisenhower had been concerned about the woeful state of American roads ever since participating in a much-publicized cross-country Army convoy in 1919, and exposure to the German *autobahns* had only reinforced his concerns. By the mid-1950s, although the number of auto-mobiles had doubled since World War II, the nation still possessed few urban expressways or dual carriageways connecting major cities. A wide variety of interest groups recognized the need for a comprehensive federal highway programme but there was no consensus as to how it should be administered and financed. In this area, Eisenhower saw a pressing need for federal activism. Modernizing the nation's roads would provide clear economic and national security advantages. Not only would it directly employ thousands of workers and spur business activity generally, but it would also facilitate the movement of men and materiel in the event of war. Only the federal government, moreover, had the necessary power and resources to direct such an undertaking.

Eisenhower delegated the task of developing the national highway programme to a blue-ribbon advisory commission whose recommendations formed the basis for the legislation that he submitted to Congress early in 1955. The administration's plan envisioned a 41,000-mile system of interstate highways linking the major cities, with a federal Highway Trust Fund footing 90 per cent of the construction bill through the issue of revenue bonds. The plan stalled in Congress for a year when Democrats insisted on financing construction through tolls on road users. Eventually, Eisenhower endorsed a compromise measure that retained the trust fund, thus keeping the programme off budget, but provided funding through pay-as-you-go taxes on petroleum, tyres and lorries. Largely unnoticed at the time, the final legislation also offered a concession to urban constituencies by providing for freeways to go directly through the heart of major urban centres. Eisenhower proudly viewed the Highway Act as a landmark of his presidency. The commission, it seemed, had overcome the narrow self-interest of car manufacturers, hauling firms, automobile clubs and oil companies that had delayed federal action for a decade and devised a plan that offered something for everyone. The final measure, however, paid no heed to the long-term impact on the urban landscape, such as inner-city decay, and ignored such environmental issues as air quality and inefficient energy consumption.

Overall, Eisenhower had good reason to be pleased with his administration's major economic programmes heading into the 1956 election. He had removed the Korean War economic controls, balanced the budget while reducing the tax burden, and presided over a modest expansion of the social welfare system while reining in federal programmes elsewhere. Most importantly, the administration had weathered the 1953–54 recession, exorcizing the ghost of Herbert Hoover and indicating that the Republican Party was indeed competent to handle the nation's economy. By 1956, economic growth averaged over 7 per cent, unemployment remained low, and inflation had been held to less than 2 per cent. With the noticeable exception of farming, it seemed that more and more Americans were sharing in the postwar prosperity.

THE ANTI-COMMUNIST CRUSADE

One of the most troubling political problems that confronted Eisenhower in his first term was Senator Joseph R. McCarthy and his crusade to purge the government of communists and fellow-travellers. The junior Republican senator from Wisconsin had exploded on to the national scene early in 1950 with sensational charges of communist subversion in the federal government. Offering a simple explanation for American reversals in the Cold War, McCarthy's outrageous allegations and effective manipulation of the mass media played on people's fears of communism and seemed to attract a powerful, popular following. The fact that none of his charges was ever proven was irrelevant as McCarthy kept his critics off balance with ever more spectacular stories of official cover-ups. In the 1950 and 1952 elections, the Republican Party effectively exploited McCarthy and the anti-communist issue to discredit Truman and the Democrats for being 'soft on communism'. In the 1952 election, McCarthy campaigned for Republican candidates in sixteen states. He easily won re-election and was credited with helping to defeat four Democratic incumbents, including the Senate Majority Leader. Even with a Republican president and Congress, however, McCarthy vowed to continue 'exposing communists' (Griffith, 1970: 208).

McCarthy soon made mischief for the administration. He first held up Senate confirmation of several of Eisenhower's nominees for top government posts, including those of Eisenhower's friend and wartime chief-of-staff Walter Bedell Smith, designated to be undersecretary of state, and Soviet expert Charles E. Bohlen, chosen for the ambassadorship to Moscow. McCarthy objected to Smith because he had commended a State Department official whom McCarthy believed to be a communist, while Bohlen was implicated in President Roosevelt's alleged 'sell-out' of Eastern Europe at Yalta. Eisenhower was furious, but worked quietly through Vice-President Richard M. Nixon and other Republican senators to get his nominees confirmed. Next, McCarthy moved on to new targets of opportunity, launching investigations into the Voice of America and the International Information Agency's Overseas Library programme. His trusted aides Roy Cohn and G. David Schine 'discovered' numerous communist and subversive publications on the shelves of official American libraries overseas, resulting in a purge of the offensive material and some book burnings.

Although Eisenhower had used McCarthy during the election campaign to discredit the Democrats, he deplored McCarthy's tactics and personally loathed the senator. His partisanship and demagoguery offended the president's sense of justice and fair play. Privately, Eisenhower suspected that McCarthy had presidential ambitions and vowed to block his way, but he resisted the entreaties of his brother Milton and others to speak out strongly against the senator's excesses. Eisenhower's reluctance stemmed in part from his philosophy of leadership. He wanted to build consensus and overtly attacking McCarthy would alienate the millions of Americans who apparently supported him. He also believed in the constitutional separation of powers and was wary of impinging on congressional prerogatives. On a practical level, with just a two-seat majority in the Senate, offending the Republican senators who most strongly supported McCarthy might destroy party unity and jeopardize the administration's entire legislative agenda. Finally, Eisenhower believed that McCarthy thrived on publicity, and cracking down against him would both demean the institution of the presidency and immediately transform McCarthy into a martyr. As he told his friends, 'I just won't get into a pissing contest with that skunk' (Ambrose, 1984: 57). Eisenhower preferred to ignore McCarthy and allow him enough rope to hang himself [*Doc.* 2].

In fact, Eisenhower's major disagreement with McCarthy was not so much over the issue of internal security but rather over the most effective means of rooting out the subversive threat to national security. Eisenhower believed that such matters were best handled quietly through appropriate administrative and judicial procedures, not in the court of public opinion or as issues in partisan politics. For his own part, Eisenhower displayed impeccable anti-communist credentials. In his first weeks in office he rejected humanitarian appeals from home and abroad to extend clemency to Julius and Ethel Rosenberg, who had been convicted and sentenced to death in 1951 for conspiring to pass atomic secrets to the Soviet Union. Eisenhower also initiated a more stringent internal security programme which dramatically expanded the criteria that federal agency heads could use to dismiss employees summarily. Like the McCarthyites, he accepted the notion that some federal bureaucracies had indeed been infiltrated by subversives and was wont to conflate liberals and New Dealers with socialists and communists. Secretary of State John Foster Dulles employed a McCarthy friend as his department's security officer and promptly fired over five hundred employees, including several prominent 'China hands' whom McCarthy blamed for the 1949 'loss' of China to the Communists. The administration, moreover, was not above conducting its own forays into red-baiting for political advantage. Attorney General Herbert Brownell scored former President Truman for employing a known communist, Harry Dexter White, as an adviser. These actions, and Eisenhower's refusal to condemn McCarthy publicly, only added credibility to the senator's dire warnings about the domestic communist menace. By January 1954, opinion polls indicated widespread approval for McCarthy and his endeavours.

Eisenhower hoped to draw a clear distinction between his administration's own calm, judicious handling of internal security and the senator's publicity-grabbing witch-hunts during the investigation of allegations against nuclear physicist J. Robert Oppenheimer. In late 1953, Federal Bureau of Investigation (FBI) Director J. Edgar Hoover passed along derogatory information about Oppenheimer, who had headed the Los Alamos National Laboratory during the Manhattan Project in World War II and had served as a consultant on atomic weapons issues ever since. Oppenheimer's association with communists among his friends and family members was already well known to security officers, who had nevertheless cleared him to work on the nuclear weapons programme in the 1940s. The principal new allegations actually reflected a major cleavage within the scientific community over nuclear weapons policy. Fellow physicist Edward Teller and others alleged that Oppenheimer, who had advised against building the hydrogen bomb in 1949 on moral and technical grounds, had hindered timely development of the weapon by influencing other leading scientists not to work on the project. In fact, Eisenhower and AEC Chairman Lewis L. Strauss had already decided to dispense with Oppenheimer's services by quietly freezing him out of his advisory positions. Eisenhower did not share Strauss's suspicions about the scientist's loyalty, but he reportedly 'just didn't feel comfortable with Oppenheimer' because of his 'hypnotic influence over small groups' (Bernstein, 1982: 206–7). The new allegations, however, forced the president's hand. Fearing that McCarthy would pounce on the information to embarrass the president and launch a new witch-hunt against the leading scientists whose cooperation was vital to the nuclear weapons programme, Eisenhower ordered that a 'blank wall' be placed between Oppenheimer and all classified material pending a full administrative review by the AEC. After a lengthy hearing, the AEC ruled that Oppenheimer was loyal but a 'security risk' and withdrew his security clearances permanently. Eisenhower quickly congratulated Strauss for tactfully handling the situation in an orderly and fair manner, but many prominent scientists did not see much distinction between the administration's actions and McCarthyism.

The final break with McCarthy only came when the senator launched an investigation into communist penetration of Eisenhower's beloved Army. After failing to prove charges of a 'radar spy ring' at the Army's Fort Monmouth research facility, McCarthy homed in on the case of Dr Irving Peress. The draftee dentist had refused to answer routine screening questions about past political affiliations but, through an administrative error, had been promoted before being honourably discharged. Early in 1954, McCarthy hauled Peress's commanding officer, General Ralph Zwicker, before his committee and ruthlessly browbeat the decorated war hero. Secretary of the Army Robert T. Stevens then met with McCarthy and several Republican leaders to ensure that future Army witnesses would be treated with dignity, but McCarthy and the press portrayed the meeting as a complete capitulation by the administration to the senator. Eisenhower was furious. He pepped up a distraught Stevens, who had offered to resign, delivered a stirring tribute to Zwicker's patriotism, and insisted that administration witnesses be treated with respect and courtesy. The administration also counter-attacked by releasing a chronology detailing efforts by McCarthy and Cohn to secure preferential treatment for their associate, Schine, who had recently been inducted into the Army. Characteristically, McCarthy retaliated with charges that the Army had held Schine hostage to blackmail the senator into halting his investigation.

Throughout the spring of 1954, several weeks of inconclusive televised hearings into the charges and counter-charges helped to precipitate McCarthy's demise, although ultimately his fellow senators, rather than Eisenhower, dealt the *coup de grace*. During the proceedings, the American people received their first prolonged exposure to McCarthy's undignified badgering of witnesses and diversionary tactics. Opinion polls soon indicated that McCarthy's support was slipping. When McCarthy attempted to expand the inquiry into the actions of White House staffers, Eisenhower boldly asserted the right of 'executive privilege' and ordered his aides not to testify, compounding the senator's frustration. Meanwhile, as the hearings wound down, moderate Republicans worried that McCarthy was alienating independent and liberal voters in the upcoming elections. In July, Republican Senator Ralph Flanders of Vermont finally introduced a censure resolution, which was referred to a special six-member committee chaired by Utah Republican Arthur Watkins. In late December, with the elections safely over, the lame duck Senate voted, 67–22, to censure McCarthy for acting in a manner that brought the Senate into 'dishonor and disrepute'. The Republican contingent split 22–22, with almost all the leadership supporting McCarthy. McCarthy's power was effectively broken. The day after the vote, Eisenhower invited Watkins to the White House to congratulate him.

Eisenhower's quiet strategy for disarming McCarthy ultimately worked, but at a price. Under the administration's stringent loyalty-security programmes, thousands of federal employees, few of whom were security risks, lost their jobs. Many people were smeared with unfounded allegations of disloyalty. Conformity became the test of loyalty. As historian Richard Fried has observed, giving McCarthy enough rope 'enabled him to hang others before hanging himself' (Fried, 1990: 135). McCarthyism, moreover, outlived McCarthy. Even as the Senate debated his fate, Congress approved and Eisenhower signed the stringent 1954 Communist Control Act, declaring the Communist Party 'an agency of a hostile foreign power' and stripping members of their civil liberties. Red-baiting would remain a feature of party politics throughout the 1950s. Only with the gradual easing of Cold War tensions and several Supreme Court decisions affirming individual liberties over national security would the loyalty-security regime be curbed.

CIVIL RIGHTS AND THE *BROWN* DECISION

When Eisenhower became president, there was no more pressing moral issue than the African-American struggle for civil and political rights, yet in this area Eisenhower's philosophy of government and style of leadership proved to be wanting. Although he periodically stated his support for the principle of full equality for all United States citizens, Eisenhower's actions as president emphasized temporization and gradualism. He was reluctant to use the full authority of the federal government to compel southern states to change their discriminatory practices, even after the Supreme Court had spoken. He repeatedly called on black citizens, who had waited for almost a hundred years for enforcement of the Fourteenth and Fifteenth Amendments to the Constitution, to exercise patience and restraint, characterizing the most ardent opponents of racial segregation as extremists. Only in those limited areas where the federal government had undisputed authority did he exercise his executive powers to dismantle racial discrimination. In short, by pursuing a 'middle way' on the issue of civil rights, the Eisenhower administration left a decidedly mixed legacy in race relations.

By the early 1950s, a number of factors had combined to push black civil rights on to the national political agenda and stimulate rising expectations among African Americans for racial melioration. Since the turn of the century, hundreds of thousands of blacks had migrated out of the rural South, where segregation and disfranchisement were enshrined in state and local statutes, in search of economic opportunity. The two world wars, the boll weevil and the increasing mechanization of agriculture exacerbated this trend. In the North, while still enduring discrimination, African Americans nevertheless found a political voice. Increasingly, both Republicans and Democrats competed for their votes, gradually transforming race relations from a regional into a national issue. The ideological crusades against Nazi racism and Soviet totalitarianism further fuelled the struggle for black equality as theories of scientific racism fell into disrepute and African-American leaders demanded that the nation confront the disparity between its democratic ideals and its discriminatory practices. In 1948, President Harry S. Truman secured his surprising re-election in part by cultivating black political support through a civil rights plank in the Democratic Party platform, causing some Southern Democrats to bolt the party. Meanwhile, the National Association for the Advancement of Colored People (NAACP), aided by rising membership rolls and greater black participation in the general postwar prosperity, initiated a series of increasingly effective legal challenges to segregation, particularly in the field of education. Thus, by 1952, civil rights had become a political issue that could no longer be ignored.

Eisenhower, like many leaders of his generation, held generally conservative views on civil rights. Born and raised in a racially-segregated society, and professionalized in a similarly segregated military establishment, he largely accepted the *status quo*. He shared common prejudices against blacks, believed them to be generally inferior soldiers and occasionally swapped 'darky' stories with his close friends and family (Larson, 1968: 126–7). When President Truman ordered the desegregation of the armed forces in 1948, Eisenhower concurred but urged a gradualist approach. As a candidate in 1952, moreover, Eisenhower courted southern white conservative voters. He endorsed 'equality of opportunity for all men' and further desegregation of the armed forces, but emphasized that real progress in race relations could only be achieved by changing long-held attitudes (Burk, 1984: 17). He explicitly rejected the notion of federal compunction, however, arguing that it would promote statism and provoke disorder. Significantly, Eisenhower won backing from several Southern Democratic governors and became only the second Republican presidential candidate to carry Florida, Texas and Virginia since Reconstruction.

As president, Eisenhower moved cautiously on civil rights, confining his speeches to generalities and taking action only where the federal government had clear authority, such as in the armed forces and the District of Columbia. His administration's measures, however, were often designed for symbolic purposes. He eliminated the last segregated military units but did little to address ongoing discriminatory practices regarding postings and promotions. In the nation's capital, concerned at the international embarrassment caused by discrimination against non-white foreign visitors, Eisenhower exerted influence behind the scenes to persuade local business leaders to integrate their restaurants, hotels and movie theatres voluntarily. These quiet initiatives, reinforced by a Supreme Court ruling that barred racial discrimination in the district's restaurants, largely eradicated racially-segregated public accommodations in the nation's capital by late 1953 (Hughes, 1963: 200–1).

Eisenhower was far more reluctant to become involved in the five public school desegregation cases pending before the Supreme Court, known collectively as *Brown vs Board of Education of Topeka, Kansas.* Beginning in the late 1930s, the NAACP's Legal Defense Fund had waged a series of court challenges to racially-segregated schools, aimed at ultimately reversing the 1896 Supreme Court ruling in *Plessy vs Ferguson* that had sanctioned 'separate but equal' educational facilities. In the last days of the Truman administration, the Court heard oral argument on the *Brown* case, and the administration submitted an *amicus curiae*, or friend of the court, brief arguing that segregation was unconstitutional. The justices, however, remained divided on the issue, and in an effort to build consensus on such a momentous constitutional matter, Chief Justice Fred Vinson asked the parties, now including the Eisenhower administration, to re-argue their briefs in 1953, focusing specifically on the applicability of the Fourteenth

Amendment's requirement for equality of the laws for all citizens to the case at hand. Eisenhower, worried about the political consequences for the Republican Party in the South, initially wanted to decline the invitation, but Attorney General Herbert Brownell, a supporter of civil rights, persuaded the president that it was his constitutional duty as an officer of the court to submit a brief. The president relented, but prohibited Brownell from collaborating with the NAACP. In its December 1953 presentation, the Justice Department argued that segregated public schools violated the Fourteenth Amendment and urged a gradual transition to integrated schools, but Eisenhower publicly distanced himself from the brief.

Eisenhower's most important contribution to the eventual *Brown* ruling was unintentional. He appointed Earl Warren as chief justice following Fred Vinson's fatal heart attack in September 1953. The Republican Governor of California had helped to secure Eisenhower's nomination at the 1952 Republican convention, and in return had been promised the first vacancy to occur on the Supreme Court. Eisenhower admired Warren's progressive record as governor, and believed that he would provide the necessary statesmanship to build consensus on the Court. True to form, after re-argument in December, Warren delayed a decision for several months as he crafted unanimity among his colleagues. In the interim, Eisenhower made his own views known to Warren at a White House stag dinner, telling him that white southerners were 'not bad people. All they are concerned about is to see that their little girls are not required to sit in school alongside some big overgrown Negroes' (Warren, 1977: 291). The president's words apparently had no effect. On 17 May 1954, the Supreme Court ruled unanimously that 'in the field of public education, the doctrine of "separate but equal" has no place. Separate educational facilities are inherently unequal.' Segregated education violated the Fourteenth Amendment's provision for equal protection of the laws to all citizens [*Doc.* 3].

The *Brown* ruling greatly troubled Eisenhower. Although the Supreme Court had thrown the full moral weight of the Constitution on the side of integration, he pointedly refused to endorse the decision. Privately, he believed that it was a mistake. He worried that some states would simply close down their publicly-funded school systems and divert resources to 'private' all-white institutions, to the detriment of both blacks and poor whites (Ferrell, 1983: 54). He also believed that forced integration by federal order would provoke a backlash by white segregationists, setting back the cause of racial equality for years. Publicly, he remained noncommittal on the subject, merely promising to uphold his constitutional duty to enforce the law. Yet Eisenhower's silence spoke volumes and undoubtedly encouraged white segregationists to circumvent the Court's ruling.

When the Supreme Court requested further argument before ruling on the implementation of *Brown*, Eisenhower again counselled gradualism. He directly participated in the drafting of the Justice Department brief and personally edited the text to strike language urging immediate integration in favour of a more deliberate process that would allow white southerners time to adjust to the new reality (Mayer, 1986: 67–9; Brownell and Burke, 1993: 196). In marked contrast to his silence on the *Brown* ruling, Eisenhower also lobbied for his gradualist approach at press conferences. The Court's unanimous ruling on *Brown II* in May 1955 closely followed the Justice Department's brief. The justices declared that desegregation should proceed 'with all deliberate speed', but refused to establish a time-table for compliance and required each school district to submit its own desegregation plan to federal district court for approval.

The administration hoped that its 'middle-of-the-road concept of moderation with a degree of firmness' would ensure peaceful progress towards school integration, but the reality proved different (Burk, 1984: 150). As early as 1954, the first white citizens' councils, dedicated to resisting school integration by both legal and extra-legal means, had begun to appear in the Deep South. Initial school desegregation efforts in several border states encountered violent opposition. Early in 1956, the University of Alabama expelled its first black student after white mobs protested against her presence. And in March 1956, almost a hundred southern congressmen and senators from eleven states signed the Southern Manifesto denouncing the Supreme Court's 'unwarranted decision' in the *Brown* case and pledging to employ 'all lawful means' to reverse it [*Doc. 4*].

In all these instances, Eisenhower refused to interfere or endorse the Court's decision, and his silence encouraged further acts of defiance. He was quite right to assert that the federal government could not change people's beliefs and prejudices, but he missed a clear opportunity to exert moral leadership and provide immediate redress. During the 1956 election, he carefully avoided any discussion of civil rights whatsoever. He even vetoed a statement in the 1956 Republican Party platform that credited him with the *Brown* decision, noting that the Supreme Court was not part of his administration. For Eisenhower, civil rights was just not a pressing moral issue.

THE 1956 ELECTION

By 1956, the prospects for Eisenhower's re-election seemed to be good. Despite the ongoing controversy over school desegregation, his personal popularity remained robust. A healthy economy and low inflation, pop-ularly dubbed 'the Eisenhower prosperity', helped, as did a generally successful foreign policy. As the year began, however, there was consider-able speculation about whether the president had the will or the physical ability to run for a second term in office.

Early in his presidency, Eisenhower had confided to close associates his intention of being a one-term president. He had run in 1952, he claimed, to reinvigorate the Republican Party and save the nation from the mess in Washington, but expected to step aside in 1956, barring any unforeseen international crisis. He initially hoped to institutionalize his 'middle-way' philosophy among a younger generation of Republican leaders who could be groomed to succeed him (Griffith, 1984: 117–18). By 1954, however, Eisenhower was becoming increasingly frustrated with the Old Guard leaders who still dominated the congressional party and seemed more determined than the opposition Democrats to obstruct his 'progressive moderate' legislation and his internationalist foreign policy. Eisenhower attributed the Republicans' electoral reversals in that year, when the Democrats narrowly regained control of Congress, to his party's failure to establish its middle-of-the-road credentials; the Old Guard retorted that Eisenhower's abandonment of traditional Republican principles was the determining factor. In reality, the lingering effects of the 1953–54 recession were probably more decisive. Still, while not yet declaring himself a candidate, the president was determined to thwart any move by right-wing, Old Guard Republicans to capture the party's nomination in 1956.

Eisenhower's heart attack in September 1955 added a complicating factor to his thinking about whether to seek re-election. Although the president made a steady recovery, he was incapacitated for several days and only resumed a normal work schedule early the following year. In the interim, he continued to meet individually with Cabinet members and issue instructions, while Vice-President Richard Nixon chaired regular Cabinet and National Security Council meetings. During this prolonged convalescence, Eisenhower again contemplated his political future. Admitting his own failure to develop someone 'on our side within our political ranks who can be elected or run this country', he mulled over several possible presidential candidates, including Nixon, California Senator William F. Knowland, Chief Justice Earl Warren, Deputy Secretary of Defense Robert Anderson and Brownell, before finding a reason to rule out each of them (Ferrell, 1983: 239–46). Gradually, Eisenhower came to the inexorable conclusion that only he commanded the necessary public support and party unity to defeat the Democrats and preserve his legislative accomplishments. He also worried that handing the reins of power over to an inexperienced successor might weaken the nation's international standing. After receiving a clean bill of health, Eisenhower officially announced his candidacy on 29 February 1956.

Eisenhower had rather more difficulty selecting a running mate. Although he had never developed a close personal relationship with Nixon, he admired his loyalty and yeoman efforts on behalf of Republican candidates and considered him 'a darn good young man' (Ambrose, 1987: 377). At the same time, Eisenhower complained that Nixon had not yet matured, remained too partisan, and lacked widespread popular support outside the ranks of Republican regulars. In short, he was not yet presidential material. Late in 1955, Eisenhower mortified Nixon by suggesting that he broaden his administrative experience by taking a Cabinet post. Nixon disagreed with Eisenhower's assertion that this would strengthen his presidential chances in 1960, particularly in light of Eisenhower's questionable health, but he loyally offered to do whatever the president ordered. Eisenhower, however, could never quite bring himself to fire Nixon directly. Instead, he used various intermediaries to hint that Nixon should step down and speculated with his inner circle as to an appropriate replacement. Eisenhower hoped that Robert Anderson, an Eisenhower Democrat from Texas who served as undersecretary of defense, might accept the vice-presidential slot, but Anderson declined. Meanwhile, Nixon quietly accumulated commitments from delegates to the Republican National Convention. Although Eisenhower remained coy about his vice-president, the party convention eventually settled the matter by selecting Nixon with only one dissenting vote.

Compared with the drama surrounding Nixon's renomination, the 1956 presidential election campaign was anti-climactic. The Democrats again nominated Adlai Stevenson for president and chose liberal Tennessee Senator Estes Kefauver as his running mate, a ticket that Eisenhower contemptuously dubbed 'about the sorriest and weakest ... ever' (Griffith, 1984: 173). Confident of victory from the outset, Eisenhower hoped to win decisively, thereby strengthening his ability to reform the Republican Party along moderate lines and exact cooperation from congressional Democrats. His campaign emphasized his administration's solid achievements, primarily peace and prosperity, and blasted congressional Democrats for their narrow partisanship. Meanwhile, Stevenson's criticism of Eisenhower's foreign policy backfired badly when he suggested that the United States should pursue a Soviet proposal to halt nuclear weapons tests as a means of jump-starting disarmament talks. Nixon labelled the Democrat an appeaser. The simultaneous Suez and Hungarian crises on the eve of the election, moreover, merely reinforced many voters' sense that the national security was already in capable hands.

On election day, Eisenhower won his sweeping personal mandate. His almost ten million-vote margin of victory nearly doubled his 1952 plurality. He carried forty-one states, and made further inroads into the formerly solid Democratic South by picking up Louisiana. Despite the president's tremendous popularity, the Republican Party fared less well, dropping two additional seats in the House of Representatives and one in the Senate. Nevertheless, Eisenhower proclaimed his victory a vindication of the principles of Modern Republicanism and vowed to continue his pursuit of the 'middle way' into his next term.

CHAPTER THREE

WAGING PEACE

During the 1952 election campaign, the Republicans excoriated President Truman and the Democrats for their inept handling of the international communist menace. The Republican platform, drafted by John Foster Dulles, denounced the concept of containment as 'negative, futile, and immoral' for condemning 'countless human beings to a despotism and godless terrorism' (Porter and Johnson, 1956: 499). For many conservatives, the failure to pursue victory in Korea epitomized containment's shortcomings. In its stead, the Republicans vowed to pursue a 'policy of boldness' that would 'roll back' the communist tide and 'liberate' the captive peoples of Eastern Europe and Asia from totalitarianism (Dulles, 1952).

Despite the bold campaign rhetoric, Eisenhower's foreign policy views actually had much in common with his predecessor's. Unlike the more strident unilateralists and Asia-firsters in the Republican ranks, he strongly supported the principle of collective security and generally endorsed the strategy of containment. He remained sceptical about the prospects for roll-back and liberation, but echoed the need for a more positive foreign policy and agreed with Dulles's view that 'peace must be waged just as war is waged' (Bowie and Immerman, 1998: 65). Where the Truman administration had most seriously erred, Eisenhower believed, was in its failure to devise a coherent strategic concept that balanced America's international commitments with its limited resources. Eisenhower repeatedly argued that true national security entailed defending 'a way of life' rather than just territory. He therefore set out to devise a strategy of containment that would be sustainable indefinitely. In effect, he sought a 'middle way' between the Fortress America isolationism of the Taft Republicans and the unrestrained globalism that had characterized Truman's policies since 1950.

Eisenhower's efforts to rationalize foreign policy encountered a series of complicating factors. Old Guard members of the Republican Party remained largely unreconciled to containment and multilateralism, and could not be counted on to support military and economic aid packages. Within the administration itself, Eisenhower had difficulty developing consensus for his 'security with solvency' approach to national security policy, particularly among members of the military. The death of Soviet leader Josef Stalin, meanwhile, introduced both new opportunities and uncertainties into Soviet–American relations and the conduct of the Cold War, and the escalating arms race entered a new era of danger with the advent of thermonuclear weapons. Finally, the emergence of powerful nationalist forces in the so-called Third World added immeasurably to Eisenhower's difficulties. Not surprisingly, the administration's record in handling these various challenges over the next four years proved to be rather uneven.

THE NEW LOOK

Eisenhower entered office determined to bring greater coherence to national security policy-making. A firm believer in the importance of sound organizational arrangements and good staff work for decision-makers, he set about reorganizing the national security bureaucracy inherited from Truman in order to achieve a more systematic approach to policy-making. At the same time, alarmed at the long-term impact of high levels of defence spending on the American economy and democratic institutions, Eisenhower revisited Truman's $45 billion military budget request for 1954 and initiated a thoroughgoing review of overall national security policy. Out of these deliberations came the New Look, the strategic concept designed to deliver security with solvency over the long haul. It would form the basis of Eisenhower's national security policy for the remainder of his presidency.

Eisenhower first moved to reorganize the national security establishment. He reinvigorated the National Security Council (NSC), the statutory group of foreign policy advisers to the president established in 1947, which had so far operated with only limited effectiveness. Whereas Truman had rarely presided over its meetings, Eisenhower intended the council to become the principal forum for vigorously debating foreign policy issues and developing consensus behind presidential decisions. To that end, he established a Planning Board, composed of the chief planning officers in each department or agency, to draft policy statements for NSC discussion and presidential approval and to identify 'splits' between agencies requiring resolution. He also set up the Operations Coordinating Board to ensure compliance with NSC decisions. He established the new post of special assistant to the president for national security affairs, with responsibility for managing the NSC staff and following up on NSC actions. In order to encourage his advisers to take a broader view of national security matters, Eisenhower required all new policy proposals to include a budgetary annexe and regularly invited the budget director and chairman of the Council of Economic Advisers, as well as the treasury secretary, to participate in the

NSC's deliberations. Most importantly, Eisenhower usually presided over the regular weekly meetings in person and fostered freewheeling discussion.

Eisenhower's drive to rationalize national security policy-making and achieve economies in the defence budget extended to the Pentagon. He appointed General Motors president Charles E. Wilson as secretary of defense, mainly because of his managerial expertise as head of the nation's largest corporation. Wilson's primary task was to achieve greater efficiency and economy in the world's biggest bureaucracy while Eisenhower drew on his own military experience to handle larger strategic questions. Eisenhower also attempted to strengthen civilian control over the armed services, which had been feuding since the late 1940s over roles and missions and funding levels. He appointed service chiefs whom he hoped would divorce themselves from narrow service viewpoints and take a broader, corporate perspective on national security policy. Admiral Arthur W. Radford, Commander-in-Chief, Pacific, seemed to fit the bill, and became Eisenhower's first chairman of the Joint Chiefs of Staff (JCS), the president's top military advisers. Finally, in mid-1953, the president won congressional approval for a series of administrative reforms designed to strengthen the civilian secretary of defense's authority over the individual services.

Even before the bureaucratic reorganization had been completed, the administration also set out to modify the Truman administration's strategic posture and achieve significant economies in Truman's last defence budget. Eisenhower rejected the alarmist assumptions of National Security Council Paper 68 (NSC–68), the strategic concept adopted by Truman shortly after the outbreak of the Korean War in 1950. According to NSC–68, the Soviet Union was an implacable foe intent on world domination, and would achieve the military capability to risk all-out war in 1954, the 'year of maximum danger'. In order to contain this threat, NSC–68 had advocated a rapid build-up of 'political, economic, and military strength in the free world' (FRUS, 1950: 1.282). This pessimistic analysis, coupled with the Korean War, had propelled defence spending from $13.5 billion in 1950 to $50 billion by 1953, a level that Eisenhower considered unjustified and unsustainable. While acknowledging that the Soviet Union represented a real threat to United States interests, he doubted that Soviet leaders would jeopardize their regime by risking a general war. Rather than a moment of 'maximum danger', Eisenhower believed that the nation faced a prolonged period of international tension. High levels of defence spending, moreover, undermined American economic strength by exacerbating budget deficits, fuelling inflation, increasing the tax burden, and ultimately requiring economic controls that hindered the free enterprise system and accelerated the drift towards statism. In short, failure to balance means and ends in national security policy might result in a 'garrison state' at home, effectively destroying the American way of life rather than preserving it (FRUS, 1952–

54: 2.469). Eisenhower defined the basic problem as achieving 'a reasonable and respectable posture of defense' without 'bankrupting the nation' (FRUS, 1952–54: 2.236–7).

During the early months of 1953, Eisenhower's NSC grappled with this 'great equation', and significant differences surfaced among the president's inner circle. Secretary of the Treasury George Humphrey led the economizers. He viewed a balanced budget as sacrosanct and predicted dire economic consequences, not to mention electoral defeat, if Truman's 1954 budget request, with its projected $9.9 billion deficit, were not slashed immediately. He urged drastic cuts in military and foreign aid programmes. Predictably, Truman's appointees on the outgoing JCS opposed any cuts whatsoever, arguing that existing funding levels were already inadequate to meet global requirements. Wilson and Dulles took the middle ground, recognizing the need for economies, but cautioning that the massive cutbacks in defence and foreign aid programmes required to balance the budget would seriously weaken the free world position against communism.

Eisenhower ultimately decided the question in a manner that prefigured the New Look. In April 1953, he approved an interim statement of national security policy that incorporated the economizers' concerns. It forthrightly stated that 'the survival of the free world' depended on 'the maintenance by the United States of a sound, strong economy' which in turn required balanced budgets and reasonable taxes. But given the current international context, with an ongoing war in Korea and the need to strengthen the free world positions in Europe and Asia, Eisenhower rejected the large cutbacks in spending that would be needed to balance the budget immediately, fearing that it might convey a lack of resolve and embolden communist adventurism. Rather, the administration envisioned moving towards a balanced budget only 'as rapidly as is consistent with continuing our leadership in the free world' (FRUS, 1952–54: 2.307–16). By planning for a 'floating D-Day' instead of a 'year of maximum danger', however, Eisenhower was able to reduce force levels and slow the planned Air Force build-up, achieving economies of some $7.4 billion over Truman's original spending request (PPP, 1953: 238–42). Even so, Old Guard Republicans who wanted immediate tax cuts were far from happy. Taft dismissed Eisenhower's economies as 'puny' and accused him of taking the nation 'down the same road Truman traveled' (Morgan, 1990: 53). Although they were unable to push through tax reductions, congressional Republicans pruned a further $2.5 billion from Eisenhower's national security appropriations. Nevertheless, the battle over the 1954 military budget indicated Eisenhower's determination to balance economic and military strength over the long haul.

Having addressed the immediate question of the next year's fiscal expenditures, Eisenhower initiated a more systematic effort to devise a comprehensive national strategy and forge consensus among his administration. Operation Solarium, conducted in May 1953, evaluated the existing containment policy in comparison with more aggressive options suggested by Secretary Dulles. One option contemplated drawing 'a continuous line around the Soviet bloc beyond which the U.S. will not permit Soviet or satellite military forces to advance without general war'. A second advocated rolling back the Soviet tide to produce 'a climate of victory' that would bolster the West, encourage the liberation of captive peoples, and throw the Soviet bloc into disarray (FRUS, 1952–54: 2.326, 365). Three teams staffed out each of these alternatives and their financial implications. The containment and rollback options envisaged raising annual defence spending to $40 billion and $60 billion respectively, while the deterrence option offered the prospect of economies by de-emphasizing large conventional forces and involvement in peripheral wars in favour of air-atomic power. When the task forces reported their findings to the NSC in mid-July, Eisenhower drove home his point. He warned that increased spending would require 'more and more controls' and that 'the more you do this, the more you lose the individual liberty which you are trying to save and become a garrison state'. He also seemed to rule out the aggressive rollback policy, remarking that the 'only thing worse than losing a global war was winning one'. He then charged the three task forces with producing a 'unified policy' (FRUS, 1952–54: 2.397).

Meanwhile, Eisenhower similarly requested his new JCS appointees to provide a 'fresh view' of the nation's military capabilities in light of its global responsibilities and limited economic resources (Jurika, 1980: 320–1). In August, JCS Chairman Radford presented two major recommendations to the NSC: greater emphasis should be placed on the deterrent power of strategic and tactical nuclear weapons; and 'over-extended' American forces in Europe and Asia should be redeployed back to the United States, where they could bolster continental defences and constitute a mobile reserve in the event of general war. Wherever possible, indigenous troops should replace American forces overseas, while the United States would supply air and naval support. Recognizing the significant savings that would accrue from this capital-intensive strategy, Humphrey called the document 'terrific'. Dulles agreed that America's allies should bear a greater share of the free world defence burden, but worried that redeployment might revive allied fears of an American retreat to isolationism (FRUS, 1952–54: 2.443–55). Eisenhower insisted that American troop deployments overseas had always been a 'temporary expedient', but agreed that any withdrawal would have to be 'very carefully handled'. He then added the JCS concept to the Solarium deliberations (FRUS, 1952–54: 2.455–7).

At the end of October, the administration thrashed out its new national security policy, NSC–162/2, designed to meet the Soviet threat without

'seriously weakening the U.S. economy' or undermining the nation's 'fundamental values and institutions' [*Doc. 5*]. It advocated a capital-intensive
strategy that emphasized the massive retaliatory power of nuclear weapons
to deter general war with the Soviet Union and a readiness to employ such
weapons should deterrence fail. It also reiterated the importance of
collective security, stressing the necessity for overseas air bases and the
importance of the military and economic resources of the major industrialized states to the free world cause. Thus, there could be no major
redeployment of American troops from overseas 'under present conditions'
because these forces signalled America's commitment to its allies and
strengthened the 'cohesion of the coalition' (FRUS, 1952–54: 2.592–3). The
allies might be progressively weened from American aid, however, by
promoting measures to stimulate international trade and encourage global
economic growth and prosperity. Finally, the new strategy urged 'feasible
political, economic, propaganda and covert measures' to create and exploit
problems for the Sino-Soviet bloc (FRUS, 1952–54: 2.595).

The administration began implementing the New Look in its 1955
budget. The end of hostilities in Korea and the new emphasis on air-atomic
power allowed for an immediate $4 billion reduction in estimated military
expenditures to some $37.5 billion. By 1957, moreover, the administration
expected military spending to stabilize at around $33.5 billion annually. The
major savings would be effected by progressive reductions in conventional
forces. The Army would be reduced from twenty-two divisions to fourteen
and have its service and support units depleted, while the Navy would
endure a 125,000 personnel cut and be limited to 1,000 ships. The Air
Force, the major beneficiary of the New Look, would increase from 115 to
137 combat wings, but at a slower pace than earlier conceived. In addition,
Eisenhower requested $5.4 billion for economic and military assistance
programmes. Although congressional conservatives denounced the foreign
aid 'giveaways' and Democrats accused Republicans of putting tax relief
ahead of national security, final congressional action on the 1955 defence
budget provided most of what Eisenhower requested. For the remainder of
his presidency, the New Look's emphasis on 'security with solvency' over the
'long haul' would remain at the core of Eisenhower's grand strategy, but he
would find it increasingly difficult to keep the armed forces, Congress, and
even his own administration in line behind that concept.

NUCLEAR BRINKMANSHIP IN ASIA

Eisenhower delegated the task of articulating the implications of the New
Look strategy to Secretary of State John Foster Dulles. In a January 1954
address to the Council on Foreign Relations, Dulles explained that hence-
forth the United States would deter further communist aggression by

bolstering local defences and developing 'massive retaliatory power'. Under this asymmetrical strategy, potential aggressors would no longer be free 'to pick the time, place, and method of warfare'. Rather – employing a phrase that Eisenhower himself had drafted for the occasion – the United States would develop 'a great capacity to retaliate, instantly, by means and at places of our choosing'. This increased emphasis on nuclear weapons, moreover, would provide 'maximum deterrent at a bearable cost' [*Doc. 6*]. In response to critics who suggested that the Soviet Union and its allies might not view the threat of massive retaliation and general war as credible in some local conflicts, Dulles refined his position to explain that the United States would not necessarily revert to all-out nuclear war to meet every contingency, but would develop 'the flexibility and the facilities which make various responses available'. Local defences might be supplemented by 'more mobile deterrent power', such as tactical nuclear weapons (Dulles, 1954: 358). To make the nuclear deterrent credible, moreover, both Eisenhower and Dulles asserted their resolve to go to war and employ nuclear weapons if necessary. As Dulles later described it, being prepared to go 'to the brink' of war without getting into one was 'the necessary art' (Shepley, 1956: 78). Indeed, Dulles and Eisenhower would later claim that on three separate occasions in Asia – in Korea, Indochina and Taiwan – the administration had resolutely 'walked to the brink' and, by threatening war, faced down communist aggression.

Eisenhower and Dulles first employed the art of nuclear brinkmanship to the most pressing foreign policy issue confronting the administration in 1953, the ongoing war in Korea and the deadlocked armistice talks at Panmunjom. They worried that the war drained American resources and that the failure to achieve a decisive conclusion raised doubts about the credibility of the United States to contain communist aggression, under-mined NATO cohesion, and fostered neutralism among non-aligned countries. Before his inauguration, Eisenhower fulfilled his campaign promise to 'go to Korea' to view the situation firsthand, and he spent much of his first months in office debating policy options for ending the war. Several of the president's military advisers urged expanding the war, using tactical nuclear weapons if necessary, should the stalled armistice talks break down entirely. Dulles emphatically agreed, noting that Soviet propaganda had promoted a 'false distinction' between nuclear and conventional weapons that hamstrung American policy options (FRUS, 1952–54: 15.769 –70). In mid-May, Eisenhower approved contingency plans to expand the war with a new ground offensive up the waist of the peninsula accompanied by tactical nuclear air strikes against Chinese air bases in Manchuria, but he remained deeply concerned about adverse allied reaction to such a scheme and the possibility of Soviet nuclear retaliation against Japanese cities (Eisenhower, 1963: 180).

Eisenhower and Dulles believed that their grim determination to resort to nuclear war ultimately broke the diplomatic impasse and persuaded the Communists to accept an armistice in Korea. In May, during a visit to Indian Prime Minister Jawaharlal Nehru, Dulles warned that if the armistice negotiations in Korea collapsed, the United States might widen the war and hinted at the use of nuclear weapons. Nehru, Dulles believed, would relay this information to Beijing. Meanwhile, the administration conveyed similar messages through Taiwan and United Nations negotiators at Panmunjom. Two weeks later, the Communist side formally relented to the Western demand for the voluntary repatriation of prisoners-of-war, removing the last major obstacle to an armistice. On 27 July 1953 the two sides concluded an agreement (Steuck, 1995: 325–9). 'Danger of an atomic war', Eisenhower later remarked, had finally brought the Communists to their senses (Adams, 1961: 48–9).

In retrospect, it seems clear that Eisenhower and Dulles overestimated the efficacy of their nuclear brinkmanship in Korea. In all probability, their indirect warnings through Nehru and other channels never reached their intended audience. Certainly, the Chinese knew of Eisenhower's campaign statements calling for a more aggressive policy in Korea, but they also believed that their 1950 alliance with the Soviet Union and the latter's own nuclear weapons would deter the United States from a nuclear strike. Rather, sustained high casualties and a general war-weariness in China and North Korea predisposed the Communists to accept a truce by mid-1953. In addition, after Josef Stalin's death in March, the new leaders in the Kremlin, anxious to consolidate their position at home and address the mounting economic and political problems in Eastern Europe, pressed their allies for 'the soonest possible conclusion of the war in Korea' (CWIHP, 1995–96: 6–7.80). Finally, having staved off the forcible reunification of the Korean peninsula, Chinese leader Mao Zedong could portray the armistice agreement as a 'victory' over Western imperialism. Thus, it seems that the Eisenhower administration's veiled nuclear threats were only one of several factors pushing the Communists towards a truce in Korea (Gaddis, 1997: 108–10). That said, the Korean armistice and its provision for voluntary rather than forcible repatriation of POWs represented an important diplomatic accomplishment for the new administration.

The Eisenhower administration's emphasis on massive retaliation and brinkmanship faced a second major test in Indochina, where a crisis had been brewing since 1945. During World War II, the Japanese had occupied the former French colony of Vietnam, but after Japan's defeat in August 1945, Vietnamese Communist leader Ho Chi Minh had proclaimed independence. When the French attempted to reimpose colonial rule, Ho's Viet Minh launched a highly effective insurgency. In 1949, in an attempt to establish a credible nationalist alternative to the Viet Minh, France had extended nominal independence to Vietnam, Cambodia and Laos, and installed a pro-French puppet emperor as 'head of state' in Vietnam. In 1950, after Mao Zedong's victory in the Chinese civil war and his formal recognition of Ho's Democratic Republic of Vietnam, the Truman administration had recognized the State of Vietnam and extended military aid to France to contain the communist contagion in Southeast Asia.

The Eisenhower administration shared its predecessor's assessment of the strategic importance of Vietnam and Indochina to the larger Cold War struggle and envisioned dire consequences should it fall [*Doc. 7*]. Although Eisenhower and Dulles privately expressed contempt for colonialism and urged the French to extend meaningful independence to Indochina, the latter could not be allowed to go communist. Indochina 'was the first in a row of dominoes', and its loss might trigger the fall of Thailand, Burma and even British Malaya, Indonesia and the Philippines to communism (FRUS, 1952–54: 13.1261). The repercussions of such a setback could be far-reaching. Japan, the new bulwark of American containment policy in Asia, would lose access to important sources of raw materials and markets, and might even question the value of the recently-signed American security commitment. The loss of Malayan rubber and tin would hurt Britain's ability to earn the dollars essential for its economic recovery. A French defeat, meanwhile, might jeopardize ongoing efforts to strengthen the Western military alliance by devising an acceptable formula for German rearmament. Finally, any loss of territory to communism in Asia would be politically damaging to the administration. The Republican Party had excoriated Truman for the 'loss' of China in 1949, and the party's Old Guard would not brook further reverses. In effect, the final domino in the sequence might be the White House itself (FRUS, 1952–54: 13.419–20).

The Vietnam crisis came to a head in early 1954, when a large Viet Minh force surrounded the 12,000-man French garrison at Dien Bien Phu, a remote village in northwestern Vietnam that had been used as a staging area for the Viet Minh operations against Laos (Map 1). The French had sought a decisive pitched battle where they could bring their superior fire-power to bear, but Dien Bien Phu was a poor choice of battlefield. Viet Minh forces quickly seized the high ground overlooking the French outpost and, aided by Chinese materiel, gradually tightened the noose. Heavy artillery knocked out the airstrip, and by March Viet Minh troops had overrun the defenders' outer perimeter. As the situation deteriorated, the French sought American air strikes to relieve the beleaguered garrison.

Eisenhower and Dulles responded cautiously to the French overtures. Although French and American military staffers in Saigon had developed a plan for such a contingency, the president's top military advisers disagreed over the efficacy of air strikes. Within the JCS, Chairman Radford and Air Force Chief of Staff Nathan Twining believed that tactical nuclear weapons might turn the tide at Dien Bien Phu, but Army Chief of Staff Matthew Ridgway worried that air strikes would have to be followed up with deployments of American ground troops, possibly as many as seven divisions, and warned that such massive intervention would seriously over-extend existing military capabilities. Eisenhower shared Ridgway's scepti-cism. The New Look strategy, moreover, was supposed to avoid another Korea-type conflict by relying on local forces to bear the brunt of regional defence while the United States supplied air and naval power. Eventually, Eisenhower and Dulles agreed that the United States would only intervene in Indochina as part of a multilateral force.

In late March, Dulles unveiled just such a plan, dubbed United Action. He proposed a regional coalition consisting of the United States, Great Britain, France, Australia, New Zealand, Thailand, the Philippines and the Associated States of Indochina to contain communism throughout South-east Asia. United Action would hopefully stiffen the resolve of the French both on the battlefield and in the upcoming Geneva Conference on Indo-china, and also deter direct Chinese Communist intervention in the area. Should military intervention still be required, however, United Action would ensure the most favourable environment possible for the United States. Multilateral intervention would require the French to surrender a share of decision-making in Indochina to the allies, undermine communist propaganda about a colonial war, and assuage congressional concerns that the United States not intervene alone in another Asian war. The scheme also comported with the New Look doctrine by requiring regional allies to provide the bulk of the manpower while the United States performed a supporting role.

United Action quickly ran into difficulty at home and abroad. Con-gressional leaders refused to contemplate an open-ended authorization of American military intervention in Southeast Asia without prior com-mitments of support from the allies, especially the British, and a French promise to grant full independence to Indochina. The British balked. They worried that multilateral military intervention might actually escalate the conflict by provoking Chinese or Soviet involvement, thereby risking a third world war. They also rejected the dire predictions of the domino theory and preferred to negotiate a compromise peace in Indochina at the scheduled Geneva Conference. Without a British commitment, Australia and New Zealand refused to sign on. Finally, the French insisted that France could not be expected both to give up Indochina and continue the war against the Viet Minh. Although their position softened somewhat as the military situation became more desperate, British opposition to eleventh-hour military intervention remained firm. On 7 May, after fifty-five days of gallant but futile resistance, the remnants of the French garrison at Dien Bien Phu surrendered.

The fall of Dien Bien Phu the day before the opening of the Indochina phase of the Geneva Conference convinced Eisenhower and Dulles that only the continued threat of American or multilateral military intervention would secure an acceptable outcome in the negotiations. Throughout the proceedings, Dulles projected an air of unrelenting hostility towards the Soviets, the Chinese Communists, and the Viet Minh, famously refusing even to shake hands with Chinese Foreign Minister Zhou Enlai or be seated near any of the Communist delegates. For several weeks, he conducted detailed but ultimately fruitless negotiations with the French government about the precise conditions under which American military intervention in Indochina might occur. The administration also signalled that the prospect for United Action was still alive by hosting military staff talks with potential participants. Fearing allied appeasement at Geneva, Eisenhower and Dulles even hoped that the conference might collapse. In mid-June, however, a new socialist government came to power in France determined to reach a settlement in Indochina, and the British drafted a series of compromise agreements, based on a plan worked out in Washington, that would allow for the integration of non-communist governments in Southeast Asia into a regional security system.

The Eisenhower administration's tough stance apparently paid dividends when the 1954 Geneva Accords proved less onerous than originally feared. Neither the Soviets nor the Chinese welcomed the prospect of American intervention and a wider war, and both pressed Ho to make concessions. The Soviets calculated that conciliatory gestures in Indochina might soften French support for the European Defence Community and German rearmament. Ho, also wishing to forestall American intervention that might prolong the independence struggle, accepted terms that he believed would pave the way for the eventual reunification of Vietnam by political means. Under the accords, Cambodia and Laos gained independence, and the Viet Minh agreed to withdraw their forces from those two countries. Vietnam was temporarily divided at the 17th Parallel. The Viet Minh withdrew to the North and the French to the South pending the outcome of national reunification elections to be held in 1956 under an international control commission. In the interim, neither party was to introduce new forces or equipment into the area, allow the establishment of foreign military bases, or join a military alliance. Dulles regretted the loss of North Vietnam to the Communists, but thought the arrangements the best deal possible under the circumstances. Nevertheless, the administration insulated itself from right-wing criticism and preserved its freedom of action by not signing the accords and agreeing only 'not to disturb' them.

After Geneva, Dulles moved quickly to reformulate United Action into a regional collective security system to deter further communist expansion in Southeast Asia. In September, he engineered the Southeast Asia Treaty

Organization (SEATO), or Manila Pact, comprising the United States, France, Great Britain, Australia, New Zealand, Pakistan and the Philippines. The members agreed to consult in the event of common danger. Although the Geneva Accords prohibited the formal participation of Cambodia, Laos and southern Vietnam in SEATO, a separate protocol emphasized that the allies would consider any threat to those areas as a danger to their 'peace and security'. In effect, SEATO established a mechanism for United Action in Southeast Asia and, in violation of the spirit of the Geneva Accords, extended a measure of independence to the 'State of Vietnam'.

At the same time, the Eisenhower administration acted to shore up the non-communist regimes of Southeast Asia and gradually displace French influence. American military advisory groups headed to Laos and Cambodia, and in Vietnam the Eisenhower administration threw its support behind Ngo Dinh Diem. A Catholic in a largely Buddhist society, and a staunch nationalist who had opposed both the French and the Japanese, Diem became Prime Minister in 1954 after securing extensive powers from the emperor. The following year, Diem consolidated his rule. With support from the Army and Central Intelligence Agency operatives, he moved ruthlessly against his political enemies, ousted the emperor in a referendum that elected him president, and proclaimed the creation of the Republic of Vietnam. The French detested Diem's Francophobia and open defiance of the Geneva Accords, but Dulles viewed him as the most effective nationalist leader available. When the French withdrew, the Eisenhower administration stepped up military and economic assistance to Diem and supported his decision to block the scheduled 1956 elections. For Eisenhower and Dulles, Diem became the key to maintaining an independent South Vietnam and holding the line against communism in Southeast Asia. In the short term, they avoided direct American military intervention in Vietnam and prevented any further loss of territory to communism, but, in the words of two students of the entire affair, 'the decision not to intervene militarily may well loom as less important than the political commitments made after the fall of Dien Bien Phu' (Herring and Immerman, 1984: 363).

Even as the Eisenhower administration was concluding the SEATO arrangements, it faced another severe test of its policy of massive retaliation and brinkmanship in East Asia. On 3 September 1954, the People's Republic of China (PRC) commenced a sustained bombardment of the Nationalist-held island chain of Quemoy (Jinmen), two miles from the mainland port of Amoy (Xiamen) (Map 2). Quemoy and some thirty other offshore islands had been retained by Chiang Kai-shek's fleeing Nationalist forces as they abandoned the mainland to the Communists at the end of the Chinese civil war. The islands held no great strategic value for the defence of Taiwan itself, but as long as they remained in Nationalist hands they lent credibility to Chiang's oft-stated promise to return and liberate the mainland. By 1954, Chiang had garrisoned some 70,000 troops on Quemoy and Matsu (Mazu) and used the islands as bases for raids against the mainland and PRC shipping. Indeed, the Chinese civil war effectively continued in these coastal regions.

The shelling of Quemoy caused great concern within the Eisenhower administration because it represented a direct challenge to American credibility and prestige in East Asia. In 1953, partly in response to pressure from the 'China lobby' within the Republican Old Guard, the administration had vowed to 'unleash' Chiang against the PRC and continued to recognize the Nationalists as the legitimate government of China. This support for Chiang, moreover, was part of the administration's larger strategy of applying unrelenting pressure to the PRC in order to hasten the collapse of the regime from within. Eisenhower and Dulles also hoped to drive a wedge between the PRC and its Soviet ally by exploiting mutual suspicions and contradictory priorities between the two communist powers (Mayers, 1986). By attacking Quemoy, however, the PRC deliberately flouted Secretary Dulles's recent warning that a Communist move against the offshore islands might provoke American military action. Thus, for the Eisenhower administration, the credibility of 'massive retaliation' seemed to be on the line (FRUS, 1952–54: 14.545–7).

Eisenhower's advisers were uncertain about Communist intentions towards Quemoy. Although a direct attack on Taiwan did not appear to be imminent, some saw the shelling as a preliminary probe of American resolve in the region. In fact, Chinese sources indicate that Mao had no immediate territorial designs on Quemoy. Rather, his army was preparing for an all-out assault against the Tachens, offshore islands some two hundred miles northwest of Taiwan. Mao's pressure on Quemoy was part of his 'armed propaganda' campaign to draw attention to Nationalist and American provocations in the area and promote his 'Liberate Taiwan' message before world opinion. Mao also hoped to deter the United States from concluding a mutual security treaty with Taiwan, which was rumoured to be under discussion, by indicating that any American commitment to Nationalist-held territory risked all-out war with the PRC. The local military commander actually initiated the bombardment on 3 September to coincide with the expected arrival of a Nationalist supply ship, and possibly also to draw attention away from the impending action against the Tachens.

Unsure of Mao's intentions and concerned about allied and domestic reaction to a firm commitment to defend the offshore islands, Eisenhower determined on a policy of deterrence through uncertainty. The administration would 'keep the Reds guessing' by explicitly stating its commitment to the defence of Taiwan and the nearby Pescadore Islands, but saying nothing about Quemoy, Matsu and other offshore islands (FRUS, 1952–54:

14.982). Dulles believed that Mao would not call the American bluff and risk 'massive retaliation'. As the shelling continued intermittently and Nationalist aircraft raided the mainland, Dulles also negotiated the long-anticipated Mutual Defense Treaty with Chiang, committing the United States to the defence of Taiwan, the Pescadores, and 'such other territories as may be determined by mutual agreement' (Immerman, 1990: 242). Chiang reciprocated by secretly pledging not to launch major operations against the mainland without American approval. At the same time, Dulles also worked behind the scenes at the United Nations to introduce a cease-fire resolution. The UN initiative, Dulles believed, would both placate world opinion and serve the additional purpose of straining the Sino-Soviet alliance. If the USSR blocked the resolution, it would give the lie to its recently-announced 'peace offensive', but if it supported the resolution, it would alienate the PRC. The UN approach floundered when Chiang, anxious to avoid any semblance of *de facto* recognition of Mao's regime, refused to cooperate.

Eisenhower's deterrence through uncertainty failed miserably in the face of Mao's own version of brinkmanship. In November, the PRC responded to news of the impending Mutual Security Treaty by announcing the conviction on espionage charges of several American airmen captured during the Korean War. More seriously, Mao interpreted the treaty's ambiguous territorial provisions to mean that the United States would not defend any of the offshore islands, and he instructed his military commanders to press ahead with the campaign to seize Yijiang island in the Tachens. Still, Mao did not seek war with the United States, and he postponed the invasion for a month in order to avoid a clash with American naval forces conducting manoeuvres in the area. Only on 18 January, after American forces had vacated the environs, did some 10,000 Communist troops overwhelm the Yijiang garrison, inflicting heavy casualties (Chang and He Di, 1993: 1512–14).

Confronted with the failure of deterrence through uncertainty, and concerned both about Nationalist morale and political pressure from the China lobby, Eisenhower decided to 'draw the line' unambiguously in the Taiwan Strait (FRUS, 1955–57: 2.42, 69–82; Eisenhower, 1963: 466). The day after the fall of Yijiang, Dulles informed the Nationalists that the United States would publicly announce its commitment to defend Quemoy and Matsu if Chiang would withdraw from the exposed Tachens. Chiang reluctantly agreed. Meanwhile, the administration solicited congressional support for a resolution authorizing the president to employ American forces for the defence of Taiwan, the Pescadores and 'related positions and territories of that area now in friendly hands'. In late January, with only three dissenting votes in each chamber, Congress gave Eisenhower a blank cheque to act as he saw fit in the region. Significantly, however, the Formosa

(Taiwan) Resolution still made no specific reference to Quemoy and Matsu, which Eisenhower had belatedly decided to omit. Dulles privately reassured an anxious Chiang that the United States remained committed to their defence (FRUS, 1955–57: 2.89, 182–4). Early in February, American naval vessels assisted the Nationalists' evacuation from the Tachens, and days later the islands fell to Communist forces without a shot being fired.

The conclusion of the Tachens campaign ended the PRC's immediate military operations in the Strait, but Mao's unrelenting hostility to any form of negotiated settlement in the region convinced Eisenhower's advisers that the danger was far from over. Mao, like Chiang, adamantly opposed any diplomatic solution that would tacitly recognize the existence of two Chinas, and he rejected all third-party mediation efforts. The 'Liberate Taiwan' propaganda offensive continued unabated, and the PRC pronounced America's Taiwan Resolution a 'war message' and warned that China would fight to defend its interests (FRUS, 1955–57: 2.157). After a visit to Taiwan in March, Dulles became convinced that there was 'at least an even chance' that the United States would have to go to war (FRUS, 1955–57: 2.345–50). Eisenhower's advisers were so certain of Mao's aggressive designs that they interpreted the lack of intelligence concerning Chinese troop deployments opposite the offshore islands to mean that hostilities were imminent! In fact, Mao had no immediate designs on Quemoy, and his army lacked the capability for another amphibious operation so soon after the Tachens campaign. Nevertheless, the Eisenhower administration prepared for the worst. The JCS drafted contingency plans for war with China and top administration officials launched a publicity campaign to prepare domestic and world opinion for the possible use of nuclear weapons. At a news conference on 16 March, Eisenhower remarked that he saw no reason why nuclear weapons 'shouldn't be used exactly as you would use a bullet or anything else' against military targets (PPP, 1955: 332).

While Eisenhower was quite prepared to use nuclear weapons, he hoped that the threat alone would deter further PRC adventurism. He was also acutely aware that brandishing nuclear weapons over the tiny offshore islands caused considerable unease both at home and abroad, and he continued to pursue a diplomatic solution to avert war [*Doc. 8*]. In mid-April, he and Dulles encouraged Chiang to abandon Quemoy and Matsu in return for an American air and naval blockade of the Chinese coastline opposite the Taiwan Strait and the stationing of American nuclear weapons on Taiwan. Chiang was dumbfounded. He accused the United States of reneging on its earlier secret pledge to defend the islands. Even without American support, he insisted, his troops would stand and fight on Quemoy and Matsu. Chiang's rejection of the proposal rescued the Eisenhower administration from potential disaster. A blockade would have amounted to an act of war against the PRC, which would undoubtedly have provoked a military response by Mao and possibly a general war.

The crisis unexpectedly ended a few days later when the Chinese announced their willingness to discuss a peaceful resolution of the conflict in the Taiwan Strait. Dulles quickly followed up by offering direct talks between American and PRC representatives, and the shelling of Quemoy ceased. Having succeeded in bringing the issue of Taiwan to world attention and securing his limited territorial objectives in the Tachens, Mao was ready to ease tension in the region by diplomatic means. He had no desire to provoke a war with the United States, particularly a nuclear one, and the ongoing crisis undermined Chinese efforts to promote peaceful coexistence and Asian solidarity among non-aligned nations. Meanwhile, the Soviet leadership, which was seeking improved relations with the West at this time, also encouraged Beijing to pursue a peaceful resolution. By August, Sino-American talks were underway in Geneva, and the convicted American flyers had been freed.

The Eisenhower administration's handling of the offshore islands crisis was far less efficacious than Dulles and Eisenhower later claimed, and indicated some of the pitfalls of atomic diplomacy and nuclear brinkmanship. The threat of massive retaliation did not deter the PRC from seizing the offshore islands. Mao had no immediate designs on Quemoy, and he was able to take the Tachens as planned. Interestingly, Mao's own brinkmanship backfired when his coercive diplomacy brought about the very mutual security treaty between Taiwan and the United States that he had sought to deter, and which effectively accomplished one of Chiang's major diplomatic objectives. The Eisenhower administration's brandishing of nuclear weapons might have been one of several factors in Mao's decision to ease tension in the region by diplomatic means, but it also led him to initiate China's own atomic bomb programme. Those same threats, moreover, seriously strained relations between the United States and its European allies, most of whom saw no logical reason to risk a global war over tiny islands of little strategic value. The offshore islands crisis dramatically illustrated how quickly events could spin out of control and, given the New Look strategy, bring the world to the brink of nuclear war.

CONTAINING THIRD WORLD NATIONALISM

As the Asian crises demonstrated, the Eisenhower administration entered office at a time of political ferment in the so-called Third World. Eisenhower and Dulles understood that the old European colonial empires were in decline and nationalism was 'on the march'. Between 1946 and 1960, thirty-seven new nations came into existence. But such changes presented the administration with a difficult dilemma. While anxious to retain British and French cooperation in Europe and elsewhere, neither Eisenhower nor Dulles wanted to align the United States with the forces of colonialism and reaction in the newly-emerging nations of Asia, Africa and the Middle East. To frustrate legitimate national aspirations might play into the hands of the Soviets, who sought to exploit 'racial feelings and anti-colonialism' to foment unrest and weaken NATO. In the administration's view, the 'vast manpower' and 'essential raw materials' of these areas were vital to the prosperity and strength of the free world, and their loss to communism might 'decisively' alter the world balance of power (FRUS, 1952–54: 2.587). The problem, then, became one of 'walking a tightrope' between the effort to maintain close relations with traditional allies and convincing Third World peoples that their long-term interests would best be served by aligning themselves with the United States and the free world (FRUS, 1955–57: 16.906). In practice, however, Eisenhower's avowed intention to accommodate 'slower and more orderly' change in developing nations ran up against Cold War perceptions and geopolitics. Eisenhower and Dulles too often conflated reformist nationalism with communism and intervened to preserve the pro-Western *status quo* in a way that frustrated popular movements (Ferrell, 1981: 223–4).

Eisenhower quickly confronted the complexities of Third World nationalism in Iran, where a long-running dispute over control of the oil industry had been brewing since 1951. In that year, the nationalist government of Prime Minister Dr Mohammed Mossadeq, having failed to renegotiate an earlier agreement that had granted the British-owned Anglo-Iranian Oil Company (AIOC) a virtual monopoly over Iran's oil industry, nationalized the company's holdings and offered compensation. The British government, a major shareholder in AIOC, responded by withdrawing technicians, closing down the major refinery at Abadan, and organizing an international embargo of Iranian oil. The boycott devastated the Iranian economy, but hardened Mossadeq's resistance to any re-imposition of colonial control over Iran's natural resources. For the British, however, Iranian actions not only jeopardized an important supply of oil and a major source of revenue, but they also set a dangerous precedent for Western concessions elsewhere. When Shah Mohammed Reza Pahlavi tried to remove Mossadeq in mid-1952 and replace him with a pro-British candidate, riots and demonstrations by nationalists and the Iranian Communist Party forced the monarch to reverse himself. Indeed, Mossadeq exploited his confrontation with the Shah and foreign interests to win greatly enhanced powers from the Iranian parliament. Shortly before Eisenhower's election, Mossadeq broke off diplomatic relations with Britain.

Both Mossadeq and British Prime Minister Winston Churchill hoped that the new American president might resolve the crisis, although by rather different means. Mossadeq urged Eisenhower to extend economic assistance to his embattled nation and break the British embargo by purchasing Iranian oil. The British, meanwhile, highlighted Mossadeq's increasing reliance on the Communists and pressed the administration to support a covert operation to engineer a *coup d'état* against the prime minister by pro-Western forces in the Iranian military. Eisenhower soon decided in favour of the latter. Mossadeq's intransigence in negotiations with the British, his deteriorating relations with the pro-Western Shah, his flirtation with Iranian communists and hints that he might sell oil to the Soviets settled the matter. Mossadeq, it seemed, was leading Iran down the slippery slope to communism and Soviet domination. Although Eisenhower publicly urged Mossadeq to continue negotiations with the British, as early as February he agreed in principle to the British scheme to remove him.

When Mossadeq opened trade negotiations with the Soviets in August, Eisenhower authorized the covert operation planned jointly by the CIA and Britain's Secret Intelligence Service to proceed. American agents cultivated the support of military officers loyal to the Shah and organized street demonstrations against Mossadeq. Although the Shah initially panicked and fled to Italy, several days of riots and street fighting resulted in Mossadeq's surrender, his replacement by a general, and the Shah's triumphant return. The Eisenhower administration quickly extended $45 million in economic aid to the new government.

In the short term, the Anglo-American covert operation seemed to be a remarkable success. With Mossadeq imprisoned and the communists crushed, Iran had apparently been delivered from communism. The new government restored diplomatic relations with Britain and reopened negotiations on the oil dispute. In 1954, Iran agreed to pay AIOC $25 million compensation for the assets seized three years earlier and accepted an American-brokered agreement for a new international consortium to develop its oil industry in which the AIOC and American oil companies each enjoyed a 40 per cent stake. Under the new agreement, the consortium accepted a fifty-fifty profit-sharing arrangement with the Iranian government but effectively controlled the level of production. Covert operations, it seemed, might be an efficient and cost-effective means of securing American interests.

The success of the operation in Iran encouraged the administration to employ similar methods in Guatemala, where the left-leaning, reformist government of President Jacobo Arbenz Guzmán also appeared to jeopardize American interests. A wealthy landowner and former army colonel, Arbenz sought to modernize Guatemala by encouraging economic diversification, allowing workers to organize, expanding the franchise, and enacting land reform. In 1952, the Guatemalan National Assembly unanimously approved his agrarian reform plan, which called for the expropriation and redistribution of uncultivated land on the large estates that accounted for 70 per cent of the nation's arable land. Landowners would be compensated with interest-bearing government bonds in the amount that they had declared the land to be worth for tax purposes. Guatemala's largest landowner and employer, the Boston-based United Fruit Company, immediately objected to the assault on its privileged position in the nation's economy and insisted that the $3 per acre offered in compensation was inadequate. Company officials also began lobbying Washington about the growing communist menace in Guatemala.

United Fruit found a sympathetic audience in the Eisenhower administration, where several members had close ties to the company. Dulles's former law firm had represented United Fruit in earlier dealings with the Guatemalan government, and Assistant Secretary of State for Inter-American Affairs John Moors Cabot was a major stockholder in the company. More importantly, however, top administration officials were convinced that Guatemala was slipping under communist control and endangering United States hegemony in the Western Hemisphere. Although the Guatemalan Communist Party had only several thousand members and communists held no major cabinet positions, Arbenz's critics noted that his majority coalition in the National Assembly included four communists and that communists played important roles in the government's land and labour reform programmes. Even Arbenz, himself, fell under suspicion. Cabot accused him of 'openly playing the Communist game', and the American Ambassador reported to Dulles that the Guatemalan president 'thought like a Communist, talked like a Communist, and if not actually one, would do until one came along' (Eisenhower, 1963: 422). In mid-1953, Eisenhower decided that Arbenz had to go.

The Eisenhower administration employed a two-part strategy of covert action and diplomacy against Arbenz. First, following on the heels of the successful coup against Mossadeq in Iran, the CIA initiated preparations for a similar operation in Guatemala. The plan entailed training and arming a small invasion force of Guatemalan exiles in neighbouring Honduras, led by Colonel Carlos Castillo Armas, who had been exiled following an unsuccessful coup in 1950. The CIA also set up a radio station to broadcast anti-Arbenz propaganda and publicize the impending military action. The goal of the exercise was to pressure the Guatemalan army into joining forces with conservative landowners and Church leaders and forcing Arbenz to resign. Secondly, the administration worked assiduously to isolate Arbenz diplomatically, pressuring its European allies to join the boycott of economic and military assistance to Guatemala and seeking to rally support for collective action against the communist threat to the hemisphere through the Organization of American States (OAS).

The diplomatic offensive against Arbenz, spearheaded by Dulles himself at the March 1954 meeting of the OAS in Caracas, Venezuela, achieved only a qualified success. Despite an intense propaganda offensive throughout the hemisphere by the United States, few Latin American governments shared the fear of a communist menace in Guatemala. At the OAS forum, Latin American delegates actually displayed 'more fear of U.S. interventionism than of Guatemalan communism' (FRUS, 1952–54: 4.1148). While the conference overwhelmingly approved Dulles's resolution declaring communist domination or control of any American state a threat to the entire hemisphere, it stopped short of endorsing unilateral or collective intervention in such cases. Guatemala cast the sole dissenting vote. The Eisenhower administration came away from Caracas sceptical about the utility of the OAS as an anti-communist bulwark in the Western Hemisphere, but many of Arbenz's supporters now worried about Guatemala's diplomatic isolation and the wisdom of maintaining such a defiantly anti-United States stance.

As the United States stepped up the psychological pressure, Arbenz became increasingly desperate. Unable to obtain weapons from the United States or Western Europe, he purchased Czech materiel, apparently with the intention of arming a militia against the anticipated invasion. The Eisenhower administration portrayed the weapons shipment as further proof of Guatemala's plan to foment communist revolution in the region, extended military assistance to neighbouring Honduras and Nicaragua, and, over British objections, initiated an illegal blockade of Guatemalan ports. On 18 June, Castillo Armas's force of 150 men 'invaded' and CIA pilots bombed the capital. Arbenz made a last-ditch appeal to the United Nations Security Council for help. Britain and France appeared willing to hear Guatemala's case and consider a cease-fire resolution, but Dulles bluntly warned them that failure to follow the American lead would free the United States to pursue 'an independent line concerning such matters as Egypt and North Africa' (FRUS, 1952–54: 4.118–85; Ferrell, 1983: 74–5). The Council eventually voted 5–4 to exclude Guatemala from its agenda, with Britain and France abstaining. Meanwhile, the psychological offensive worked. The Guatemalan Army refused to fight and called on Arbenz to resign. The hapless president fled into exile, and Castillo Armas emerged as the new president.

The administration depicted events in Guatemala as 'the biggest success in the last five years against Communism' (Immerman, 1982: 179). Although the CIA's role obviously remained secret, Eisenhower was delighted with the agency's success and became further convinced of the efficacy of covert operations. Within Guatemala, meanwhile, Castillo Armas oversaw a counter-revolution that outlawed the Communist Party, reversed the recent reforms, and restored lands to their previous owners, including United Fruit. Elsewhere in Latin America, student and labour groups organized protests against Arbenz's overthrow, and several governments issued condemnations of United States aggression. The State Department concluded that the United States had lost a measure of prestige and good will throughout the region. What mattered most to the Eisenhower administration, however, was that 'the evil purpose of the Kremlin to destroy an inter-American system' had been defeated (Smith, 1994: 87). In 1955, Castillo Armas received a hero's welcome in the United States and several honorary degrees for his contributions to the cause of 'freedom'. Under Eisenhower, containing communism took precedence over progressive reform and economic development in Latin America.

THE SUEZ CRISIS

The British and French soon became disabused of the notion that deference to the United States in Central America would be reciprocated by the Eisenhower administration in the Middle East, where Egyptian president Gamal Abdel Nasser stoked the fires of radical Arab nationalism and political turmoil seemed to invite Soviet intervention. After overthrowing the corrupt, pro-Western monarchy in 1952, Nasser had embarked on an ambitious programme to remove the vestiges of imperialism, modernize Egypt, and assert his leadership over the Arab world. Eisenhower and Dulles had already concluded that Anglo-French decline in the region was irreversible and that the United States would have to assume greater responsibility for maintaining order in an area that held two-thirds of the world's known oil reserves and supplied two-thirds of Western Europe's oil requirements. They therefore urged their Western allies to accommodate progressive change in the region in an effort to overcome the bitter legacy of colonialism, promote peace and prosperity, and forestall the expansion of Soviet influence.

The Eisenhower administration initially tried to steer Nasser's nationalism into acceptable channels, but gradually came to view him as a 'complete stumbling block' to stability and Western interests in the region (Ferrell, 1981: 319). In 1954, under American pressure, the British reluctantly agreed to Nasser's demand to abandon their military bases around the Suez Canal, the traditional lifeline of the British Empire. The following year, the United States sponsored the Baghdad Pact, a military alliance between Britain, Turkey, Iran, Iraq and Pakistan, intended to deter the Soviets from moving into the power vacuum created by the British departure. The Americans hoped that Nasser might eventually join the pact, but he denounced it as a Western imperialist scheme and extended support to anti-colonial movements throughout the region. Secret Anglo-American diplomacy to secure a comprehensive Arab–Israeli peace similarly ran afoul of Nasser's pan-Arabist ambitions and hostility to Israel. When the West refused to assist Nasser's arms build-up following the February 1955 Israeli attack on Gaza, he struck a deal with Czechoslovakia to supply Soviet weapons (Map 3).

The Czech arms deal stung Eisenhower and Dulles, who still hoped to woo Nasser into the Western camp with economic aid. In late 1955, the United States and Britain offered a $400 million package of grants and loans for Nasser's massive Aswan Dam project, which would provide irrigation and flood control for the Nile valley and supply half of Egypt's electrical power needs. Nasser stalled over the terms of the loan, fearing continued Western interference in the Egyptian economy. Meanwhile, congressional leaders in the United States also expressed strong reservations. Southerners questioned the wisdom of indirectly subsidizing Egyptian cotton that would compete with the American crop, anti-communists objected to extending aid to such an independent-minded neutralist, and the pro-Israel lobby opposed any aid to a leader bent on Israel's destruction. By March 1956, the administration decided to use economic aid as a stick rather than a carrot. By withholding economic aid already approved, stepping up aid to pro-Western Arab regimes in the region and delaying further negotiations over the Aswan Dam, Dulles would 'let Colonel Nasser realize that he cannot cooperate as he is doing with the Soviet Union and at the same time enjoy most-favored-nation treatment from the United States' (Mayers and Melanson, 1987: 213). In May, Nasser applied pressure of his own by defiantly recognizing the People's Republic of China. When Dulles withdrew the aid package, Nasser nationalized the Anglo-French Suez Canal Company and announced that he would use the revenues to finance the Aswan Dam project.

Nasser's action provoked a sharp split between the Western allies. Britain and France immediately contemplated military intervention to recover their property and topple Nasser. British Prime Minister Anthony Eden equated Nasser with Hitler and Mussolini, arguing that he should no longer be appeased. Such a dangerous and unreliable character could not be allowed to jeopardize the major supply route for Western European oil from the Middle East. The French also hoped to strike a blow against Nasser for his support of the rebellion in their Algerian colony. Eisenhower and Dulles deplored Nasser's seizure, but they preferred to step up the economic and diplomatic pressure on him to provide adequate compensation. Military intervention, they warned, would be counter-productive. It would inflame Arab nationalism against Western interests throughout the region, open the door for the expansion of Soviet influence, and possibly lead to the canal's closure and disruption of oil supplies from the Middle East. Thus, Eisenhower simultaneously pursued a diplomatic solution with Egypt to internationalize control of the canal and urged restraint on the Anglo-French.

In late October, without informing the Americans, the British and French hatched a plot with Israel to recover the canal and bring down

Nasser. On 29 October, Israel attacked Egypt in the Sinai peninsula and advanced on the canal. The following day, an Anglo-French ultimatum warned the belligerents to withdraw their forces from the Canal Zone. When Nasser predictably refused, Anglo-French aircraft began bombing Egyptian bases and an invasion fleet moved towards Port Said, ostensibly to ensure that the canal remained open. Before the invasion force could land, Nasser blocked the canal by scuttling dozens of ships and Syrian forces cut the oil pipeline from Iraq to the Mediterranean. Now faced with the prospect of an oil shortage and a financial panic, and suffering defections in his own government, Eden accepted a United Nations cease-fire resolution on 6 November, the day of Eisenhower's overwhelming re-election in the United States.

Eisenhower was furious, and incredulous, at the Anglo-French military adventure, and threw the full weight of the United States behind United Nations efforts to impose a cease-fire. The Anglo-French actions offended Eisenhower's anti-colonial sensibilities, but he was also driven by Cold War considerations. The Suez crisis diverted world attention from the Soviet Union's brutal crushing of the Hungarian reform movement and undermined what should have been a major propaganda coup for the West. The United States also had to distance itself from Anglo-French colonialism in order to prevent the newly-independent nations and the Arab world from aligning with the Soviet Union [*Doc. 10*]. By taking the lead in drafting UN resolutions, moreover, the United States forestalled even more critical resolutions from being passed. After the cease-fire went into effect, Eisenhower kept up the pressure on the British, French and Israelis to secure a swift withdrawal. He blocked financial aid to stabilize the pound and delayed implementation of a plan to offset oil shortages in Western Europe by stepping up production in the Western Hemisphere. In December, Anglo-French forces finally withdrew from Egypt, and the Israelis followed suit in March 1957.

Eisenhower's handling of the Suez affair temporarily bolstered American standing in the Arab world, but failed to contain Nasserism. Although Egypt suffered a humiliating military defeat, Nasser won a political victory by standing up to Western imperialism and hanging on to power. He became a heroic figure for Arabs throughout the region. As the Western allies had feared, the Soviets soon expanded their influence in the Arab world. A well-timed warning to Britain and France that they risked attack by Soviet rockets unless they withdrew from Egypt won widespread Arab approval, and the Soviets stepped in to finance the Aswan Dam. Israel, meanwhile, benefited from its military victories by ending the Egyptian blockade of Eilat. As for Britain and France, they drew quite different lessons from the crisis. Prime Minister Harold Macmillan, who replaced the ailing Eden in January 1957, recognized Britain's dependence on American economic support and worked assiduously to repair the 'special relationship'. The French, already upset over American handling of Indochina, came to the conclusion that the United States could not be trusted to support vital French interests.

THE EUROPEAN SETTLEMENT

By 1953, Europe was divided into Western and Soviet spheres of influence (Map 4). At its heart lay a divided Germany and, as historian Marc Trachtenberg has recently argued, 'the problem of German power lay at the heart of the Cold War' (Trachtenberg, 1999: vii). Neither the United States nor the Soviet Union – nor the Germans for that matter – was willing to contemplate German reunification on the other's terms. Since the Korean War, American military planners had concluded that some form of West German rearmament would be essential for Western European security, and thus reunification would only be acceptable if the new Germany aligned squarely with the West. On the Soviet side, although Josef Stalin suggested the possibility of German reunification and neutralization in 1952, in reality he had no intention of abandoning his socialist protégé, Walter Ulbricht, and the German Democratic Republic (GDR) in the East. But Stalin's death in March 1953, the accelerating pace of the nuclear arms race and growing sentiment in favour of negotiations between East and West seemed to hold out prospects for an easing of tensions and some sort of diplomatic settlement. Eisenhower tried to exploit these developments through a series of well-publicized initiatives, but resistance to arms control measures in his own administration, alliance politics and continued mistrust between East and West conspired against any dramatic breakthroughs in the Cold War.

Even as the Eisenhower administration fashioned its New Look concept, news of Stalin's death and noises from the new collective Kremlin leadership about 'peaceful coexistence' prompted Eisenhower to seek an opening to Moscow. His instincts suggested that the time was right to 'do something' to break the Cold War deadlock, but his closest advisers, such as Dulles, remained highly sceptical of Soviet intentions (Hughes, 1963: 104–6). The result was a major speech in April, 'The Chance for Peace', that fell rather short of Eisenhower's original intentions [*Doc. 9*]. The president eloquently lamented the human cost of the Cold War and the arms race. Humankind, he warned, was being sacrificed upon a 'cross of iron'. But Eisenhower offered no real basis for ending the nightmare. Reflecting his advisers' preference for waging psychological warfare and scoring propaganda points, he called on the Kremlin to 'help turn the tide of history' by undertaking concrete steps to end the Cold War. Specifically, he suggested an Austrian peace treaty, an armistice in Korea, free elections and reunification of Germany, the liberation of Eastern Europe and verifiable arms control agreements. In short, complete Soviet capitulation to Western demands represented the only 'chance for peace'. A bellicose speech by Dulles two days later and Eisenhower's refusal to countenance Churchill's calls for an early summit meeting with the new Soviet leadership dashed any hopes for a *détente* in the immediate post-Stalin era.

The Eisenhower administration soon developed a consensus that the Soviet 'peace offensive' was nothing more than a cynical tactic to undermine West European unity and any strengthening of NATO through West German rearmament. Both Eisenhower and Dulles strongly supported Western European integration, with the ultimate objective of creating a 'third great power bloc' that would be strong enough to mount its own defence without American assistance (FRUS, 1955–57: 19.150–1). To that end, the administration promoted the Pleven Plan for rearming the Federal Republic of Germany (FRG) and integrating its forces into a supranational European Defence Community (EDC) under NATO command. The EDC would be a desirable step towards the larger goal of full European economic and political integration, and only an integrated Europe could contain both Soviet and German power and eventually allow for the withdrawal of American troops from the continent. Although the EDC agreements had been signed in 1952, however, lingering French anxiety about German rearmament and the level of Anglo-American commitment to French security had prevented a ratification vote. Thus, until the EDC had been finalized and German rearmament achieved, Dulles believed, the Soviet 'peace offensive' had to be deflected.

Mounting international concern about the escalating nuclear arms race also troubled Eisenhower. Indeed, even as his administration increased American reliance on nuclear weapons and oversaw the introduction of thermonuclear weapons into the stockpile, Eisenhower privately worried that the world was 'racing towards catastrophe' (Ferrell, 1981: 262). He groped for a way to break the log-jam in nuclear disarmament talks and reduce the danger of nuclear war, and also convince world opinion that the United States desired peace. In September 1953, a month after the Soviet Union's detonation of a thermonuclear device, Eisenhower hit upon an idea to get the disarmament talks moving and 'bring some hope to replace fear in the world' (Chandler and Galambos, 1996: 15.760). Given the dim prospects for a comprehensive arms control agreement, the president suggested more limited steps that might build a degree of mutual trust and pave the way for more consequential measures later. At the United Nations General Assembly in December, Eisenhower called on the nuclear powers to join the United States in donating a set amount of fissionable material from their weapons stockpiles to peaceful purposes under UN auspices. 'Atoms for Peace', as it became known, received a warm reception at the UN, and again scored propaganda points for the United States, but failed to elicit a positive response from the Soviets. They recognized, as Eisenhower knew all along, that the scheme would actually prolong American nuclear superiority by diverting fissionable material from the much smaller Soviet stockpile (FRUS, 1952–54: 2.1213). More obviously, the plan neither limited the use of nuclear weapons nor halted the arms race.

Eisenhower briefly considered more substantial measures to limit the nuclear arms race in March 1954, after the unexpectedly high yield of the Atomic Energy Commission's (AEC) thermonuclear test in the Pacific generated adverse public reaction. The fifteen megaton blast obliterated Eniwetok atoll and spread deadly radioactive fallout hundreds of miles downwind, contaminating dozens of Marshall Islanders and the crew of a Japanese fishing boat. World opinion was stunned and angered. For a few weeks, Eisenhower confidentially explored the prospect of a nuclear test moratorium, but stiff resistance from the Pentagon and AEC led him to drop the notion. Even Dulles, however, recognized that the United States could not continue developing bigger bombs 'without any regard to the impact of these developments on world opinion' (FRUS, 1952–54: 2.1428). Like Eisenhower, the foremost spokesman for 'massive retaliation' was rapidly coming to the conclusion that a general nuclear war would be so destructive as to be unthinkable. Still, the administration deflected Churchill's renewed calls for a summit meeting with the Soviet leaders to alleviate international tensions and 'lift this nuclear monster from our world' until German rearmament had been finalized (Boyle, 1990: 124).

The German question dramatically came to a head in August 1954 when, despite intense pressure from the United States, the French National Assembly decisively rejected the EDC treaty. Dulles was momentarily distraught, and worried that further delaying the restoration of German sovereignty would undermine the pro-Western government of Chancellor Konrad Adenauer. The British, who had foreseen such an eventuality and had always been cool towards the European concept anyway, quickly suggested that Germany simply become a member of NATO, subject to certain restrictions. Reluctantly, the Eisenhower administration now followed the British lead. The Paris Accords of October 1954 provided for the restoration of West German sovereignty and the creation of a national army fully integrated into the NATO structure. The Federal Republic of Germany undertook not to develop atomic, bacteriological or chemical weapons, and the Western powers retained the right to station military forces on German territory. Adenauer also promised that Germany would never use force to achieve reunification and the Western powers reserved the right to veto any all-German settlement. The Paris Accords successfully reconciled French security concerns with German sovereignty and rearmament. They also met Adenauer's insistence that the FRG be tied to the West in order to safeguard the development of German democracy, even at the expense of postponing unification indefinitely. In May 1955, the Federal Republic of Germany formally entered NATO; the Soviet Union responded by creating the Warsaw Pact. After years of delay over the EDC, German rearmament within NATO was finalized within a matter of months.

The resolution of West German rearmament and the Soviet Union's surprise accession to an Austrian peace treaty and neutralization in 1955 made it increasingly difficult for Eisenhower to resist European demands for a summit conference with the Soviet Union. Churchill had pressed for just such a meeting since 1953, and his successor, Anthony Eden, had campaigned on the theme in the 1955 British election. Now, the French and Germans joined the chorus. The Soviets, moreover, seemed to have met the essential preconditions laid down by Eisenhower in his 'Chance for Peace' speech; the Korean War had ended, the Soviets now appeared willing to discuss comprehensive disarmament and verification measures at the United Nations, and an Austrian peace treaty had been signed. Doubtful about the prospects for any significant agreements, and cautioned by Dulles to avoid a communist trap, Eisenhower nevertheless consented to a summit meeting at Geneva in July.

The Geneva Summit achieved nothing of substance, but that in itself represented a triumph for American strategy. Eisenhower and Dulles worried that the allies might accept a flawed agreement merely for the sake of easing Cold War anxieties. They therefore worked to prevent any agreement on German reunification or European security that might undo the recent NATO arrangements and sought 'every opportunity to weaken or break the Soviet grip' on Eastern Europe (FRUS, 1955–57: 5.292–6). At the same time, Eisenhower hoped to follow up on recent Soviet disarmament overtures to determine how far they were willing to go on the matter of verification. As he saw it, the summit's primary value would be to 'create a new spirit' in international affairs that might ease tensions and make possible future agreements (Eisenhower, 1963: 515). At Geneva, the president castigated Soviet behaviour in Eastern Europe and insisted that German reunification could only occur on the basis of free elections and Germany remaining within NATO. The most dramatic moment occurred on 21 July, when Eisenhower introduced the 'Open Skies' concept developed by a team of academics working under Nelson A. Rockefeller, the president's special assistant for Cold War strategy. He proposed that the United States and Soviet Union exchange blueprints of military installations and permit mutual aerial surveillance. As with 'Atoms for Peace', 'Open Skies' would redound to the advantage of the West by penetrating the Iron Curtain. Britain and France signed on to the initiative, but Soviet Communist Party Secretary Nikita Khrushchev quickly rejected it as 'a bald espionage plot' (Eisenhower, 1963: 521). As intended, Geneva produced no agreements, but Eisenhower welcomed the more cordial atmosphere in superpower relations generated by the talks. Informal conversations between American and Soviet leaders developed a better appreciation that neither side considered nuclear war a viable policy option (Gaddis, 1997: 229).

The American reluctance to pursue diplomatic agreements at Geneva derived in part from the administration's conviction that the Soviet Union was on the defensive in the Cold War and might soon be pushed towards complete capitulation. Plagued by economic problems, the Soviets had failed to block West German rearmament and incorporation into NATO, had meekly accepted the Western position on Austria, and had been upstaged as peacemakers at Geneva by 'Open Skies'. The administration therefore sought to keep up the psychological pressure by adopting a hard line in subsequent talks at the Council of Foreign Ministers and using radio broadcasts to encourage 'captive peoples' in Eastern Europe to seek 'liberation' from the Soviet yolk. Khrushchev's secret February 1956 speech to the Twentieth Party Congress of the Soviet Union reinforced the impression that the Soviet empire was in disarray. Khrushchev acknowledged socialism's failures and denounced Stalin's crimes, repudiated the Marxist-Leninist doctrine of inevitable conflict between socialism and capitalism in favour of 'peaceful coexistence', and accepted the need for diversity among local communist parties. The Eisenhower administration obtained a copy of the speech and released it to the *New York Times* in June.

For a few months it seemed as if the administration's policy of 'liberation by peaceful means' might bear fruit. Khrushchev's de-Stalinization programme, abolition of the Cominform and acceptance of national variants of communism unleashed centrifugal forces in Eastern Europe. In June, riots erupted in Poland, eventually resulting in the installation of a reformist communist leader. Khrushchev initially tried to block the reforms, but relented when the Poles reassured him that Poland would remain within the Soviet bloc. In October, a popular insurrection in neighbouring Hungary brought another communist reformer, Imre Nagy, to power. As the Budapest movement took on an increasingly anti-Soviet tone, the Eisenhower administration tried to forestall a violent Soviet reaction by signalling that the United States had no intention of incorporating Hungary into the Western alliance. When Nagy precipitously announced Hungary's withdrawal from the Warsaw Pact, however, Khrushchev exploited the West's preoccupation with the Suez crisis to crush the rebellion. Over 20,000 Hungarians and 3,000 Russians perished; Nagy was arrested and later executed. Plaintive Hungarian appeals for Western help went unanswered.

The Hungarian crisis exposed the hollowness of 'peaceful liberation'. The Eisenhower administration was quite willing to wage psychological warfare through propaganda and covert actions, but the United States lacked the military means or the will to achieve liberation in Hungary by force of arms. Overt intervention would almost certainly have precipitated a general war with the Soviet Union. The president thus vetoed last-minute CIA plans to airlift arms to the insurgents on the grounds that such action would merely postpone the inevitable. Instead, the United States condemned Soviet aggression at the United Nations, circulated newsreels of the violent repression, and extended aid to the refugees. Unfortunately, most Hungarians failed to appreciate that the administration's reckless rhetoric about liberation was essentially a political fop to the Republican Party base and a ploy to secure the votes of Americans of East European origin. Eisenhower would not risk a global war to detach a satellite state from the Soviet bloc.

Eisenhower's major foreign policy achievements during his first term were to fashion the New Look strategic concept that put national security policy on a sustainable basis and to prevent a variety of international crises from erupting into all-out war. A combination of nuclear threats, covert actions, diplomatic skill and good fortune kept the peace. In Europe, West German rearmament was finally achieved. But, by 1956, the Cold War seemed to be as dangerous as ever. If anything, the failure to relax Cold War tensions, the Suez crisis and the Hungarian uprising convinced Americans that they needed Eisenhower's experienced hand on the national tiller more than ever. While his international achievements were hardly an unalloyed success, his calm, reassuring leadership was precisely what the nation wanted and no doubt contributed to his overwhelming re-election in 1956.

CHAPTER FOUR

HOLDING THE LINE

Eisenhower's overwhelming re-election in 1956 represented a resounding vote of confidence in his leadership. The Eisenhower prosperity, rising expectations about the 'Geneva spirit' in superpower relations, and Eisenhower's sure handling of the Suez and Hungarian crises propelled the president's approval ratings to unprecedented heights. Yet, as one pair of observers has noted, this high point of his personal popularity proved to be 'a pinnacle rather than a plateau' (Pach and Richardson, 1991: 136). Eisenhower's coat-tails were non-existent in the 1956 elections. The Democrats picked up one seat in the Senate and two in the House of Representatives to solidify their congressional majority. Within a year, a series of domestic and international crises dealt the Eisenhower administration serious blows from which it was never quite able to recover. The Eisenhower prosperity slipped into the Eisenhower recession; white defiance of school integration forced the president's hand at Little Rock, Arkansas; the Soviet Union destroyed Americans' faith in their technological superiority by launching Sputnik, the first artificial earth satellite; and the Republican Party suffered dramatic reversals in the midterm elections. Under pressure from an ever more assertive Congress, Eisenhower reluctantly approved a significant expansion and reorganization of the national security state, even as he began to shift from the middle of the road to the right in order to hold the line against the increasingly ambitious designs of his critics.

THE BATTLE OF THE BUDGET

Eisenhower suffered a serious personal defeat in his battle with Congress over the 1958 budget. In January 1957, the president submitted a $71.8 billion spending plan, the highest peacetime budget ever. Even with expected revenues of $73.6 billion, Eisenhower found himself in the unusual and uncomfortable position of defending his budget from economizing efforts by normally spendthrift congressional Democrats. The whole episode turned into a major embarrassment for the administration and seemed to indicate poor planning and leadership on the president's part.

Relentless upward pressure on spending derived from several sources, but the single largest culprit was defence. Despite the New Look's reduction of conventional forces and an emphasis on strategic weapons, continental defence and a mobile reserve, Eisenhower could not hold military spending to the $34 billion annually anticipated in 1953. Inflationary pressures and faster than anticipated deliveries pushed expenditures above $38 billion by 1957, and even then the services pressed for additional funds to develop the first generation of strategic missiles. Air power advocates in Congress, such as Democratic Senator Stuart Symington of Missouri, warned that the United States was falling behind in the strategic arms race and pressed for additional B-52 bombers and accelerated missile development. Eisenhower's budget request also included expanded foreign aid programmes designed to promote development and contain Soviet economic penetration of the Third World. Finally, domestic spending, mostly on the new farm programmes enacted the previous year, rose modestly. To some observers, Eisenhower's huge 1958 budget seemed to be a first instalment on his much-anticipated Modern Republicanism.

In fact, both Eisenhower and Humphrey were deeply disturbed over the long-term trends evidenced in the budget request, but their clumsy efforts to convey their views to the public created the impression of an administration in disarray. They were especially worried by numerous budgetary built-ins that, even without additional spending programmes from the Democratic-controlled Congress, would entail ever greater expenditures for the remainder of Eisenhower's presidency. Such spending increases would further fuel the inflationary pressures already evident in the economy and force indefinite postponement of the Republicans' long-promised tax cut for business. They therefore attempted to signal their determination to hold the line against any additional spending increases from Congress and pressure the Democrats to be more frugal. In early January, Humphrey released a statement, edited by Eisenhower, warning against the twin dangers of high tax rates and inflationary federal spending, and calling on the administration and the Congress to find additional economies in the 1958 budget that would facilitate a tax cut the following year. In extemporaneous remarks accompanying the document's release, however, Humphrey warned that the long-term result of failing to economize and reduce taxes would be 'a depression that will curl your hair' (Howard, 1965: 254). The press immediately interpreted Humphrey's remarks as a repudiation of the president's budget. Eisenhower's own comments compounded the problem when he endorsed Humphrey's analysis in full and suggested that if congressmen could find places to cut the budget it was 'their duty to do it' (PPP, 1957: 19–21).

Eisenhower's political blunder allowed economizers in Congress to declare open season on the administration's budget. Conservative Republicans, who had never reconciled themselves to Eisenhower's Modern Republicanism and blamed their party's congressional reverses on Eisenhower's abandonment of the traditional Republican commitment to reducing spending, balancing the budget, lowering the national debt and cutting taxes, now followed up on Eisenhower's admonition and demanded spending cuts of several billion dollars. Business groups, anxious to achieve a corporate tax cut, pressed for even greater economies. In this climate, Eisenhower's $3.8 billion foreign aid request became particularly vulnerable. What Eisenhower viewed as a wise long-term investment to contain communism was denounced by conservatives on both sides of the aisle as an expensive foreign 'give-away'. The Democrats capitalized on the president's discomfiture and public concern about inflationary spending by adopting the cause of eliminating government waste. By presenting their own economizing measures, some Democrats hoped to earmark additional funds for social welfare programmes while others were anxious to avoid later Republican charges that failure to cut spending had made a tax cut impossible. Ironically, Eisenhower's strategy to make the Democrats more frugal worked all too well, and he now found himself defending the integrity of his budget from parsimonious congressional leaders on both sides.

Eisenhower's last-ditch appeals to spare vital national security programmes from the budgetary axe had little effect. Congress pruned defence expenditures by $2.4 billion, with the Army taking the biggest hit. A further $1 billion came out of the mutual security programme. Domestic spending also suffered, most notably a plan to aid overcrowded schools by constructing new classrooms. The end result was that Congress eliminated some $4 billion in spending from the president's budget and Eisenhower suffered a major political setback. To add insult to injury, actual federal spending in 1958 still came in at $71.9 billion, some $100 million above Eisenhower's original estimate!

CIVIL RIGHTS AND LITTLE ROCK

Eisenhower also ran into difficulties with Democratic congressional leaders as he struggled to maintain his 'middle way' on race relations. When the administration submitted a moderate civil rights bill in 1957, staunch opposition from conservative Southern Democrats and uncertain leadership from the White House resulted in a greatly watered-down measure. Eisenhower's ambiguous public utterances on school integration, moreover, encouraged continued white resistance in the South. No sooner had the Civil Rights Act been signed than violence erupted at Central High School in Little Rock, Arkansas, where a demagogic governor played the race card to secure re-election. Rather against his own inclinations, Eisenhower was compelled to intervene with federal troops to enforce a federal court order. Even then, the president refused to endorse the *Brown* decision and justified his actions on the more narrow ground of upholding the authority of a federal court.

The Eisenhower administration's interest in civil rights legislation dated back to late 1955. In the immediate aftermath of the *Brown* case, Brownell had pressed Eisenhower to support a measure that would both square with the president's convictions about limited government and exploit the North–South split in the Democratic Party in the upcoming general election. Recognizing the president's desire to avoid direct federal intervention in civil rights issues, Brownell emphasized voting rights. Since the late nineteenth century, African Americans had been systematically disfranchised across the South by a variety of legal and extra-legal devices, including poll taxes, literacy tests and overt intimidation. Throughout the South, only a small percentage of the almost six million non-whites of voting age were registered to vote. After the *Brown* decision, moreover, White Citizens' Councils had begun to purge even these voters from the rolls, which had larger legal implications because many southern states selected juries from the pool of registered voters. If voting rights could be protected, Brownell reasoned, then enfranchised African Americans would have the power to protect their interests without turning to the federal government for redress. To that end, he outlined a legislative programme including a bipartisan Civil Rights Commission to investigate black–white relations, the creation of a Civil Rights Division within the Justice Department, and modifications to the federal code reinforcing voting rights protections and granting the attorney general authority to seek injunctive relief. With Eisenhower's limited endorsement, the package passed the House of Representatives in May 1956, but Senate Majority Leader Lyndon Johnson bottled up the bill in committee to avoid an embarrassing split in Democratic ranks before that year's election.

Eisenhower believed that his 1956 electoral triumph, in which he made gains among both black and southern white voters, vindicated his moderate approach to civil rights, and he resubmitted the civil rights bill to Congress early in 1957. Northern Democrats, who were concerned at the recent Republican inroads among black voters, supported the legislation; Southern Democrats, who foresaw the possibility that federal troops might be used to enforce desegregation in the South, opposed it. Eisenhower met privately with congressional opponents in an effort to allay their fears while publicly confessing that he 'didn't completely understand' some of the language in his own bill, thus opening the door for white southerners to go on the offensive against it (PPP, 1957: 520–1). Lyndon Johnson, who now saw an opportunity to boost his presidential ambitions, championed a compromise civil rights bill and forced amendments to the administration's measure.

Thus the final bill eliminated the stringent provisions concerning the role of the attorney general in upholding civil rights and emasculated the voting rights protections by permitting all-white southern juries to adjudicate such cases. Eisenhower's lack of commitment to the cause and political ineptitude resulted in a significantly weaker bill than originally conceived.

The 1957 Civil Rights Act was nevertheless the first federal civil rights legislation since 1875, and its general tenor conformed to Eisenhower's corporate commonwealth philosophy. The president intended the bipartisan Civil Rights Commission to be an impartial investigating body that would take controversial and divisive racial issues out of the political arena. But the president's awkward efforts to reconcile African-American demands for justice with white southern efforts to defend their way of life continued to send mixed messages. In the midst of the debate over the civil rights bill, for example, Eisenhower stated that he could not imagine 'any set of circumstances' under which he would send federal troops 'into any area to enforce the orders of a Federal court' (PPP, 1957: 547). Rather than promoting a 'middle way' on race relations, such utterances undoubtedly left the impression with many white southerners that Eisenhower tacitly supported their continued acts of defiance.

Governor Orval Faubus of Arkansas apparently believed that he had little to fear from the Eisenhower administration. Following the *Brown* ruling, the school board of Little Rock, Arkansas, had developed a plan to integrate the city's public schools gradually, beginning with Central High School in September 1957. When private white segregationist groups filed suit to block the entry of nine black students into the school, local school officials obtained an injunction from a federal judge against all those seeking to interfere with the integration process. But Faubus, citing the prospect of violent resistance to the school's integration, ordered units of the Arkansas National Guard to maintain law and order by preventing the black children from entering Central High School. Faubus calculated that the Eisenhower administration would not interfere with his actions and that his opposition to integration would lock up the segregationist vote in his 1958 re-election bid. On the first day of school, Arkansas guardsmen turned the black students away. As the presiding judge prepared to charge Faubus with obstruction of a federal court order, the governor took his case directly to the president. He telegraphed the vacationing Eisenhower and requested his assistance in ending the 'unwarranted interference' by federal agents in his state's affairs (Branyan and Larsen, 1971: 1121–2). Eisenhower had little desire to intervene in the matter, and privately blamed the victims, 'the people who believe you are going to reform the human heart with the law', for the crisis (Duram, 1981: 145). Nevertheless, Eisenhower insisted that he would uphold federal authority. At the same time, he sought a negotiated, compromise solution that would avoid a direct confrontation with the governor and agreed to meet Faubus at the vacation White House in Newport, Rhode Island.

At their 14 September meeting, Eisenhower believed that he had persuaded Faubus to comply with the federal court order requiring the integration of Central High School. The president suggested that Faubus could save face by simply changing his orders to the guardsmen to allow black children to enter the school rather than withdrawing the troops entirely. In return, Eisenhower promised that the Justice Department would not pursue federal contempt charges. Faubus apparently agreed but, on his return to Little Rock, double-crossed the president by refusing to change his orders to the guardsmen and keeping the black children out of school. When Faubus failed to show up at a scheduled legal hearing, the judge in the case barred Faubus and the Arkansas Guard from taking any further actions to prevent desegregation at Central High School. Faubus thereupon withdrew the guardsmen and disclaimed any further responsibility for maintaining law and order in Little Rock.

Eisenhower's appeals for calm fell on deaf ears, leaving him no choice but to resort to the sort of military force he had hoped to avert. On Monday, 23 September, an angry mob milled around Central High School to prevent its integration. Although the black students managed to enter the building through a side door, the increasingly menacing crowd convinced the school board to send them home early. Eisenhower issued a cease and desist order against everyone interfering with the federal court's integration order and warned that he would use 'whatever force may be necessary' to implement the court's orders. The next day, when a similar mob assembled, Eisenhower responded to the mayor's desperate pleas for help by dispatching a thousand paratroopers to Little Rock and federalizing the Arkansas National Guard. That evening, Eisenhower addressed the nation. Mob violence, he explained, had necessitated the use of federal troops to uphold the law, not to enforce integration. Even now, however, he refused to endorse the *Brown* ruling, stating that 'personal opinions about the decision have no bearing on the matter of enforcement'. He also drew attention to the international repercussions of events in Little Rock, which supplied fuel for communist propaganda and embarrassed the United States in its dealings with Third World nations. He concluded by appealing to the citizens of Arkansas to return to their business so that 'a blot upon the fair name and high honor of our nation' could be removed [*Doc. 11*] (PPP, 1957: 689–94).

Eisenhower's conciliatory words failed to appease diehard segregationists, who were outraged that federal troops had 'invaded' the South. While troops escorted the black children to school and patrolled the campus, Senator Richard Russell of Georgia condemned the president's 'highhanded and illegal methods being employed … to mix the races in the public schools of Little Rock', and accused the military of behaving like Hitler's storm troopers (Duram, 1981: 159–60). Eisenhower vigorously rejected the allegations but nonetheless worked to remove the troops and return law and order responsibilities to local authorities as quickly as possible. As passions in Little Rock abated, he greatly reduced the Army presence and de-federalized most of the guardsmen. On 23 October, the black students were able to attend school for the first time without a military escort, and the following month Eisenhower withdrew the remaining paratroopers. The unrelated resignation of Brownell, widely perceived in the South as the villain of the piece, helped to appease white southern anger. But Faubus had the last word. In September 1958, when the United States Supreme Court upheld the federal integration order, Arkansas implemented a programme to close its public schools and reopen them as white-only private institutions.

For the remainder of his presidency, Eisenhower continued to avoid overt intervention in all civil rights issues other than voting rights. The Justice Department refused to pursue legal action against other states that adopted 'private' school systems or pupil placement laws to circumvent integration. Eisenhower rejected calls to employ the FBI to investigate continuing southern resistance on the grounds that he did not want to contribute to 'a Gestapo around here' (PPP, 1958: 403). In May 1958, he tactlessly informed an audience of black newspaper publishers that he was anxious for them to achieve first-class citizenship, but that they should 'be patient' (Burk, 1984: 238). In his only meeting with prominent black civil rights leaders the following month, Eisenhower was unmoved by Reverend Martin Luther King, Jr's call for a strong presidential statement endorsing desegregation as a moral issue.

The continuing violence against African Americans in the South and evidence of systematic disfranchisement uncovered by the newly-appointed Civil Rights Commission persuaded the administration to undertake a second round of civil rights legislation in 1959. The commission found that in forty-nine southern counties with black majorities, less than five per cent of voting-age blacks were registered to vote. Meanwhile, southern obstructionism and cautious leadership at the Justice Department had resulted in few voter discrimination suits being filed under the 1957 Civil Rights Act. The major innovation of the 1960 law, passed amidst partisan manoeuvring for the upcoming elections, was a provision for court-appointed referees to supervise voting procedures in counties where discrimination had prevented blacks from voting. It had little immediate effect. The Eisenhower administration employed the referee provision only twice, resulting in the addition of fewer than a hundred black voters.

The Eisenhower administration's civil rights record was modest at best. In his private criticism of the *Brown* decision, his refusal to endorse school desegregation, and his counselling of patience to African-American activists, Eisenhower clearly indicated his preference for only a gradual adjustment to the *status quo* in race relations. True, his philosophy of government militated against greater federal activism in this field, but his personal sympathies seemed to be entirely with white southerners. He only took decisive action at Little Rock when he felt constitutionally bound. Roy Wilkins of the NAACP provided a fitting epitaph when he said: 'President Eisenhower was a fine general and a good, decent man, but if he had fought World War II the way he fought for civil rights, we would all be speaking German today' (Sitkoff, 1993: 36).

SPUTNIK

The third major crisis to overtake the Eisenhower administration in 1957 erupted on 4 October when the Soviet Union launched the first artificial earth satellite, Sputnik. The dramatic Soviet space achievement shocked most Americans and shattered their complacent assumption of American superiority in science and technology. The psychological blow forced the Eisenhower administration on to the defensive in the one area where the president's expertise had previously shielded him from partisan attack, national security. Democrats seized the initiative to lambast the administration's defence policies, and presidential hopefuls, such as Senators Stuart Symington, John F. Kennedy and Lyndon Johnson, tried to exploit the issue to promote their respective candidacies. The military services, which had grown increasingly dissatisfied with Eisenhower's restrictive New Look budgetary ceilings, compounded the administration's difficulties by engaging in competitive publicity to promote their own pet projects and break free of the tight fiscal restraints. For the remainder of his presidency, Eisenhower found himself on the defensive, seeking to preserve his 'long haul' defence policy against alarmist demands for expensive crash programmes to close various 'gaps' with the Soviet Union.

Sputnik was not a complete surprise to Eisenhower. Both the United States and the Soviet Union had undertaken to launch earth satellites as part of the International Geophysical Year, an international cooperative scientific endeavour. In August 1957, the Soviets announced the successful test flight of an intercontinental ballistic missile (ICBM), indicating that they probably already possessed the capability of putting a satellite into orbit. Eisenhower also had hard intelligence on Soviet missile progress from U-2 reconnaissance flights, which had begun in July 1956, and long-range tracking radar based in Turkey. What did surprise the president was the extent to which he had seriously underestimated the profound psychological shock that such an achievement would have on the American people. Back in 1955, psychological warfare expert Nelson Rockefeller had warned that the first earth satellite would symbolize scientific and technological superiority to the world, and that the United States could not afford to lose such a contest. Eisenhower, however, had insisted that the United States not get into an overt space race with the Soviet Union. He had deliberately made Project Vanguard, the American scientific satellite, a civilian enterprise, both to convince world opinion of the peaceful nature of the American space programme and to establish the principle of 'freedom of outer space', which would smooth the way for military reconnaissance satellites already under development. As a result, the administration selected a privately-produced rocket, rather than a military missile, as the satellite booster. A combination of technical problems with the rocket and the relatively low priority assigned to the civilian project by the Pentagon allowed the Soviets to get into space first.

Most of the public and press viewed the Soviet Sputnik with alarm. Physicist Edward Teller claimed that the United States had 'lost a battle more important and greater than Pearl Harbor' (Killian, 1977: 7–8). *Life* magazine, normally supportive of the administration, agreed that Sputnik was a clear 'defeat for the United States' and pressed for greater federal aid to scientific and technical education. Various senators expressed similar concerns. Some predicted that the Soviets had established a dangerous lead in long-range missile technology and wanted an emergency session of Congress; others blamed Sputnik on the administration's misguided commitment to balancing the budget over providing adequate resources for defence. Even Minority Leader Knowland called for a complete review of the nation's military and satellite programmes. Khrushchev's boast that missiles would soon render manned bombers obsolete only exacerbated public apprehension about the Soviet achievement (Eisenhower, 1965: 205–6; McDougall, 1985: 142–5).

Eisenhower attempted to allay public anxiety by embarking on a deliberately low-key response to Sputnik and quietly reassuring Americans about the overwhelming strength of the nation's defences, but to no avail. After extensive briefings on the Soviet and American satellite and missile programmes, the president used his first press conference after Sputnik to explain that the Soviet satellite made no difference to the strategic balance between the superpowers. He emphasized that the American scientific satellite programme had been conceived to avoid interference with the 'top priority' missile programmes, and that the first satellite launch would take place in March 1958. He admitted that the Soviets had scored a 'great psychological advantage', but reminded his listeners that manned bombers would constitute a vital element in the nation's strategic deterrent for the indefinite future and that the American military missile programmes were already adequately funded at $5 billion a year. In short, Sputnik imposed 'no additional threat to the United States' and did not raise his concerns about the nation's security 'one iota' (PPP, 1957: 719–35). The nation, however, seemed to be unconvinced. Indeed, Eisenhower's restrained comments created the impression in some quarters that the ageing president was perhaps out of touch with new technological realities.

Behind the scenes, Eisenhower took positive steps to ensure that he did, indeed, receive the best technical advice on matters of science and national security and that the nation undertook appropriate, measured responses to the Soviet satellite. Eisenhower acted on the long-standing recommendation of several prominent scientists to appoint a science adviser to the White House. James R. Killian, Jr, president of the Massachusetts Institute of Technology, became Eisenhower's special assistant for science and technology, and Eisenhower established the President's Science Advisory Committee (PSAC), a part-time board of distinguished scientists and engineers, to advise the administration on a broad array of scientific matters. Shortly after the launch of Sputnik II on 3 November, Eisenhower adopted his science advisers' recommendations to deliver a series of broadcasts detailing the administration's own efforts in the realm of science and national security. Eisenhower also announced plans to maintain the free world's technological edge by encouraging greater scientific exchanges with the allies, rationalizing the Pentagon's burgeoning missile programmes under a single manager, and promoting high-quality scientific and technical training to produce the next generation of scientists and engineers.

Eisenhower's efforts to calm public anxiety and sustain his security with solvency approach to defence policy suffered a further blow the day after Sputnik II with the presentation of the Gaither Report. A group of civilian consultants, headed by H. Rowan Gaither of the Ford Foundation, prepared this top secret study of the nation's passive and active defences for the NSC. The group painted a grim picture of relative Soviet and American military and economic strength. Most seriously, the panel argued that the vulnerability of the American manned bombers to a Soviet surprise missile strike undermined the credibility of the nuclear deterrent. The Gaither panel recommended a comprehensive overhaul of defence policies, ranging from expanded missile programmes to greater dispersal and protection of bomber bases, speedy development of an ICBM early warning system, improved conventional war-fighting capabilities and a national system of fallout shelters to protect the civilian population in the event of nuclear war. Eisenhower found the entire report to be unduly pessimistic and rejected many of the panel's findings, not least because the price tag of an additional $40 billion for defence over the next five years threatened to bust the budget and push the United States further down the road to the dreaded garrison state (FRUS, 1955–57: 19.620–4, 630–5, 638–61). When portions of the classified report leaked to the press, critics renewed the charge that Eisenhower was sacrificing the nation's security to fiscal considerations.

Eisenhower's refusal to release the full report to Congress on the grounds of 'executive privilege' did nothing to alleviate that impression.

Shortly thereafter, Lyndon Johnson exploited the administration's discomfiture and bolstered his presidential prospects for 1960 by opening an ostensibly non-partisan senate inquiry into the missile and satellite programmes. The Texas senator allowed 'expert witnesses' from the military and scientific communities to describe how the United States had fallen behind in space technology and offer their own prescriptions, thereby criticizing the administration's actions implicitly. Scientists like Edward Teller and Vannevar Bush called for a renewed sense of urgency in military technology and science generally, others pinpointed inter-service rivalries and unnecessary duplication as reasons for delay in the missile programmes, and military witnesses used the forum to criticize the administration's rigid budget ceilings. By December, the developing theme of the hearings was that tight budgets and poor planning in the Pentagon had allowed the Soviets to open a 'missile gap' with the United States.

The cumulative strains of 1957 took their toll on Eisenhower, both personally and politically. On Monday 25 November, the very day that Johnson opened the Senate investigation, Eisenhower suffered a minor stroke. Vice President Richard Nixon filled in for the president at a state dinner that evening, and within a matter of days Eisenhower had recovered sufficiently to resume his normal duties. His illness, however, only added to the sense that the sixty-seven-year-old president was perhaps too old and infirm to lead the nation in its time of trial. Several columnists even suggested that he resign. Such criticism, coupled with the stroke, only steeled Eisenhower's resolve to continue. In mid-December, against the advice of his close aides, he attended the NATO meeting in Paris to boost European morale by offering American intermediate-range ballistic missiles (IRBMs) to the allies to counter any Soviet missile threat. But all his exertions to restore American and allied confidence came crashing down with the first, inglorious attempt to launch an American satellite. Before the world's press, the rocket barely lifted off the launchpad, then collapsed in a fireball. Wags variously labelled it 'Flopnik', 'Stayputnik' and 'Kaputnik' (McDougall, 1985: 154). Anxiety about the space race and the missile gap remained as high as ever, and Eisenhower's personal approval rating sank to a record low. After Sputnik, Eisenhower was very much on the defensive, fighting a rearguard battle against the growing cacophony of voices demanding dramatic increases in space and military programmes to close the 'gap' with the Soviet Union.

REORGANIZING THE NATIONAL SECURITY STATE

Eisenhower began 1958 in political difficulty. Not only did the Sputniks erode public confidence in the president's previously unchallenged leadership on national security issues, but a serious economic slowdown that began in mid-1957 compounded the administration's problems. Leaks of the secret Gaither Report's recommendations, Senator Johnson's preparedness investigation into missiles and space programmes, and a critical January 1958 report on national security by the Rockefeller Brothers Fund indicated a growing consensus among military experts and defence intellectuals for dramatic increases in military spending on the order of several billions of dollars a year. In early January, on the eve of the so-called Sputnik Congress, Johnson denounced the administration's obsession with balancing the budget at the expense of national security and argued that the race for control of space would ultimately determine the outcome of the Cold War. Eisenhower's emphasis on security with solvency over the long haul was in jeopardy, but the president determined to make a stand.

Eisenhower publicly acknowledged that he had underestimated the psychological impact of Sputnik on American and world opinion, but he remained convinced of the essential wisdom of the New Look and developed a three-pronged strategy to preserve its essentials. First, he accepted modest increases in defence spending and a reallocation of resources to ensure the adequacy of the strategic deterrent. He authorized the new secretary of defense, Neil H. McElroy, a Procter and Gamble executive who had replaced the outspoken and controversial Charles Wilson in October 1957, to seek a supplemental appropriation of $1.26 billion for the remainder of 1958. The additional funds would accelerate the existing ICBM and IRBM programmes, disperse B-52 bombers, and improve readiness, all of which had been recommended by the Gaither group. Privately, Eisenhower and McElroy believed that two-thirds of the supplementary funds were 'more to stabilize public opinion than to meet the real need for acceleration' (FRUS, 1955–57: 19.703). In addition, the administration's $73.9 billion 1959 budget raised the original $38 billion ceiling for defence spending to $39.8 billion and included over $5 billion for missiles. The administration covered these increases by making economies elsewhere, such as reducing procurement of older weapons systems and cutting back on civilian programmes. The administration's adjustments reflected Eisenhower's determination to adopt only appropriate, measured responses to the changing military balance and retain his commitment to fiscal responsibility and a sound economy.

The second part of Eisenhower's strategy comprised a package of limited federal aid to education. Sputnik had reopened a long-simmering debate over the state of the nation's schools and the growing disparity between the number of scientists and engineers produced in the Soviet Union compared with the United States. At the urging of his new science advisers and the Department of Health, Education and Welfare, Eisenhower focused on improving scientific education. He proposed a threefold increase in the National Science Foundation budget to $140 million to support the agency's efforts to raise the quality of science education by sponsoring summer institutes for school teachers, producing textbooks by the nation's leading scientists, and promoting curriculum reform. He also requested $1 billion over four years for up to 40,000 scholarships for well-qualified but needy high school students to attend college, fellowships to increase the supply of college teachers, and matching funds to the states to promote training in mathematics, the sciences and foreign languages. The scholarship plan provoked the most debate in Congress, where Democratic leaders engaged in political one-upmanship by introducing their own scheme for 40,000 scholarships based on merit rather than need and a fund to provide loans of up to $1,000 a year for college students. Eisenhower resisted the Democratic plan because of its expense and the assumption of a long-term federal involvement in education that might undermine local control of schools. After much partisan wrangling, Congress finally enacted a measure that satisfied Eisenhower's major requirements. The National Defense Education Act dispensed with the scholarship provisions entirely and created a $295 million loan fund for student loans to be granted on the basis of need, $280 million in federal matching funds to promote the teaching of science, mathematics and foreign languages in the schools, and almost $60 million for graduate fellowships in subjects related to national defence. Many commentators and educators regretted the limited nature of the bill, but Eisenhower had reluctantly established the precedent of federal involvement in education (Eisenhower, 1965: 241–3).

The third element in Eisenhower's strategy required a reorganization of the national security bureaucracy. Long an advocate of greater unification in the defence establishment, Eisenhower had attempted to strengthen the secretary of defense's control over the military services in a 1953 reorganization plan. The results had been far from satisfactory, particularly in the realm of research and development, where each service had initiated competing projects to gain a foothold in the strategic mission favoured under the New Look. By 1957, Eisenhower and his science advisers believed that inter-service rivalry fostered waste and duplication that hindered overall development of new weapons systems by exacerbating shortages of scientific and technical manpower and facilities. The Johnson hearings reinforced this diagnosis. Eisenhower and his scientists preferred a systems approach, whereby military functions would be assigned to unified commands and the individual services would be confined to training and administrative matters. Following Sputnik, Eisenhower believed that 'a giant step towards unification could be made', and initiated planning between McElroy, Killian and a group of civilian consultants under Nelson Rockefeller (FRUS, 1955–57: 19.598–601).

The administration made two forays into defence reorganization in 1958. In February, McElroy centralized control of all military space programmes and anti-missile projects in a new agency in his own office. Two months later, Eisenhower presented comprehensive legislation to improve overall efficiency and economy in the Pentagon. He planned to remove the service secretaries from the chain of command, encourage the JCS to take a corporate view of national defence matters by relieving them of some of their service responsibilities and expanding their staff, and centralize co-ordination of all research and development in the Pentagon under someone 'known nationally as a leader in science and technology' assisted by a 'highly qualified' staff (PPP, 1958: 284–5). Eisenhower had to abandon his more controversial idea of having all defence appropriations made directly to the secretary of defense rather than the individual services in the face of congressional reluctance to surrender the power of the purse over the armed forces. Uncharacteristically, Eisenhower became deeply involved in the legislative process, meeting with key congressional leaders to smooth the passage of the bill and undertaking a massive letter-writing campaign to mobilize support for his plans from the private sector. His efforts paid off. The 1958 Defense Reorganization Act provided most of what Eisenhower requested. The only objectionable features were provisions that reserved to Congress the power to veto any transfer of major combat functions among the services and protected the right of service secretaries and military chiefs to present dissenting views before Congress, dubbed 'legalized insubordination' by Eisenhower (Eisenhower, 1965: 252). Nevertheless, the president was satisfied with the overall result.

Eisenhower was somewhat more reluctant to undertake a reorganization of space responsibilities, but eventually acquiesced in a new civilian space agency. After the Army successfully launched the first American satellite, Explorer I, in January 1958, the administration turned its attention to the appropriate organization for future space endeavours. Eisenhower initially preferred to channel all space activity through the Pentagon rather than establish a new federal bureaucracy that would inevitably add to the burdens on the Treasury. Eventually, however, he accepted his scientists' position that assigning all space functions to the Department of Defense would entail military control of space science and undermine the notion that American activity in outer space was motivated by peaceful purposes. The administration therefore submitted a bill that envisioned two parallel space programmes, one devoted to scientific research and the other to military applications. While the Pentagon retained control of military space activities, a new National Aeronautics and Space Administration (NASA) would direct the civilian space effort. Reluctantly, Eisenhower also accepted Senator Johnson's insistence on a Space Council, composed of Cabinet members and chaired by the president, to ensure that the space programme received high-level consideration.

After creating NASA, the administration grappled with the problem of developing an appropriate mission for the new agency. Eisenhower and his science advisers preferred a modest civilian space programme that would emphasize scientific research over space spectaculars. At the same time, the administration remained acutely aware that space had now become a battleground in the Cold War competition with the Soviet Union for international prestige. The United States already trailed the Soviet Union in the development of large rocket boosters, partly because the Soviets had been less successful in miniaturizing nuclear warheads, and the administration did not want to endure any more Sputniks. Eisenhower concluded that, for psychological reasons, the United States would have to develop a manned spaceflight programme, which in turn necessitated developing big rocket boosters beyond anything required for purely military purposes. He assigned this mission to NASA and approved the transfer of various Army facilities to the civilian space agency. Still, Eisenhower intended to compete with the Soviets on a selective basis and opposed crash programmes of dubious scientific or technical merit. The objective of the administration's space policy would be 'to achieve and demonstrate an overall US superiority in outer space without necessarily requiring US superiority in every phase of space activities' [*Doc. 12*]. The problem was that once NASA's mission was defined in terms of enhancing international prestige, it became increasingly difficult to hold down the space budget. Even under the relatively parsimonious Eisenhower administration, NASA's appropriations leapt from $250 million in 1959 to almost $1 billion by 1961. The Democrats, however, continued to charge that the administration was not doing enough to win the 'space race'.

Despite his oft-stated desire to avoid a garrison state, Eisenhower's responses to the Sputnik crisis nudged the United States farther down that road. While he continued to insist that the purpose of American national security policy was to defend a 'way of life', he also recognized that the Soviet Union was waging total Cold War. Reluctantly, under Eisenhower's leadership both space and education became battlegrounds in the larger Cold War struggle, and his halting expansion of the national security state in these areas set precedents that his less cautious successors would be unable to resist.

RECESSION AND RETRENCHMENT

Public anxiety over national security was one of the two major issues that dogged Eisenhower for the remainder of his presidency; the other was growing dissatisfaction with the administration's overall economic policies. The Sputnik crisis coincided with the onset of a recession, which exacerbated the president's political difficulties. As in the case of the Sputniks, however, Eisenhower remained determined to hold the line against unwise crash programmes. To a large extent, he succeeded, but the Republican Party paid a high political price.

In the late summer of 1957, the economy slipped into a sharp recession. By March 1958, over five million people were out of work, the worst figures since World War II, and the industrial states of the Midwest and Northeast were especially hard hit. A cyclical downturn in new housing starts, a dramatic decline in new automobile sales following the record model year of 1955, and a major slump in spending on capital goods put the brakes on the economy. Government policies, however, contributed to the downturn. In August, at the very moment when the economy was on the brink of a recession, the Federal Reserve Board raised interest rates to dampen inflationary pressures. This tightening of credit coincided with cutbacks in federal spending caused by the 1957 'battle of the budget'. For the next eight months, the economy remained mired in the deepest slump of the decade.

The administration responded ineffectually to the recession, partly because Eisenhower's overriding concern was to hold down creeping inflation, which was hovering at around 3 per cent. Eisenhower's economic advisers developed a series of limited anti-recession measures, most of which the president gradually implemented. He reversed earlier cutbacks in defence procurement and public works, accelerated construction of federally-funded projects already authorized or underway, and liberalized federal mortgage insurance requirements. But he resisted all suggestions to increase federal spending in the upcoming 1959 budget. Higher defence spending precipitated by the Sputniks and reduced revenues caused by the recession meant that the administration's $73.9 billion 1959 budget would likely end in the red anyway, and Eisenhower refused to countenance additional anti-recession spending measures that would worsen the deficit and further fuel inflationary pressures (Ferrell, 1981: 352–3).

The recession highlighted a major philosophical difference between the administration and congressional Democrats. The president preferred to rely on the automatic stabilizers in the economy to counter the recession, but many Democrats wanted to increase spending on public works in order to stimulate employment. Eisenhower exhibited concern for the unemployed and introduced legislation, which Congress quickly enacted, to extend unemployment insurance payments from the usual twenty-six weeks to thirty-nine weeks in order to sustain personal disposable income, but he resisted a variety of Democratic spending proposals that he regarded as being of dubious economic merit. In April, he vetoed an omnibus public works bill for harbours and rivers on the grounds that many of the proposed projects would get underway too slowly to have any impact on the recession and others were simply pork barrel measures designed for partisan political gain rather than economic recovery. When the president eventually accepted a scaled-down bill, the revised measure came too late to have any impact on the recession.

The economic downturn also revived public discussion over the merits of tax cuts, and again Eisenhower played spoiler. Some conservative business groups called for tax cuts to stimulate investment. Arthur Burns, who had recently stepped down as chair of Eisenhower's CEA, lobbied for a temporary $5 billion tax cut as an anti-recessionary measure. Meanwhile, liberal Democrats favoured a $3 billion tax cut targeted to boost consumption among low-income consumers. Eisenhower's own advisers were divided. Nixon, with an eye on the upcoming congressional elections and the 1960 presidential race, most strongly advocated Burns's position within the Cabinet, but Treasury Secretary Robert Anderson, who had replaced George Humphrey in 1957, held fast. Anderson sympathized with the notion of corporate and individual tax cuts to stimulate investment, but counselled against any action during the recession for two primary reasons: he feared that congressional Democrats would be unable to resist the temptation to expand any administration plan for tax relief beyond fiscally sound levels; and he worried that a deficit-boosting tax cut would further stimulate inflation, which had not yet abated. As the economy began to pick up again in April, moreover, Eisenhower viewed the mounting deficit and creeping inflation as the most serious economic problems. There would be no major tax cut.

The administration's farm proposals similarly raised questions about the president's economic leadership. Faced with continuing agricultural surpluses, Eisenhower made another attempt to reduce the costs of the farm programme by obtaining greater flexibility in price supports and acreage allotments. A coalition of farm state Democrats and Republicans, however, pushed through a farm bill that froze high federal price supports for a year to insulate farmers against the effects of the recession. Midwestern Republicans urged Eisenhower to sign the bill and remove the acerbic Benson, whose outspoken efforts to eliminate federal subsidies had made him extremely unpopular in the farm belt. Without the freeze, they warned, the party would lose dozens of seats in the upcoming elections. Eisenhower recognized the political danger of blocking the popular bill, but he loyally backed Benson and remained true to his own free market preferences by vetoing it anyway. The legislative battle over farm policy dragged on until August, when Congress finally approved a bill that provided the lower price supports and flexibility preferred by the administration. By that time, the worst of the recession had passed and an unexpected rise in commodity prices cushioned the blow to farmers somewhat.

Although the economic downturn was over by April, lingering concern about the economy played an important role in the 1958 congressional elections. The unemployment rate finally dipped slightly in May, but remained stubbornly at 6.8 per cent for the rest of the year. Indeed, the unemployment rate would only revert to its early 1957 level in 1965. Democrats exploited the sluggish economy and Benson's unpopularity to denounce the administration for failing to act in a timely or effective manner to counter the recession. They also reminded voters of the improprieties of Sherman Adams, Eisenhower's chief of staff, who resigned in September 1958 amid allegations of influence-peddling. As opinion polls suggested a major setback for the Republicans, Eisenhower belatedly entered the political fray to campaign for Republican candidates on the familiar issue of fiscal responsibility. Uncharacteristically, the president, who so vehemently denounced political demagoguery by the opposition, engaged in his own oratorical excesses. The Democratic Party, he claimed, had been captured by 'radicals' dedicated to reckless spending that would entail higher taxes, inflation and increased centralization. The choice for the voters, he believed, was clear cut: 'either … left-wing government or sensible, forward-looking government – spendthrift government or responsible government' (PPP, 1958: 760).

On election day, the Republicans suffered their worst defeat since the 1930s. The Democrats emerged with majorities of 64 to 34 in the Senate and 282 to 154 in the House. Several prominent Old Guard Republicans lost their seats. Although former aide Nelson Rockefeller won the governorship of New York, Democrats prevailed in most of the other governors' races, most notably in California, where Senate Minority Leader Knowland went down to defeat despite last-minute campaigning by Eisenhower. The 'spenders', it seemed, had gained ascendancy. The results angered and depressed Eisenhower, but also renewed his determination to hold the line on federal spending. In his first press conference after the election he pledged: 'for the next two years, the Lord sparing me, I am going to fight this as hard as I know how' (PPP, 1958: 828).

To the surprise of many political pundits, Eisenhower waged an extremely effective battle to hold down spending during 1959 by cultivating a conservative coalition of Republicans and Southern Democrats. Although Eisenhower denounced the 'spenders' in the Democratic Party, he actively courted conservative Democrats who largely shared his economic views on the necessity of a balanced budget and holding the line against massive new social programmes. Their alarm over the record peacetime deficit of $12.4 billion for 1959 drew them to the president's side. Adverse international reaction to the massive deficit and a drain on gold reserves also solidified Eisenhower's determination to balance the 1960 budget and restore foreign confidence in the dollar. Thus Eisenhower forged an effective bipartisan coalition for fiscal discipline.

From the outset, Eisenhower decisively seized the initiative in the 1960 budgetary process. After the elections but before Congress reconvened, he declared that the next budget would be balanced at $77 billion, entailing a $3 billion reduction in spending from the previous year. As usual, Eisenhower pressured the service chiefs to recognize that national security required a sound economy, and approved a defence estimate of $40.1 billion, some $10 billion less than the Pentagon had originally sought. Assisted by his new science advisers, Eisenhower weeded out unnecessary military projects while reinforcing the New Look's overall emphasis on high-technology strategic weapons systems at the expense of conventional war capabilities. His defence decisions established the nuclear triad of delivery systems – manned bombers, land-based missiles and submarine-launched ballistic missiles – that would form the basis of the American nuclear deterrent well into the future. Eisenhower cut back even further on domestic spending. He produced savings of $2.4 billion over the previous year primarily by slashing the housing and farm programmes. Having forced the administration into line, Eisenhower then set out 'to convince Americans that thrift is not a bad word' and educate them to the dangers of inflation (Ambrose, 1984: 496). He also made effective use of the presidential veto to block Democratic legislation that threatened to bust the budget. With support from Republicans and conservative Democrats, Eisenhower successfully turned back several unacceptable bills and only had one veto overridden. The president's exertions paid off handsomely. After one of the most effective legislative battles of his presidency, the 1960 budget came in with a $1.3 billion surplus.

The administration achieved similar success in the field of labour reform. Since entering office, Eisenhower had periodically called for a revision of the landmark 1947 Taft–Hartley Act, which labour unions criticized as too restrictive and business groups regarded as too lax. Eisenhower's efforts to find common ground for reform failed to achieve anything for several years, but the political climate changed in 1958 when a Senate investigation uncovered serious abuses in the conduct of union affairs by a handful of labour leaders. Early in 1959, Eisenhower called for legislation to safeguard workers' union contributions, ensure secret ballots in union elections, and protect the public interest during labour disputes. Senator Kennedy introduced a bill to address some of these concerns, but Eisenhower and business groups criticized it for not going far enough to eliminate union corruption. The administration then worked with its congressional coalition of Republicans and conservative Democrats to pass a substitute bill, the Landrum–Griffin Act, that outlawed secondary boycotts, restricted picketing, and extended federal regulation of internal union affairs. The final act signified that labour would remain very much a junior partner in Eisenhower's 'corporate commonwealth'.

Eisenhower's only major political defeat of 1959 involved his nomination of Lewis L. Strauss to be secretary of commerce. Strauss had chaired the AEC since 1953, but his arrogant manner and handling of the controversial Dixon-Yates contract had won few friends in Congress. He had also frequently clashed with congressional advocates of public power facilities, and his role in the Oppenheimer affair had earned the undying animosity of many scientists, some of whom lobbied hard to defeat his nomination. Unfortunately for Strauss, Senate Democrats, who had been frustrated on almost every legislative initiative by presidential vetoes, saw the nomination as a way to retaliate against Eisenhower. The president was outraged by the personal attacks on Strauss but could not muster the votes to save him. In June, the Senate voted 49 to 46 against confirmation, making Strauss the first presidential nominee in over thirty years to be rejected for a Cabinet post.

Despite the setback of the Strauss nomination, Eisenhower's vigorous 1959 campaign for fiscal responsibility and legislative restraint was remarkably successful. He overcame his status as a lame-duck president, huge Democratic majorities in both Houses of Congress and continued inter-service sniping over the defence programme to rein in federal spending and achieve a balanced budget. Such would not be the case in his last year in office. As politicians in both parties jockeyed for partisan advantage in the upcoming general election, Eisenhower's brand of fiscal conservatism became increasingly difficult to sustain.

THE 1960 ELECTION

The shadow of the 1960 general election loomed large over Eisenhower's last year in office. The Twenty-Second Amendment to the Constitution, passed by vengeful Republicans as a retroactive slap against Franklin D. Roosevelt, barred Eisenhower from seeking a third term. By 1959, in fact, some Republican leaders rued the fact that they had inadvertently blocked a generally popular Republican president from running again. Although not himself a candidate, Eisenhower took great interest in the election campaign, viewing it as a referendum on his presidency. He also intended his last budget to be a final statement of his economic principles of fiscal restraint and limited government. But congressional leaders similarly took note of the approaching elections, and Democrats launched a blistering partisan attack on the administration's failure to generate adequate economic growth and maintain a sound military posture. In this context of renewed partisan warfare, Eisenhower's efforts to hold the line on spending were rather less effective than in the previous year.

In January 1960, Eisenhower unveiled a $79.8 billion 1961 budget that envisaged a modest increase in overall expenditures and a substantial surplus of $4.2 billion. Eisenhower fashioned the budget according to the stabilizing budget theory, whose objective was to balance the budget over the course of the business cycle by accumulating sufficient surpluses to stem inflation during times of prosperity and offset shortfalls during downturns. Eisenhower and Anderson intended to apply most of the surplus towards debt retirement, which would boost confidence in the dollar abroad and stimulate economic growth at home by freeing up additional funds for private sector investment. To the dismay of many Republicans, the emphasis on a large surplus and debt retirement once again precluded a major tax cut (PPP, 1960–61: 38–40).

The most bitter partisan attacks honed in on the administration's defence budget. In the Senate, Democratic presidential hopefuls Kennedy and Symington excoriated the administration for allowing the Soviets to open a 'missile gap' or a 'deterrent gap' with the United States. In a major speech on defence policy, Kennedy admitted that, until the extent of the Soviet missile programme was fully known, he was willing to risk 'spending money unnecessarily', but those who resisted increased expenditures were 'taking a chance on our very survival as a nation' [*Doc. 13*]. In addition to missiles, Kennedy echoed Army demands for improved conventional warfare capabilities. During congressional hearings on the defence budget, Symington exploited confusion among administration witnesses about intelligence estimates of future Soviet missile strength to claim that: 'The intelligence books have been juggled so that the budget books can be balanced' (Roman, 1995: 139).

The assault on his defence expertise and his integrity infuriated Eisenhower, as did end-runs to Congress by several military witnesses who lobbied for pet projects that had been slighted in the administration's budget. Eisenhower's third secretary of defense, Thomas S. Gates, had no more success than his predecessors in keeping the armed services in line. Throughout the early weeks of 1960, Eisenhower faced a barrage of hostile questions in his press conferences detailing alleged deficiencies in the defence programme. In vain did Eisenhower remind his interlocutors that the United States possessed secure and adequate deterrent forces and that real national security required a strong economy. Finally, at a February press conference, Eisenhower snapped. Visibly angry, he responded to yet another question implying that he had not been forthright about the Soviet missile programme and had put a balanced budget ahead of needed weapons by declaring: 'If anybody – anybody – believes that I have deliberately misled the American people, I'd like to tell him to his face what I think about him. This is a charge that I think is despicable' (PPP, 1960–61: 198–9). Notwithstanding the president's repeated assurances that the nation's defences were fundamentally sound, the intense political climate inevitably resulted in some upward revision of military spending by Congress, although the results were not as bad as Eisenhower had feared. Congress eventually allocated only $661 million more for missiles and conventional forces modernization than Eisenhower had sought. Rather than impounding the additional funds, as he had done in the past, Eisenhower tried to defuse anxiety over the military programme and help Nixon's candidacy by spending most of it.

The opposition similarly criticized the administration's domestic programmes for failing to generate adequate economic growth. While careful to endorse a balanced budget, Democratic leaders called for a relaxation of monetary policy and a reordering of priorities. Specifically, they favoured increasing spending on education and area redevelopment by making economies in the farm programme and reforming the tax code to eliminate loopholes. Their goal was to achieve an annual economic growth rate of 5 per cent. Eisenhower fended off most of the new spending measures with a series of real or threatened presidential vetoes, but his actions inadvertently hurt Nixon's political chances. The vice president had to cast a tie-breaking vote in the Senate to uphold the administration's opposition to a generally popular measure providing federal support for teacher salaries. In May, against Nixon's wishes, Eisenhower vetoed an area redevelopment bill that commanded bipartisan support from congressmen who represented depressed areas in the Northeast and Midwest. Indeed, Nixon was already growing anxious about the health of the economy. Since March, Burns had been warning him of a possible recession on the eve of the election unless corrective measures were taken soon. When Nixon brought this up in a Cabinet meeting, however, Eisenhower and Anderson repeated their commitment to a tight money policy and a large budgetary surplus to contain inflation and restore foreign confidence in the dollar, even at the risk of a slight economic downturn. For Eisenhower, the long-term economic picture took precedence over any short-term political calculations. Unfortunately for Nixon, a mild recession did indeed hit in May, and by the time of the election unemployment had risen once again to more than 6 per cent.

While Eisenhower was largely unwilling to undertake short-term measures for the sake of political expediency, the Democratic assaults on his military and domestic programmes reinforced his conviction that a Republican victory in 1960 was essential for the nation's welfare, although he remained uncertain as to the best candidate. Nixon seemed to be the obvious choice for the Republican presidential nomination. He had served Eisenhower loyally and effectively as vice president for eight years and commanded solid support among party regulars. Even so, Eisenhower continued to harbour reservations about him. He worried that Nixon had still not matured into a statesman and that he too often examined national issues from the perspective of partisan advantage. His first choice for the Republican ticket was Anderson, but the treasury secretary had no desire to run. The only real challenger to Nixon was Rockefeller, who had bucked the Democratic trend in 1958 to win the governorship of New York and had served the president in several advisory capacities. Rockefeller's willingness to employ deficit spending and dramatically expand military programmes, however, made him unacceptable to Eisenhower. By default, then, Nixon became Eisenhower's choice for the Republican nomination. Even so, Eisenhower tried to foster party unity by maintaining the appearance of scrupulous neutrality in the Nixon–Rockefeller contest until after the Republican Convention had decided on the party ticket. Unfortunately for Nixon, by resisting press efforts to reveal his preference and withholding an official endorsement until July, Eisenhower unwittingly conveyed the impression that he had reservations about Nixon's candidacy.

When the Democrats nominated Kennedy as their presidential candidate and Lyndon Johnson for the vice presidency, Eisenhower became even more determined to achieve a Republican victory. He viewed Kennedy as 'incompetent' and his constant harping about the 'missile gap' as the worst kind of alarmism and demagoguery. Johnson was not much better. Eisenhower variously described him as 'the most tricky and unreliable politician in Congress', and a 'small man ... superficial and opportunistic' (Kistiakowsky, 1976: 402–3; Ambrose, 1984: 596–7). If the Democrats won, the result would be an unmitigated economic disaster: unrestrained spending, huge deficits, declining foreign confidence in the dollar and a drain on gold reserves. When Nixon finally obtained the Republican nomination and selected UN Ambassador Lodge as his running mate, Eisenhower immediately endorsed the ticket and set out to help the party's cause.

Eisenhower's belated intervention in the 1960 campaign was both awkward and occasionally embarrassing for Nixon. The president unintentionally delivered Nixon a mortal blow during a news conference in August. A major theme of Nixon's campaign was that his eight years of vice-presidential experience, particularly his meetings with foreign dignitaries and participation in high-level decision-making, had thoroughly prepared him for the role of president. The press repeatedly tried to elicit from Eisenhower specific instances when he had followed Nixon's advice on a major policy decision, but the president equivocated. Stung by recent criticism that he was out of touch and had not been fully informed about the U-2 affair, Eisenhower resisted any suggestion that he had not made his own decisions. Finally, after persistent questioning for an example of one of Nixon's ideas that he had adopted, an irritated Eisenhower blurted out: 'If you give me a week I might think of one. I don't remember' (PPP, 1960–61: 658). On that note, the press conference concluded. Eisenhower immediately recognized his *faux pas* and telephoned Nixon to apologize, but the damage had been done. Democrats exploited the president's slip to undermine Nixon's credentials and suggest that Eisenhower lacked enthusiasm for Nixon's candidacy.

A degree of tension between Eisenhower and the Nixon campaign further complicated the president's role in the election. Part of the problem was that Eisenhower viewed the election as a referendum on his presidency, and his campaign appearances therefore stressed his administration's achievements and the need to stay the course. Nixon, however, implicitly accepted much of the critique of the Eisenhower presidency by prescribing a more activist federal role in such areas as defence, space, education and civil rights. Eisenhower offered to campaign actively for his vice president, but Nixon's advisers were anxious to establish Nixon's own identity before the voters and to distance their candidate from recent criticism of the administration's defence and foreign policies. Eventually, it was agreed that Eisenhower would delay his major appearances until late in the campaign. Such a strategy also accorded with the wishes of Mamie Eisenhower, who worried that strenuous campaigning might jeopardize her husband's health. In fact, in the final days of the race, at Mamie's urging, Nixon turned down Eisenhower's offer to deliver a flurry of last-minute campaign speeches in several borderline states. The president was stung and angered by Nixon's stance, and only learned of Mamie's intervention much later.

Kennedy's narrow victory on election day dealt a body blow to Eisenhower. Having viewed the contest as a referendum on his administration, he was bitterly disappointed by what seemed to be a popular repudiation of his policies. The 'spenders' had triumphed, and Eisenhower feared the worst. 'All I've been trying to do for eight years has gone down the drain', he complained (Eisenhower, 1974: 285). Throughout the administration, others shared the sense of rejection. When suspicion of voting irregularities surfaced in Texas and Illinois, where the Democrats had secured victories, the president even considered launching a Justice Department investigation. Nixon, however, decided not to press the issue and Eisenhower let the matter drop. Instead, he began to prepare for a smooth transition to the next administration and worked on one last major speech to recapitulate his views about security with solvency and limited government.

CHAPTER FIVE

EXPANDING THE COLD WAR

Just as Eisenhower experienced mounting domestic difficulties during his second term, so too did his administration encounter increasing international problems. In the oil-rich Middle East, the Anglo-French débâcle at Suez not only strained relations among the Western allies but also opened the door for the expansion of Soviet influence. The Eisenhower administration sought to contain communist penetration in the region, but seemed to conflate Arab nationalism with communism. No sooner did the administration direct its attention to that area than a second crisis flared up in the Taiwan Strait over the offshore islands. In the aftermath of the Sputniks, moreover, the United States and its allies had to deal with an increasingly belligerent Nikita Khrushchev, who tried to parlay Soviet achievements in rocketry into a propaganda and diplomatic advantage over the West. The Soviet leader tested the Western resolve to defend West Berlin and undertook an economic aid offensive in the Third World. In Latin America, Fidel Castro led a successful revolution against the pro-American Cuban dictator Fulgencio Batista, and pursued an increasingly provocative and independent foreign policy. Despite these confrontations, Eisenhower refused to give up hope for a limited *détente* with the Soviet Union, especially in the area of arms control. By the last year of his presidency, there seemed to be a prospect for a genuine breakthrough. Ultimately, however, Eisenhower's inability to build consensus within his own administration doomed the nuclear arms control efforts, and the shooting down of an American spy plane over the Soviet Union scotched the long-anticipated Paris summit. By the time he left office, Eisenhower had managed to keep the peace, but he had failed to ease Cold War tensions significantly and bequeathed a series of unresolved international difficulties for his successor.

THE EISENHOWER DOCTRINE AND THE MIDDLE EAST

Eisenhower and Secretary Dulles spent the first days of 1957 contemplating the significance of the Suez episode for regional stability in the Middle East.

In their estimation, the Anglo-French demise created a power vacuum that the Soviets might readily exploit. Furthermore, Nasser's brand of radical Arab nationalism was on the rise, and the remaining pro-Western Arab regimes in the area had to be assured of continued support. Finally, tension between the Arab states and Israel threatened to erupt into a regional war at any moment. Eisenhower and Dulles concluded that only the United States had the necessary economic, military and diplomatic means to contain communism in the region and extinguish any sparks that might ignite the whole powder keg. Under their guidance, the United States became deeply embroiled in the labyrinth of Middle Eastern politics.

In January 1957, the White House unveiled the Eisenhower Doctrine for the Middle East. Building on the precedents of the Truman Doctrine formulated during the Greco-Turkish crisis of 1947 and the more recent Formosa (Taiwan) Resolution, Eisenhower requested discretionary authority from Congress to disburse up to $200 million of military and economic aid in the region over the next two years. He also sought congressional approval to send American troops to any nation that requested assistance when threatened with 'overt armed aggression by any country controlled by international communism' (PPP, 1958: 6–17). Such an American commitment was necessary, he argued, because the Soviet Union was poised to extend its influence in the region and the creation of communist satellites in the Middle East might threaten vital sea lanes and the supply of oil to the West. A clear indication of America's willingness to intervene would bolster the confidence of pro-Western regimes and deter 'ambitious despots' and 'power-hungry Communists'. Not all congressional leaders agreed with the administration's analysis. Some questioned the wisdom and constitutional propriety of granting the president a blank cheque to use American armed forces. Others opposed additional foreign aid expenditures, especially to Arab nations. Ultimately, however, the Middle East Resolution passed both Houses of Congress with only minor amendment and Eisenhower signed it into law on 9 March [*Doc. 14*].

Although the Eisenhower Doctrine stressed the menace of external communist aggression, Eisenhower recognized that the most pressing threat to Western interests in the Middle East was the spread of Nasserism. Under the guise of containing international communism, Eisenhower soon deployed the Middle East Resolution against the Egyptian president's adherents. In April 1957, Jordanian elections resulted in a victory for the Nasserites, who quickly moved to break ties with the West. King Hussein, fearful for his throne, dismissed his prime minister and declared martial law. The ousted leader established a government-in-exile in neighbouring Syria, while his supporters took to the streets in Amman. King Hussein appealed to the Eisenhower administration for help against the 'communist' subversion threatening his country. Under the authority granted him by the

Middle East Resolution, Eisenhower quickly allocated $20 million in aid to Jordan and moved the US Sixth Fleet into the Eastern Mediterranean as a precaution. Shortly thereafter, the king and his conservative allies restored order. The Eisenhower Doctrine, it seemed, had effectively preserved a pro-Western regime from radical Arab nationalism (FRUS, 1955–57: 13.104–7).

The administration was rather less successful containing Nasserism in Syria, which Eisenhower adjudged to be drifting into the communist camp. When the leftist Syrian government signed an arms deal with the Soviet Union, Eisenhower approved CIA plans to foment a military coup by pro-Western army officers. The Syrian government thwarted the operation in August and expelled several American diplomats. The State Department pessimistically concluded that Syria was becoming 'a base for military and subversive activities' designed to establish 'Soviet Communist domination' in the Middle East (FRUS, 1955–57: 13.685–9). But Eisenhower's efforts to use the Eisenhower Doctrine to mobilize a coalition of pro-Western Arab states to contain Syria ran afoul of inter-Arab politics and Arab nationalism. As a last resort, the administration encouraged Turkey to move troops menacingly along the Syrian border, but the manoeuvre backfired when even friendly Arab states proclaimed their solidarity with Syria against Turkish military intervention in the region. The crisis dissipated in October when King Saud offered to mediate a settlement and the Turks withdrew their forces. Nasser trumped Saud's diplomatic efforts, however, by dispatching a token force of Egyptian troops to Syria to defend his Arab brothers against external aggression and bolster the political fortunes of pro-Nasser elements there. In this case, Eisenhower's meddling simply drove the Syrians closer to the Soviet Union and Nasser. Early in 1958, Egypt and Syria united under Nasser's leadership as the United Arab Republic.

These developments greatly troubled the government of neighbouring Lebanon, where pro-Western president Camille Chamoun's scheming to amend the constitution and secure a second consecutive term threatened to undermine that country's delicate political balance between Christians and Muslims and precipitate a civil war. Chamoun had aligned Lebanon closely with the United States in the Cold War and vocally supported the Eisenhower Doctrine in 1957, but Lebanese Muslim leaders sympathized with Nasser. With help from the CIA, Chamoun's forces swept to victory in the 1957 parliamentary elections, but Muslim leaders protested the widespread fraud and agitated for new elections. Chamoun, with an eye to securing American support for his political ambitions, accused his opponents of 'playing the Kremlin's game' (FRUS, 1955–57: 13.219–20). Following the unification of Egypt and Syria, political violence between Chamoun's supporters and their opponents escalated. Nasser stirred up his followers by broadcasting increasingly strident anti-Chamoun propaganda into Lebanon.

By May, Lebanon was on the brink of civil war. The assassination of a prominent journalist by pro-Chamoun gunmen led to violent clashes in Beirut. Although some prominent Lebanese Christians attributed the crisis to Chamoun's political ambitions, Chamoun declared that his nation was under assault from the United Arab Republic (UAR) and the Soviet Union and sounded out the United States about the prospects for American military intervention under the auspices of the Eisenhower Doctrine.

Chamoun's request forced the Eisenhower administration to ponder the larger implications of the Middle East Resolution. Aware of the internal causes of Chamoun's difficulties, Dulles warned that the doctrine might not apply in Lebanon's case, given the lack of evidence that the UAR had attacked Lebanon or that the UAR was under the control of international communism. Direct military intervention, moreover, would jeopardize the good will generated among Arab nations as a result of the United States's stance against Western imperialism during the Suez crisis. Eisenhower agreed, but worried that failing to respond to Lebanon's request might be even more damaging to American interests as it would raise doubts among pro-Western regimes everywhere regarding the commitment of the United States to its friends. Eisenhower thus informed Chamoun that he would dispatch American troops on condition that he first seek United Nations help in resolving the crisis and renounce any intention of seeking a second presidential term. While Chamoun moved to meet these conditions, Eisenhower again sent the Sixth Fleet to the Eastern Mediterranean and authorized the dispatch of twenty tanks requested by the Lebanese leader. Eisenhower hoped that Chamoun would be able to stabilize the situation himself, but he had already decided that should Chamoun formally request American military help he would be compelled to respond in order to maintain American credibility, even at the price of creating 'a pro-Western dictatorship, since there is not sufficient popular support in Lebanon for Western intervention' (FRUS, 1958–60: 11.133–7).

Just as the United Nations appeared to be on the verge of mediating a settlement in Lebanon, a military coup in Iraq dramatically changed the political climate and Chamoun forced Eisenhower's hand. On 14 July, pro-Nasser forces in Baghdad overthrew the pro-Western monarchy, executing the king and the crown prince in the process. Chamoun immediately appealed for American help, warning that communism and Nasserism were about to engulf Lebanon and the entire Middle East. Turkey, Iran, Pakistan and Saudi Arabia also urged American and British intervention. Eisenhower quickly decided that American credibility necessitated military action, even at the risk of inflaming Arab opinion against the West and interrupting oil supplies. Inaction might result in the loss of Lebanon and the entire region, which would be 'far worse than the loss of China, because of the strategic position and resources of the Middle East' (FRUS, 1958–60: 11.211–15).

Eisenhower and Dulles met with congressional leaders to obtain their endorsement of a decision that had, in effect, already been taken. When several senators questioned Dulles's assessment of the Lebanese crisis as communist-inspired and the applicability of the Eisenhower Doctrine, the president interjected that it was more important to consider 'what the victims believe' and that Chamoun was convinced that he was battling 'Soviet Communism' (FRUS, 1958–60: 11.224). Shortly after the first of some 14,000 Marines and Army personnel went ashore in Beirut on 15 July, Eisenhower informed the American people that the United States was acting to thwart communist aggression against Lebanon and prevent the outbreak of a larger conflict (PPP, 1958: 556–7). Two days later, the United States assisted the airlift of 3,700 British paratroopers to Amman, Jordan, to bolster the regime of an anxious King Hussein.

Eisenhower's remarks to the American people were disingenuous. He understood that 'Nasser's capture of Arab loyalty and enthusiasm', not Soviet subversion, was the real source of Western difficulties in the Middle East, but raising the communist spectre secured the necessary congressional and public support for military intervention (FRUS, 1958–60: 11.365). Fortunately, a political settlement in Lebanon allowed Eisenhower to withdraw American forces a few weeks later before sceptical congressmen could challenge the propriety of his actions. Eisenhower's envoy brokered a settlement whereby Chamoun agreed to step down as president in favour of a general. Shortly after the transition of power and dispatch of UN observers, American forces left Lebanon and the British departed Jordan. The intervention had been bloodless and had propped up pro-Western regimes in Lebanon and Jordan, but it had also aroused popular Arab antagonism towards the West and encouraged closer ties between the UAR, Iraq and the Soviet Union.

After the Lebanese intervention, the Eisenhower administration reconsidered its entire Middle Eastern policy. The president admitted that the Eisenhower Doctrine, by attempting to stem the tide of the most dynamic force in the region, Arab nationalism, had in fact alienated popular sentiment and played into the Soviets' hands. Eisenhower therefore approved a new policy whereby the United States would 'work more closely with Arab nationalism and associate itself more closely with such aims and aspirations of the Arab people as are not contrary to the basic interests of the United States' (FRUS, 1958–60: 12.189). As a first step, the Eisenhower administration moved towards normalizing relations with Nasser and extended $153 million in food aid. The Eisenhower Doctrine was shelved.

THE SECOND OFFSHORE ISLANDS CRISIS

Even before American troops departed Lebanon, a second crisis erupted in the Taiwan Strait over the offshore islands (Map 2). On 23 August, the PRC began an intensive artillery bombardment and blockade of Quemoy. Once again, the United States faced the prospect of becoming embroiled in the Chinese civil war. Eisenhower quickly concluded that Khrushchev and Mao were acting in collusion to test American resolve in East Asia, and determined to thwart the communist aggression. As in the earlier offshore islands crisis, the administration decided that Quemoy and Matsu could not be sacrificed under duress, but the ensuing American military build-up and tough rhetoric unnerved the allies and ran the risk of triggering a third world war.

Mao's decision to initiate a new offshore islands crisis apparently derived from several factors. In part, he intended to punish Chiang Kai-shek and the United States for militarizing the region. Since the 1954–55 crisis, Chiang had ignored American advice to de-emphasize the islands and instead had increased his garrison to 100,000 troops, representing about one-third of his entire army. At the same time, Chiang continued to receive American military and economic aid, including medium-range nuclear missiles that had arrived in Taiwan in 1957. Mao believed that renewed military pressure in the strait might persuade Chiang and the Americans that the offshore islands were not worth defending. He also saw military action as a means to emphasize the PRC's frustration with the stalled ambassadorial-level talks with the United States over formal diplomatic recognition, PRC representation in the United Nations and the status of Taiwan. He suspected that the United States was seeking a two Chinas solution. Finally, Mao recognized an opportunity to enhance his revolutionary credentials. He would 'pin down' American forces in Asia and thus demonstrate his support for the Arabs' anti-imperialist struggle in the Middle East. While not seeking a war with the United States, he would nevertheless prove that the PRC could not be intimidated by Dulles's threats of nuclear retaliation (CWIHP, 1995–96: 6–7.209–10).

Mao's military preparations and his renewed 'liberate Taiwan' propaganda offensive had alerted the Eisenhower administration to the possibility of PRC military action against the offshore islands. Eisenhower and Dulles mistakenly believed, however, that Mao and Khrushchev had deliberately concocted the crisis to test American resolve in light of the Soviets' new ballistic missile capability (FRUS, 1958–60: 19.50–1). In fact, Mao acted on his own initiative and had not informed Khrushchev of his intentions during the latter's visit to Beijing in early August (Zubok and Pleshakov, 1996: 220–1). As in the earlier Taiwan Strait crisis, Eisenhower concluded that the islands' real importance was more psychological than strategic.

Given Chiang's unwise concentration of forces there, their loss might destroy Nationalist morale, undermine Chiang's regime in Taiwan, and pave the way for that island's eventual reunification with the mainland under Communist rule. Such an outcome, moreover, might set off a chain reaction in South Korea, Japan, the Philippines and Southeast Asia where pro-Western governments would succumb to Sino-Soviet pressure and internal subversion. For that reason, Dulles urged a strong statement of the administration's intention to defend the offshore islands and deter a PRC assault. Eisenhower, however, preferred a more ambiguous statement. He worried that a clear American commitment would play into the hands of Chiang, who might then provoke further escalation with the PRC in order to drag the United States into a war to liberate the mainland. The president therefore placed American forces in Asia on war alert, stepped up military aid to Chiang, reinforced the Seventh Fleet and deployed it close to Taiwan, but stopped short of making the explicit statement to defend the islands requested by Chiang (FRUS, 1958–60: 19.73–6).

Eisenhower's initial actions failed to halt the PRC bombardment or lift the blockade, and as pessimistic reports on the supply and morale situation on Quemoy arrived from Taipei, he escalated American involvement. He authorized the Navy to convoy Nationalist supply vessels through international waters, arranged for the delivery of amphibious vehicles to facilitate the resupply effort, and reinforced American air forces in the Taiwan area. Eisenhower confidentially decided that an all-out PRC assault on the islands would require direct American military intervention and the JCS developed contingency plans for a graduated military response, ranging from conventional weapons to tactical nuclear strikes against PRC airfields and entrenched positions. Dulles and the military chiefs argued that the United States had to be prepared to use such weapons, even at the risk of adverse international reaction, in order to sustain the credibility of the United States and the New Look strategy. Eisenhower agreed that nuclear weapons might be required if deterrence failed, but recognized the danger of escalation and insisted on retaining final authority over their use (Craig, 1998). This apparent willingness to resort to nuclear war over the islands, however, was precisely what troubled the allies. Early in the crisis, the British reminded the administration that they did not consider the offshore islands worth a world war. Dulles's assurance that any tactical nuclear weapons used would entail 'no more than small airbursts without fallout' hardly eased British anxieties about American intentions (FRUS, 1958–60: 19.100–4, 138). The British instead suggested a quiet approach to Khrushchev to pressure Mao into negotiating an end to the crisis.

As the shelling and blockade continued into early September, Eisenhower resorted to a combination of deterrence and diplomacy to defuse the crisis. On 4 September, Dulles issued a presidentially-approved statement warning that the United States might regard any effort to seize the offshore islands by force as grounds for retaliation under the authority of the Formosa Resolution. At the same time, Dulles held out the prospect for a negotiated settlement by inviting the PRC to resume diplomatic talks to settle the status of Taiwan peacefully (FRUS, 1958–60: 19.134–6). In Moscow, this combination of overt military preparations and strong words had the desired effect on a worried Khrushchev, who dispatched his foreign minister to Beijing on 5 September to ascertain Mao's intentions and urge restraint on the Chinese leader. Although Mao reportedly boasted to his Soviet guest of China's willingness to endure a nuclear strike by the Americans, the Chinese leader actually wanted to avoid war with the United States and had instructed his commanders to avoid clashes with American forces. He had already begun to contemplate resuming the ambassadorial talks as a way of easing tension with the United States, and on 6 September the PRC declared its readiness to reopen negotiations. The following day, with the danger of war apparently averted, Khrushchev attempted to shore up his own credentials as the leader of the socialist bloc by warning Eisenhower that any attack on the PRC would be considered an attack 'on the Soviet Union'. Privately, Mao did not welcome Khrushchev's belated intervention, and he turned down a Soviet offer to extend its nuclear deterrent to the defence of the Chinese coast. Eisenhower accepted Mao's offer of negotiations, but in a belligerent address to the American people designed to reassure Asia-first Republicans and Chiang Kai-shek, he warned that there would be no 'appeasement' of Communist aggressors during the talks (PPP, 1958: 694–700).

Although Eisenhower and Khrushchev continued to exchange sharp words and the PRC continued the shelling, the reopening of ambassadorial talks in Warsaw in mid-September marked the first easing of the crisis. As promised, the United States pursued a hard line in the negotiations, refusing to compromise the security of Taiwan and keeping open the possibility of a two Chinas solution, but at the same time the Eisenhower administration pressured Chiang Kai-shek into restricting his military activities against the mainland and reducing his garrison on Quemoy. Mao, meanwhile, concluded that Chiang and the United States could not be intimidated into surrendering the islands without a major conflict and scaled back the shelling. He also recognized that the continued Nationalist presence served a useful diplomatic purpose by providing a mechanism whereby the PRC could periodically increase or relax tension with the United States [*Doc. 15*]. According to Mao's analogy, the United States had tied a 'noose' around its neck with the offshore islands and handed the other end of the rope to the PRC. On 6 October, the PRC announced a unilateral seven-day cease-fire, which enabled the United States to suspend its convoy operations, and later that month Dulles visited Taiwan and obtained a vaguely-worded commitment from Chiang to refrain from using force to 'liberate' the mainland and to reduce the Nationalist presence on the offshore islands in return for United States military aid. Mao reciprocated by restricting the shelling to alternate days for the next few weeks before finally halting the bombardment. The immediate emergency was over.

The second offshore islands crisis revealed important tensions in both the Soviet and American alliance systems and raised questions about the credibility of Eisenhower's nuclear strategy. The episode seriously strained Sino-Soviet relations. Mao was becoming increasingly critical of Khrushchev's inadequate support for wars of national liberation and his moves towards 'peaceful coexistence' with the West. To Mao, Khrushchev's caution seemed all the more curious given his post-Sputnik boasts about Soviet missile capabilities and the enhanced strategic position of the Soviet Union. For his part, Khrushchev viewed Mao's actions as unnecessarily provocative and dangerous. Aware of the hollowness of his own nuclear threats, he was anxious to avoid a general war and eventually decided to renege on an earlier promise to assist the Chinese atomic bomb project by delivering a prototype nuclear weapon. The crisis proved equally troubling for United States relations with its allies. Rather than establishing American credibility, the Europeans viewed Eisenhower's commitment to the defence of small, insignificant islands in the western Pacific as wrongheaded and dangerous. At home, developments in the Taiwan Strait generated questions about Eisenhower's leadership in national security affairs and the feasibility of massive retaliation in light of improved Soviet nuclear capabilities. Eisenhower's personal approval ratings sagged and the crisis further compounded the Republicans' difficulties in the build-up to the disastrous off-year elections. Henceforward, Eisenhower's foreign policy never quite regained the generally bipartisan support it had previously enjoyed.

BERLIN

Eisenhower hardly had time to congratulate himself over the easing of tensions in the Taiwan Strait than the United States faced a new crisis over Berlin. On 10 November 1958, Khrushchev announced that the Soviet Union intended to sign a separate peace treaty with the German Democratic Republic, which would terminate the occupation rights of the United States, Britain and France in West Berlin, and turn over to the East Germans responsibility for controlling access to the city. Later that month, Khrushchev proposed that West Berlin become a demilitarized 'free city' and gave the Western powers six months to negotiate a settlement along these lines. Should no agreement be reached by 27 May 1959, the Soviet Union would unilaterally complete arrangements with East Germany, terminating Western transit and occupation rights in Berlin. If the Western allies then resorted to force against the GDR to maintain their privileges, the Soviet Union would come to the defence of its Warsaw Pact ally. In short, Western failure to comply with Soviet demands might result in general war.

Khrushchev's belligerent stance on Berlin derived from several sources. West Berlin was an anomaly on the map of Europe – an island of capitalism located in the heart of Communist East Germany – and a cause of concern and embarrassment for Khrushchev and East German leader Walter Ulbricht. Khrushchev variously described the Western enclave as a 'thorn' and a 'bone in my throat' (FRUS, 1958–60: 8.148–52). As the West German 'economic miracle' proceeded apace in the 1950s, West Berlin dramatically demonstrated the growing political and economic disparity between the two Germanies. While Ulbricht struggled to establish a socialist state, thousands of East Germans fled to the West through the city, including many intellectuals and highly skilled workers. Khrushchev and Ulbricht wanted to stem this flow of refugees and enhance the physical security of the GDR, but Khrushchev also viewed Berlin as an important means of exerting pressure on the West to reopen negotiations on the larger German question. Berlin, he explained, was 'the testicles of the West. Every time I want to make the West scream, I squeeze on Berlin' (Gaddis, 1997: 140). By late 1958, the Soviets feared that a resurgent West Germany was becoming too powerful and was undermining the *status quo* of a weak, divided Germany. The Soviets were especially concerned about the Eisenhower administration's decision to supply tactical atomic weapons to NATO allies in order to offset the Soviet bloc's numerical advantage in conventional forces. An economically resurgent Federal Republic of Germany armed with atomic weapons might prove too powerful to be contained by NATO's political arrangements. Interestingly, Khrushchev initiated the Berlin crisis just as West German units began training for an atomic capability. The Soviet leader's timing also seems to have been influenced by his perception that Soviet missile advances had shifted the strategic balance in his favour. Finally, a forceful stance over Berlin would help to restore Soviet credibility as the leader of the international socialist movement in the aftermath of the recent offshore islands crisis [*Doc. 16*].

As Khrushchev had anticipated, his Berlin ultimatum exposed significant divisions among the Western allies. Eisenhower and Dulles believed that Western firmness and solidarity in defending their rights in the face of Khrushchev's threats would eventually convince the Soviet leader to back down. In their view, American credibility was again at stake, specifically the obligation to the Germans of West Berlin. The British, however, expressed reluctance to fight for Berliners and preferred to work out practical arrangements to conduct business with East German authorities while stopping short of extending formal diplomatic recognition to the GDR. West German Chancellor Konrad Adenauer violently objected to the British approach. Any Western dealings with GDR officials, he warned, would signify the first step down the slippery slope towards the acceptance of two Germanies. Such a development would destroy public support for his strategy of aligning the FRG with the West and deferring reunification, and might ultimately result in a united but neutralized Germany. Under intense pressure from Adenauer, the Eisenhower administration dropped consideration of its own contingency plan to treat East German officials as 'agents' of the Soviet Union.

Eisenhower and Dulles moved to resolve allied differences and forge a unified Western position at the NATO Council meetings in December 1958 and a series of bilateral talks the following January. In the Paris NATO meetings, Dulles reiterated his belief that Khrushchev would back down in the face of Western firmness and the threat of general war, and his exertions produced a strong NATO Council statement supporting Western access rights and condemning the Soviet plan to repudiate its obligations and turn them over to the GDR. But NATO also offered Khrushchev a face-saving way out by calling for renewed negotiations on the whole German question. Only with great difficulty, however, did Dulles secure Anglo-French endorsement of military contingency planning to keep the access routes to West Berlin open, and that on the strict understanding that no action would be taken without further inter-allied consultation. Armed with at least a façade of allied unity, the administration finalized its strategy for dealing with Khrushchev. In January 1959, Eisenhower and Dulles proposed negotiations on the German question at the foreign ministerial level and timed to overlap with Khrushchev's six-month ultimatum, thereby allowing the Soviet leader to manoeuvre out from under his self-imposed deadline. Meanwhile, Eisenhower approved a series of military preparations, such as increased patrols, that would signal American and allied resolve to defend their rights in West Berlin. Should the East Germans block access after the 27 May deadline, the allies would suspend traffic and seek to mobilize international opinion against the Soviets (FRUS, 1958–60: 8.292–4, 300–6). In order for this 'double-barrelled' strategy to work, the Soviets had to be convinced that, as Eisenhower put it, 'our whole stack was in this play' (Eisenhower, 1965: 338–9).

Despite ostensible allied unity, the British government's attitude continued to trouble the administration. In February, against American advice, Macmillan visited Moscow. The British prime minister remained convinced that diplomacy, rather than military confrontation, could resolve the Berlin crisis, but Dulles feared another Munich. Macmillan also had an eye on his political future, having scheduled a general election for later in the year. During the Moscow talks, however, Khrushchev could not persuade Macmillan to accept *de facto* East German control over access routes to West Berlin and, having failed to drive a wedge between the Western allies, effectively rescinded his original ultimatum by agreeing to a foreign ministers' conference on the broader German question to be followed by a summit meeting. Macmillan then visited Washington to convince Eisenhower to shelve the military contingency planning for the duration of the foreign ministers' conference and agree to a summit. Although Eisenhower refused to drop the contingency planning, he agreed to attend a summit should the foreign ministers' meeting prove productive. Indeed, Eisenhower had begun to contemplate 'startling Macmillan a little bit' by inviting Khrushchev to visit the United States (Trachtenberg, 1991: 201–2).

By the time the Geneva foreign ministers' conference convened in mid-May, Dulles had resigned. In February 1959, he had been diagnosed with a recurrence of the stomach cancer that had first afflicted him during the Suez crisis. Eisenhower initially refused Dulles's resignation and the secretary worked from his hospital bed while undergoing radiation treatments. Only in mid-April, as Dulles's condition deteriorated, did Eisenhower reluctantly accept the inevitable and elevate Dulles's understudy, former Massachusetts governor Christian A. Herter, to the secretaryship. The Geneva negotiations, however, quickly stalled. Herter rejected Soviet demands to formalize the division of Germany and withdraw all occupation forces from Berlin. The Western allies offered to reduce their forces in the city, but insisted that Germany could only be reunified after free elections. The conference thus failed to achieve any progress towards a German settlement. On 27 May, the expiration date of Khrushchev's original ultimatum, the ministers recessed their talks to attend Dulles's funeral in Washington.

As the Geneva talks deadlocked, Eisenhower followed through on his idea of a direct approach to Khrushchev to 'break the log jam' (FRUS, 1958–60: 10.308). Macmillan had pressed Eisenhower for a summit and Khrushchev desired any opportunity to enhance his international standing. Dulles had always resisted such meetings on the grounds that they artificially raised expectations and tended to encourage agreements for the sake of agreement, but after his death Eisenhower had more room to manoeuvre. In July, the State Department extended an official invitation to Khrushchev to visit the United States, but an apparent misunderstanding between the White House and the State Department failed to convey Eisenhower's precondition that progress first had to be made at the Geneva talks. Khrushchev accepted the offer before the oversight could be corrected, and Eisenhower found himself saddled with an unconditional meeting. Even so, Eisenhower believed that his personal diplomacy might serve a useful purpose. Despite condemnation from right-wing Republicans, Eisenhower welcomed the opportunity to promote a thaw in East–West relations and 'soften up the Soviet leader even a little bit' (Eisenhower, 1965: 432). The imminent prospect of a personal meeting between Eisenhower and Khrushchev, however, effectively foreclosed the possibility of any major agreements during the final month of the Geneva foreign ministers' meeting. Meanwhile, as preparations for Khrushchev's visit commenced, Eisenhower hastily visited Western Europe to reassure nervous allied leaders excluded from the proceedings that he would not sacrifice their interests for sake of an agreement.

The Western leaders need not have worried. Khrushchev's twelve-day visit to the United States in September generated a great deal of public interest but nothing of substance. Indeed, Eisenhower had little to offer the Soviet leader because Adenauer had effectively vetoed consideration of any Berlin or German settlement that would modify the *status quo*. Eisenhower's major objective was to persuade Khrushchev to lift any deadline or ultimatum for a German settlement and establish a sense of trust between the superpowers. In a private conversation with Khrushchev, Eisenhower told him that he had 'the opportunity to become the greatest political figure in history' if he exerted his power for the cause of peace. The Soviet leader reciprocated, insisting that he believed that neither nation sought war with the other, that it was necessary to establish mutual trust, and that 'there should be will and determination on both sides to do everything possible to resolve their differences' (FRUS, 1958–60: 10.394, 409–10). Two days of frank discussions at Camp David failed to produce anything more than an agreement to continue negotiating. Eisenhower consented to a summit conference on the European question and a reciprocal visit to the Soviet Union in the following spring. He also conceded that the allied position in Berlin was an 'anomaly' and that the United States had no desire to prolong its occupation indefinitely. For his part, Khrushchev agreed to drop the notion of a separate peace treaty with East Germany and negotiate a mutually satisfactory Berlin settlement without insisting on any deadline (FRUS, 1958–60: 9.45–52).

For the moment, the Berlin crisis had been alleviated. Eisenhower managed to paper over inter-allied differences and defuse Khrushchev's ultimatum. Khrushchev, however, had forced the West to reopen negotiations on the German question and obtained the unexpected bonus of a prestige-enhancing visit to the United States. Both leaders anticipated more substantive, and problematic, negotiations on the crucial issues of Berlin, Germany and European security at the Paris summit scheduled for the following spring (Eisenhower, 1965: 488–90).

DISARMAMENT AND THE NUCLEAR TEST BAN

The second major area of proposed discussion for the 1960 summit conference was disarmament, and specifically the idea of a nuclear test ban agreement. During his first term, Eisenhower had periodically expressed deep concern about the escalating nuclear arms race, but he had failed to forge consensus within his administration behind a feasible disarmament proposal. Both his 'Atoms for Peace' and 'Open Skies' initiatives had been so skewed in favour of the United States that they had never really stood much chance of forming the basis for an international agreement. The Atomic Energy Commission (AEC) and the Pentagon, meanwhile, remained steadfastly opposed to any disarmament proposal that impinged on the development of the very nuclear weapons that formed the basis of the administration's New Look defence policy. During the 1956 election campaign, Eisenhower himself had sharply criticized Adlai Stevenson for broaching the idea of a nuclear test suspension as a first step towards a more comprehensive disarmament agreement on the grounds that the Soviets might exploit American restraint to advance their own nuclear weapons programme. Until 1958, therefore, the Eisenhower administration's official disarmament position made any suspension of nuclear weapons tests contingent on Soviet agreement to a verifiable cut-off in nuclear weapons production and conventional force reductions. But early in 1958, Eisenhower's resistance to new disarmament initiatives, and especially some form of nuclear test ban, began to soften.

Several factors encouraged Eisenhower to take a new look at the disarmament problem. Adverse world reaction to the poisonous radioactive fallout generated by the continued atmospheric testing of nuclear weapons raised pressure on the administration to suspend such tests. Some nine thousand scientists from forty-four countries signed Nobel Prize-winning chemist Linus Pauling's petition to the United Nations demanding a halt to testing. Eisenhower's United Nations Ambassador, Henry Cabot Lodge, reported that the United States was taking a beating on the testing issue (FRUS, 1958–60: 3.537–8). At home, congressional hearings on the public health dangers of radioactive fallout raised public awareness of the issue. Equally important, however, were personnel changes within the administration. When Eisenhower brought in Killian as his personal science adviser and created the President's Science Advisory Committee (PSAC), he secured an alternative source of technical advice that challenged the rigid anti-test ban views of AEC scientists such as Edward Teller. Ironically, the February 1958 resignation of Eisenhower's special assistant for disarmament, Harold Stassen, who had been the administration's strongest supporter of a nuclear test suspension, also facilitated a more flexible administration position on disarmament. Dulles had always resented Stassen's appointment as an infringement on State Department prerogatives and had frequently blocked his innovative proposals. But after his rival's departure, Dulles increasingly voiced his own support for a test ban, both as a confidence-building measure towards further disarmament agreements and as a sop to increasingly critical world opinion.

The Soviets provided the final impetus for Eisenhower to explore the possibility of a nuclear test ban. On 31 March 1958, after completing a nuclear test series, they announced a unilateral test suspension and called on the United States to do likewise. Dulles had anticipated this Soviet demarche and had urged Eisenhower to deliver a pre-emptive strike by announcing his intention to halt American tests after completion of the current series, scheduled to run from April through September. Eisenhower, as usual, had deferred to the AEC and Pentagon insistence that further tests would be essential for maintaining the American advantage in nuclear weapons technology. Nevertheless, Dulles's warnings about the deteriorating American position in the court of world opinion prompted Eisenhower to urge his advisers to 'think about what could be done to get rid of the terrible impasse in which we now find ourselves with regard to disarmament' (FRUS, 1958–60: 3.572). A few days after the Soviets' announcement, Eisenhower's science advisers offered a solution. An interagency panel of experts concluded that a practical system for detecting most atmospheric, underwater and underground tests could be developed using existing technology. Such a system might provide the 'opening wedge' for a general disarmament inspection regime. The PSAC also estimated that a test ban after the current American series would actually freeze an American qualitative advantage in nuclear weapons development. As an added political bonus, early announcement of a planned suspension of nuclear testing might offset pressure to accept any Soviet proposal to halt rocket tests, which would freeze a Soviet advantage (FRUS, 1958–60: 3.603–4). These technical assessments, coupled with Dulles's diplomatic concerns, finally led Eisenhower to seek a modest step towards halting the increasingly expensive and potentially disastrous nuclear arms race. At the end of April, over the objections of the Pentagon and AEC, Eisenhower offered the Soviets technical talks on the feasibility of verifying a permanent nuclear weapons test ban. The administration had now taken the significant step of de-linking the issue of testing from a cut-off in production of nuclear weapons.

The prospects for a nuclear test ban agreement and a halt to atmospheric testing advanced considerably throughout the rest of the year. In the summer, scientists from the United States, Britain, Canada, France and the Soviet Union met in Geneva and devised a mutually acceptable control system for verifying compliance with a nuclear test ban agreement. The so-called Geneva System envisioned a worldwide network of seismic control posts, supported by shipboard stations and numerous specially-equipped aircraft. The experts believed that the system would be able to detect most nuclear explosions greater than five kilotons in yield, and on-site inspections of suspicious seismic events would minimize the potential for undetected violations of a test ban. Once the conference reported that a workable control system was 'technically feasible', Eisenhower invited the other nuclear powers, Britain and the Soviet Union, to enter into negotiations for a test ban treaty and suspended American tests for one year, provided that the Soviets reciprocated (PPP, 1958: 635–6). Eisenhower closely coordinated his announcement with the British, assuring them that recent revisions to the Atomic Energy Act would allow the United States to provide necessary technical information for the refinement of British thermonuclear weapons and timing the test moratorium to coincide with the completion of a scheduled British test series. Khrushchev quickly accepted Eisenhower's offer to negotiate. Before the conference convened in Geneva, however, all the nuclear powers engaged in one last frenzied round of testing to beat the 31 October deadline, ensuring that 1958 would witness more weapons tests and radioactive fallout than any previous year.

Eisenhower's faith in his science advisers and a technological solution to disarmament was sorely tested when American scientists analysing data from the most recent underground shots discovered that the Geneva Conference of Experts had seriously underestimated the difficulty of using seismographs to distinguish between underground nuclear explosions and natural earthquakes. The Soviets accused the United States of manipulating the data to justify a more intrusive inspection system in Soviet territory, and Eisenhower's military advisers insisted that the United States should now drop the idea of a comprehensive test ban and pursue a more modest measure confined to atmospheric tests and large-yield underground shots that could be positively identified. A scientific consultant for the Air Force further clouded the picture by suggesting that nuclear explosions in excavated underground chambers might be effectively muffled from the surrounding earth, greatly reducing the resulting seismic signal and casting further doubts about the technical feasibility of monitoring a comprehensive test ban. Reluctantly, Killian now advised Eisenhower to settle for a more limited test ban agreement. In April 1959, Eisenhower formally proposed an atmospheric test ban as an interim step, pending agreement on a verifiable comprehensive test ban (PPP, 1959: 331–2). Khrushchev rejected the offer on the grounds that it did nothing to halt the arms race, but he kept alive the hope for a comprehensive test ban by offering to accept a British proposal for an annual quota of on-site inspections and agreeing to further technical talks on the significance of the new scientific data for the detection system. In late 1959, however, the technical talks ended acrimoniously without producing a mutually acceptable monitoring system, effectively killing the prospect for a comprehensive nuclear test ban.

Despite the lack of progress, Eisenhower resisted the pressure to resume nuclear tests when the moratorium expired on 31 October 1959. The AEC insisted that renewed testing was essential to improve the yield of ballistic missile warheads, explore the potential of 'clean' nuclear weapons that produced lower levels of radioactive fallout, and ensure the safety of stockpiled weapons. George Kistiakowsky, the Harvard chemist who replaced Killian as Eisenhower's science adviser in mid-1959, disagreed. He assembled another inter-agency panel of scientific experts, which concluded that there was no pressing requirement for additional tests in the immediate future. Armed with this finding, Eisenhower extended the American test moratorium to the end of 1959. The British and Soviets followed suit. When the Geneva technical talks finally broke down, Eisenhower announced that the United States would not resume testing without advance notification, and Khrushchev declared that the Soviet Union would not resume tests unless the West did. In fact, encouraged by his science advisers and the State Department, Eisenhower refused to sanction further nuclear tests for the remainder of his presidency.

Kistiakowsky also injected new life into the test ban negotiations. Early in 1960, he suggested that the administration pursue an atmospheric and underwater test ban accompanied by a suspension of underground tests above a threshold of 4.75 on the Richter scale. Employing the Richter scale threshold would sidestep the tricky issue of establishing an international scientific consensus on the correlation between the kiloton yield of an explosion and its seismic amplitude, although American scientists believed that 4.75 on the Richter scale would correspond to an underground blast of up to 19 kilotons. The 4.75 threshold, moreover, would be sufficiently high to require a modest number of on-site inspections in the Soviet Union, thereby parting the Iron Curtain to some degree, but not so low as to impair AEC and Pentagon efforts to develop small-yield nuclear weapons through continued underground testing (Kistiakowsky, 1976: 222–3). The new initiative would have the added benefits of keeping the British in line behind the administration's insistence on a verifiable test suspension, rather than an indefinite and unpoliced moratorium, and alleviating international concern about radioactive fallout (FRUS, 1958–60: 3.825–31). Eisenhower announced the new position in February 1960, and proposed a joint research effort by American, British and Soviet scientists to improve seismic detection techniques so that the threshold might be progressively lowered (USDD, 1960: 31–2).

Despite continued opposition from the AEC and the Pentagon, the prospects for an agreement along the lines suggested by Kistiakowksy seemed to be good. In March, the Soviets accepted the threshold concept on condition that the Western powers agree to a four- to five-year moratorium on all tests below the 4.75 threshold pending completion of the joint research programme. Macmillan viewed the Soviet offer as a 'wonderful chance' for an agreement and flew to Washington to bolster Eisenhower's resolve (Macmillan, 1972: 185). Meanwhile, in a heated meeting with his top national security advisers, Eisenhower insisted that the international political advantages of a threshold agreement and a limited-duration moratorium far outweighed any inconvenience to the nuclear weapons programme. He suggested adopting a one- to two-year moratorium on condition that the other powers reciprocated, but he wanted to impose it by executive action rather than international treaty in order to by-pass potential opposition in the Senate and avoid tying the hands of his successor in the White House. When the AEC protested, Eisenhower angrily retorted that if the United States failed to explore the Soviet offer 'all hope of relaxing the Cold War would be gone' (FRUS, 1958–60: 3.861–3; Kistiakowsky, 1976: 281–2). Macmillan heartily endorsed Eisenhower's position and believed that 'the omens were good' for a test ban treaty (Macmillan, 1972: 191). The two leaders anticipated that the upcoming summit in Paris would provide the ideal forum for ironing out the remaining details regarding the composition of the international control commission, the exact quota of on-site inspections and the seismic research programme.

THE U-2 AND THE PARIS SUMMIT

Expectations were high for the Paris Summit. In the months leading up to the meeting significant progress towards a nuclear test ban agreement and Khrushchev's willingness – his heated rhetoric notwithstanding – to negotiate a mutually satisfactory agreement on Berlin augured well for the high-level meeting. Western leaders were especially optimistic about the prospects for a test ban because it appeared that Khrushchev wanted to prevent the further proliferation of nuclear weapons, particularly to the unpredictable Mao Zedong. Eisenhower, meanwhile, was determined to advance the cause of *détente* with the Soviets and conclude concrete agreements at Paris that might ease international tensions. Macmillan believed that the world was 'on the eve of a great step forward' (Macmillan, 1972: 195). Then, on 5 May 1960, just days before the conference was to convene, Khrushchev dramatically announced that the Soviet Union had shot down an American spy plane over Soviet territory.

Eisenhower had first authorized intelligence-gathering overflights of the Soviet Union by the high-flying U-2 aircraft in mid-1956. The project sprang from the recommendations of a special scientific panel headed by Killian that had reported on technical measures to safeguard against the danger of surprise attack. The panel's recommendations also spurred efforts to develop reconnaissance satellites, but these would not be operational until 1960. In the meantime, Eisenhower authorized limited overflights by the U-2. The aircraft could photograph huge swaths of territory 125 miles wide from an altitude of 70,000 feet, rendering it immune to interception by Soviet aircraft and surface-to-air missiles of the mid-1950s, although not to detection by Soviet radar. Eisenhower and Dulles calculated that the

Soviets would never publicly condemn the overflights for fear of revealing the inadequacy of their own air defences. Even so, the president recognized the provocative nature of the missions, which was partly why he assigned responsibility for the project to the ostensibly civilian CIA rather than the Air Force and insisted that every operation be cleared with him first. Indeed, by 1959, as he moved towards *détente* with Khrushchev, Eisenhower increasingly weighed the political and diplomatic risks of continued overflights against the value of additional hard intelligence on the Soviet military–industrial complex, and occasionally blocked missions for political reasons (FRUS, 1958–60: 10.260–2). In a remarkably prescient moment early in 1960, Eisenhower told his aides that his 'one tremendous asset in a summit meeting ... [was] his reputation for honesty. If one of these aircraft were lost when we are engaged in apparently sincere deliberations, it could be put on display in Moscow and ruin the President's effectiveness' (Ambrose, 1984: 568). But the hard intelligence gathered by the U-2 proved irresistible. It alleviated Eisenhower's concerns about a potential surprise attack and confirmed his hunch about the limited nature of the Soviets' long-range missile programme, steeling his resolve to hold the line on defence spending against the military services and congressional Democrats. In early 1960, Eisenhower considered suspending further overflights altogether but eventually yielded to CIA requests for additional operations to monitor Soviet progress towards deploying operational intercontinental ballistic missiles. In April, he approved one final U-2 flight before the summit, provided that it was completed by 1 May.

The Eisenhower administration's public reaction to the downing of the U-2 turned into a comedy of errors. Having been led to believe by his military and intelligence advisers that the Soviets lacked the capability to shoot down a U-2 and that, in the event of a mishap, the pilot would never be taken alive and all evidence of espionage would be destroyed by built-in self-destruct systems in the aircraft, Eisenhower authorized the release of a prearranged cover story that a high-altitude NASA weather plane was missing. When Khrushchev declared that Soviet forces had shot down a spy plane, Eisenhower sanctioned another statement suggesting that the NASA aircraft might have accidentally strayed into Soviet airspace. Khrushchev's bombshell before the Supreme Soviet on 7 May that he had both the wreckage of the spy plane and the pilot, who would be tried for espionage, caught the administration in a lie. At first, Eisenhower acquiesced with his advisers' efforts to insulate him from responsibility for the débâcle, but Herter's statement that the president had granted broad authorization to conduct intelligence gathering without specifically approving individual missions simply compounded the problem. It apparently confirmed Khrushchev's analysis that Pentagon militarists were out of control and reinforced Democrats' campaign charges that the president was out of touch. The inept cover-up fuelled press speculation at home and abroad about who ran United States policy and also caused a minor rift in the administration when the Pentagon protested against the suggestion that field commanders were acting unilaterally. Eventually, Eisenhower decided to 'endure the storm' (FRUS, 1958–60: 10.517). On 9 May, Herter revealed that Eisenhower had authorized the U-2 overflights for several years and justified them on the grounds of preventing another Pearl Harbor. In his press conference two days later, Eisenhower defended his actions and emphasized that he saw no reason why a spat over 'an unarmed nonmilitary' plane should jeopardize progress on such vital issues as disarmament and the status of Berlin that were scheduled for discussion at the forthcoming summit (PPP, 1960: 403–4).

Although Eisenhower publicly remained optimistic about prospects for the summit, Khrushchev's reaction to the U-2 episode indicated that the meeting was now in jeopardy. Indeed, by taking responsibility for the spy missions and justifying them on the grounds of the Soviets' obsession with secrecy, Eisenhower infuriated the Soviet leader. Khrushchev had overcome considerable domestic and Chinese resistance to 'peaceful coexistence' on the grounds that the communist world could gain more by negotiation with the West than confrontation and that Eisenhower was trustworthy, but now he felt personally betrayed. Khrushchev had also probably lowered his own expectations for the summit after a recent visit to France had convinced him that the Western allies could not be divided on the question of Berlin's status and would not make significant concessions. Thus, Khrushchev embarked on a series of angry public statements designed to restore his own prestige and that of the Soviet Union. He denounced American aggression, warned that the Soviets would do whatever was necessary to defend their sovereignty, and threatened retaliation against nations that provided bases for the U-2. Even so, Khrushchev only definitely decided to scuttle the summit rather than risk further humiliation minutes before he departed for Paris. On the day before the opening session, he circulated a set of demands that he knew Eisenhower could not possibly accept, including a formal apology for the U-2 incident, punishment of those responsible and a promise that there would be no further spy flights over Soviet territory (FRUS, 1958–60: 9.416).

In effect, the summit collapsed before it had ever started. At the opening session on 16 May, Khrushchev delivered an emotional harangue against the United States and insisted on receiving satisfaction concerning the U-2 before proceeding to formal discussions of other matters. He also announced that Eisenhower's planned visit to the Soviet Union would have to be postponed. Eisenhower's assurance that he had unilaterally suspended further overflights for the duration of his administration failed to placate the Soviet leader. De Gaulle and Macmillan backed up the president and unsuccessfully tried to move the conference on to more substantive issues. The next day, the Soviets refused to attend the scheduled talks and the summit collapsed.

The U-2 incident and the failure of the Paris Summit thwarted Eisenhower's ambition to achieve a significant thaw in East–West relations in the final months of his administration. Khrushchev, under mounting pressure from Mao and hardliners at home, ruled out the prospect of further negotiations on Berlin until after Eisenhower's successor had been installed, although he still managed to infuriate East German leaders by refusing to sign a peace treaty unilaterally with them and counselling continued patience on the status of Berlin. The Geneva test ban negotiations dragged on until August, but without an agreement between Eisenhower and Khrushchev on the key questions of the annual quota of on-site inspections and the duration of the moratorium on small-yield underground tests, so no formal treaty was possible. In fact, as the prospects for *détente* faded, the Soviets became less willing to accept a test ban treaty that would freeze a significant advantage in American nuclear weapons. Eisenhower was bitterly disappointed. Several weeks after the failed summit, he told Kistiakowsky that the 'stupid U-2 mess had ruined all his efforts' to end the Cold War and that 'he saw nothing worthwhile left for him to do now until the end of his presidency' (Kistiakowsky, 1976: 375).

CONTAINING CASTRO

In the final two years of the Eisenhower administration, Latin America again became a major focus of concern in the global struggle to contain communism. In the immediate aftermath of the Arbenz overthrow in Guatemala, the administration had congratulated itself on its smooth handling of hemispheric affairs and continued to provide military aid and training to militantly anti-communist regimes while largely ignoring requests from democratically-elected leaders for regional economic development aid. The extent of latent hostility towards the Eisenhower administration's hemispheric policies only became apparent to Washington in mid-1958, when Vice-President Nixon's South American goodwill tour ended in chaos. After being assailed by angry student demonstrators in Montevideo, Uruguay, and Lima, Peru, Nixon's motorcade was surrounded and attacked by a mob in Caracas. Venezuelan authorities only extricated Nixon's party with great difficulty. Although Nixon attributed his ordeal to the 'Communist conspiracy' and received a hero's welcome on his return home, the demonstrations dramatized deep regional grievances against the United States for its support of repressive regimes and its neglect of economic problems. The fracas spurred a vigorous debate within the administration over Latin American policy.

Following the Nixon débâcle and a fact-finding trip by Eisenhower's brother, Milton, to Central America, the administration revised its Latin American policies on several fronts. Over the objections of Secretary Dulles, who remained sceptical of the ability of the Latin American masses to practise democracy, Eisenhower accepted Nixon's advice to differentiate between authoritarian regimes and representative governments by offering 'a formal handshake for dictators; an *embraso* for leaders in freedom' (FRUS, 1958–60: 5.238; Nixon, 1962: 192). In February 1959, the administration's revised policy statement for Latin America called for 'special encouragement' to democratically-elected leaders. Nevertheless, the new policy ignored calls from liberal Democrats and Latin American reformers to curb the military aid programme, which still constituted the bulk of United States assistance to the region. The Eisenhower administration concluded that the Latin American officer corps constituted an important stabilizing force in the region and represented the best hope for containing communism (FRUS, 1958–60: 5.95, 102–3). Similarly, at the urging of Milton Eisenhower, the administration began to retreat from strict adherence to free-market principles in Latin American trade. The administration listened sympathetically to Brazilian President Juscelino Kubitschek's argument that regional economic development would raise living standards, encourage democratic reforms, and undercut support for left-wing revolutionaries. Given the poor infrastructure and political unrest in the area, however, such development would require government assistance to smooth the way for private capital. Recent United States import restrictions on certain Latin American commodities, moreover, had adversely affected the region during the 1957–58 economic downturn. In light of such views, President Eisenhower belatedly took modest steps to meet Latin American demands. The United States entered commodity agreement talks to stabilize the price of major Latin American exports by limiting production, and concluded a coffee agreement in 1959. That same year, Eisenhower also threw his support behind a long-anticipated regional development bank and supplied most of the initial $1 billion capitalization. Although these steps fell far short of the massive $40 billion aid package envisioned by Kubitschek, the administration remained optimistic that it would suffice to keep the hemisphere firmly aligned with the United States in the larger Cold War struggle. Indeed, in early 1959 the NSC concluded that 'none of the Latin American nations faces an immediate threat of overt Communist aggression or takeover' (FRUS, 1958–60: 5.93).

The NSC's optimistic assessment reflected the Eisenhower administration's initial difficulty in determining the significance for the United States of Fidel Castro's revolutionary triumph in Cuba over the pro-American dictator Fulgencio Batista just a few weeks earlier. Castro's movement promised political liberalization, land reform and social justice.

What began as a small insurgency against the corrupt military strongman, who had dominated the island's political life and amassed a personal fortune since the 1930s, evolved into a broad-based popular movement. At first, the Eisenhower administration attempted to safeguard the $900 million of direct American investments in the island – ranging from sugar plantations and mills to oil refineries, public utilities, mines and railroads – by encouraging Batista to adopt political reforms. But when he used his American-supplied aircraft to bomb his own people, rigged an election to preserve his political power, and refused all American efforts to step aside peacefully, Eisenhower imposed an arms embargo and withdrew diplomatic support. Although the CIA reported that Castro was no communist, concern about communist influence in his movement and uncertainty about his intentions spurred last-ditch covert efforts to create a 'third force' to thwart a Castro victory. Only after those schemes collapsed did Eisenhower accept the inevitable and recognize Castro's provisional government in January 1959 (FRUS, 1958–60: 6.347).

Whatever Castro's political philosophy, his actions soon alienated Eisenhower. Shortly after seizing power, the Cuban leader legalized the Communist Party, removed his former liberal allies from office, seized the premiership for himself, and meted out summary justice to political opponents through revolutionary tribunals. When Castro visited the United States in April at the invitation of the American Society of Newspaper Editors, Eisenhower conveyed his distaste over the executions by refusing to meet with him and delegating the task to Nixon and Herter (Eisenhower, 1965: 523). Throughout the visit, Castro sought to allay his hosts' fears. He indicated that Cuba would remain aligned with the West, acknowledged that his desire for land reform might adversely affect some American-owned enterprises, but emphasized that he would not move against the massive American naval base at Guantanamo Bay established by treaty in the aftermath of the 1898 Spanish–American–Cuban War (FRUS, 1958–60: 6.482). Nixon found Castro to be 'incredibly naive about Communism', but he and Herter agreed that his strong personality made him a natural and formidable leader whom the United States ought to try to 'orient in the right direction' (FRUS, 1958–60: 6.476). But this was precisely the problem. Castro was determined above all else to free Cuba of its traditional economic and political dependence on the United States and reassert a Cuban nationalism that had been stifled by the American intervention of 1898 and subsequent political and trade agreements. To the surprise of American officials, Castro did not request financial aid from the United States during his visit. Instead, on returning to Cuba, he quickly enacted agrarian reform that expropriated large estates and prohibited foreigners from owning land. By late 1959, most American direct investments in Cuba seemed to be threatened. More ominously for the Eisenhower administration, in February 1960 Castro moved to alleviate Cuba's dependence on the American market by concluding a trade and aid agreement with the Soviet Union.

After visiting South America early in 1960, Eisenhower returned convinced that Castro's challenge to United States hegemony in the Western Hemisphere could not be tolerated any longer. His seizures of American property were setting a dangerous precedent and his encouragement of radical revolutionary movements endangered several friendly Latin American regimes. More ominously, Castro was opening the door to Soviet economic and political penetration in an area long deemed vital to United States security. The American Embassy in Havana concluded that the Castro regime was 'bitterly anti-American' and that there was 'no hope' of ever establishing satisfactory relations with it (FRUS, 1958–60: 6.815–16, 832). Eisenhower decided that Castro would have to be removed just as Arbenz had been removed, but the United States would once again have to disguise its hand in order to accommodate Latin American sensibilities about United States intervention. On 17 March 1960, Eisenhower approved a CIA programme of covert action to replace Castro's government with one 'more acceptable to the U.S.'. The scheme entailed building up a Cuban opposition movement in exile, beaming anti-Castro radio broadcasts into Cuba, cultivating an intelligence and sabotage network within Cuba, and arming and training a paramilitary force of Cuban exiles to lead the armed resistance to Castro's regime [*Doc. 17*]. Henceforward, there would be no accommodation between the United States and Castro.

Throughout the remainder of 1960, Eisenhower increased the pressure on Castro, but to little effect. The administration engaged in economic warfare by ordering American oil refineries in Cuba not to process crude oil supplied by the Soviets, effectively prohibiting further imports of Cuban sugar into the United States, and imposing a general embargo on most trade with the island. Castro retaliated by seizing the oil refineries and other remaining American assets. The Eisenhower administration also attempted to isolate Cuba diplomatically in the Organization of American States (OAS) by offering generous financial and economic aid packages to Latin American nations willing to contain Castro, and established a new $500 million fund to promote regional economic development and short-circuit demands for radical political reform. Eisenhower even appeased democratic Latin American leaders by pressuring the Dominican Republic's long-term dictator, Rafael Trujillo, to step down. To the administration's embarrassment, however, the staunchest anti-Castro supporters in the OAS proved to be the dictatorships of Nicaragua, Guatemala and the Dominican Republic (FRUS, 1958–60: 6.977, 982). Meanwhile, the CIA's efforts to organize the anti-Castro resistance and undermine the Cuban leader, including a variety of bizarre schemes to discredit and even assassinate him, got nowhere.

Whether Eisenhower knew personally of the various assassination plots is problematic, given CIA Director Allen Dulles's care to provide the president with a degree of 'plausible deniability' regarding covert operations, but Eisenhower's subordinates had no doubt that the president wanted Castro removed (Ambrose and Immerman, 1981: 304–6). Intense factionalism among the anti-Castro exiles, however, precluded the emergence of clear alternative government and Castro's increasingly effective militia easily handled the small groups of American-trained guerrillas infiltrated into Cuba (FRUS, 1958–60: 6.1128). By late 1960, Castro's open defiance of the United States and public embrace of Khrushchev during the United Nations General Assembly meetings in New York became increasingly embarrassing for Eisenhower and Nixon. During the election campaign, while the vice president privately pressed for tougher action against Castro, Kennedy accused the administration of allowing a communist foothold in the Western Hemisphere (Eisenhower, 1965: 598).

In his waning days in office, Eisenhower became even more determined to act against Castro, and his hostility set the United States on a path that would lead directly to the disastrous Bay of Pigs invasion. Shortly after the November election, he approved CIA plans for an expanded exile guerrilla force to be trained in Guatemala and urged his advisers to 'take more chances and be more aggressive' towards Castro's regime (FRUS, 1958–60: 5.1130). By January, the CIA envisioned an amphibious landing by several hundred Cuban exiles, supported by a small air force, and the establishment of an enclave that would become the rallying point for all anti-Castro forces in Cuba. Meanwhile, the State Department sounded out Latin American support for a coordinated rupture in diplomatic relations and a trade embargo. On the military front, Eisenhower oversaw contingency plans to strike back hard should Castro move against the naval base at Guantanamo Bay, and some advisers even suggested staging an 'incident' at Guantanamo that might provide the pretext for direct military intervention. When Castro ordered a reduction in American embassy personnel in Havana, Eisenhower broke off diplomatic relations on 3 January, opening the door for the United States to extend recognition to a suitable anti-Castro alternative when one could be found (FRUS, 1961–63: 10.3–6). In his final meeting with President-Elect Kennedy before leaving office, Eisenhower urged him to step up the training of anti-Castro forces in Guatemala and do whatever was necessary to destroy Castro's government (FRUS, 1961–63: 10.44; Rabe, 1987: 171). Clearly, by the time Eisenhower left office, the United States and Cuba were embarked on a collision course.

Eisenhower found his final months in office to be extremely frustrating. The optimistic hopes for a degree of *détente* with the Soviet Union and a limited arms control agreement were dashed at Paris. Rather than *détente*, the

United States now faced an increasingly belligerent Soviet leader who appeared intent on re-establishing his communist revolutionary credentials. In the Third World, moreover, communism appeared to be on the rise. Even in the Western Hemisphere, United States hegemony was being challenged by Castro's upstart regime. Bitterly disappointed, Eisenhower handed over the problems of Berlin, arms control, Castro and falling dominoes in Southeast Asia to his young successor.

CHAPTER SIX

ASSESSMENT

On the evening of 17 January 1961, Dwight D. Eisenhower bade farewell to the American people. In his final address, he reiterated several of the themes that had preoccupied him during his eight years in office and offered guidance to his successors. Reflecting on his own inability to relax international tensions, he reminded his listeners of the overarching presence of the Cold War. The United States still faced a 'hostile ideology – global in scope, atheistic in character, ruthless in purpose, and insidious in method' for the indefinite future. Nevertheless, in a final warning about the evils of the garrison state, he emphasized the requirement for a sense of balance and perspective in addressing the communist threat; in a thinly-veiled swipe at his critics he cautioned against crash programmes offered by their promoters as panaceas for the nation's difficulties. In what would become the most memorable portion of his speech, Eisenhower noted that the 'conjunction of an immense military establishment and a large arms industry' was new in the American experience and its influence permeated 'every city, every State house, every office of the Federal government'. As a result, he called on Americans to 'guard against the acquisition of unwarranted influence, whether sought or unsought, by the military–industrial complex'. Only 'an alert and knowledgeable citizenry' could ensure that military security did not come at the expense of individual liberty, national solvency and even democracy itself [*Doc. 18*] (PPP, 1960–61: 1035–40).

Eisenhower's farewell address encapsulated the president's preoccupation with balancing means and ends in national security policy-making, or defending a 'way of life', as he put it. To a certain extent, the old general had done a remarkable job of holding down defence spending, particularly in the wake of Sputnik when he encountered growing dissent among his own military advisers and an increasingly hostile and vocal Congress controlled by the Democratic opposition. Measured in constant dollars, defence spending in calendar year 1960, Eisenhower's last full year in office, was lower than in any previous year since the Korean War. Even so, Eisenhower could not alone halt the increasing militarization of

American society. Indeed, his New Look's emphasis on high-technology weapons systems placed a premium on advanced military research and development by American industry and universities, fostering the very 'military–industrial complex' that he decried. While the overall military budget declined somewhat under Eisenhower, total federal funding for research and development grew significantly, privileging those disciplines deemed most important for national security and exerting greater governmental direction and control over the nation's research agenda. Trained manpower, moreover, came to be seen as a vital Cold War resource, providing a rationale for significantly expanded federal involvement in the nation's educational institutions. In fact, Eisenhower won the battle over military spending but lost the war against militarization. Both candidates in the 1960 presidential election pledged to do more to bolster the nation's defences and meet the communist threat, and President Kennedy embarked on a substantial military build-up even after acknowledging that the much-publicized 'missile gap' did not in fact exist.

Eisenhower's stewardship of the nation's economy similarly produced mixed results. For all his rhetoric regarding the need for fiscal responsibility and a sound dollar, Eisenhower only managed to balance the federal budget in three of his eight years in office, although inflation generally remained a modest 2 per cent throughout his tenure. Of course, Democratic control of Congress after 1954 somewhat complicated Eisenhower's efforts to hold down spending. In retrospect, his record seems much more impressive. None of his twentieth-century successors managed to match even three balanced budgets. Nevertheless, Eisenhower's determination to balance the budget and contain inflation drew increasing criticism from contemporaries by the end of his second term. Liberal economists acknowledged that the economy had steadily expanded on Eisenhower's watch, but noted that many Americans had been left behind during the 1950s' prosperity. Greater fiscal and monetary flexibility, they argued, could generate even more impressive rates of economic growth that could simultaneously solve pressing social problems at home and enable a more rigorous waging of the Cold War abroad. Eisenhower's emphasis on combating inflation rather than unemployment during the economic downturns of 1958 and 1960 seemed to run against the rising tide of public opinion. Kennedy exploited this sense of dissatisfaction by promising to get the country moving again and embracing advocates of the New Economics. Only much later, after decades of unbalanced budgets, spiralling inflation and mounting public indebtedness, did Eisenhower's fiscal views again come into general favour.

In addition to his concern about the nation's long-term finances, Eisenhower also ran for election in 1952 to rescue the Republican Party as a viable alternative to the Democrats and thereby restore the two-party system. During his first term, especially, Eisenhower sought to modernize

the Republican Party, prove that it was capable of good government, cultivate its commitment to internationalism, and widen its base of support.
These efforts to promote Modern Republicanism, however, met with
limited success. Recognizing political realities, Eisenhower stymied demands
from the Republican right to roll back the New Deal–Fair Deal welfare
state. He did eliminate the Truman administration's remaining wartime
economic regulations, but he resisted pressure from some of his party's
leaders for a massive tax cut that would have unbalanced the budget. Not
only that, he refused to dismantle the Tennessee Valley Authority and
significantly expanded Social Security coverage. He even initiated two
massive new public works programmes to construct an interstate highway
system and connect the Great Lakes to the Atlantic Ocean. If nothing else,
Eisenhower's eight years in office helped to purge the ghost of Herbert
Hoover and demonstrate that the Republicans could govern responsibly. He
made little headway, however, in cultivating a vigorous Modern Republican
movement in his own party, partly because of his inherent distaste for party
politics, but also because he actually shared many of the conservatives'
convictions about creeping socialism eroding individual freedoms and
responsibility. Indeed, Eisenhower proved to be a rather ineffective party
leader. Although his personal popularity remained high, the Republican
Party steadily lost ground after the triumph of 1952 and the conservative,
unilateralist wing of the party remained a force to be reckoned with, particularly after the débâcle in the 1958 congressional elections. Right-wing
Republicans criticized their own president for moving too close to the
Democrats, appeasing the Soviet Union, and failing to achieve longstanding
conservative goals. Senator Barry Goldwater of Arizona became the focus
for these views in Congress and he would ultimately be far more effective in
shaping the Republican Party in his own image.

On the most pressing moral issue of the day, the African-American
struggle for political and civil rights, Eisenhower was missing in action. He
personally believed that the Supreme Court's unanimous *Brown vs. Board
of Education* ruling against segregated public schools was a mistake and
worked to delay its implementation. He correctly foresaw that legal rulings
would not change people's deeply-held prejudices and convictions, but in
hesitating to enforce the law and counselling black leaders to exercise
continued patience he was overly solicitous of the diehard white segregationists. To Eisenhower's credit, when the Governor of Arkansas violated
federal authority during the 1957 Little Rock crisis, he acted decisively to
enforce the law, but the president's earlier refusal to signal his support for
the *Brown* decision precipitated the crisis in the first place. By the end of
Eisenhower's term, federal inaction and white 'massive resistance' had
resulted in little more than symbolic progress towards full civil and political
rights for African Americans.

The central issue that had caused Eisenhower's entry into presidential politics was the Cold War, and by the time he left office he had fashioned what would essentially form the basis of American grand strategy for the duration of the conflict. Viewing the Cold War as a long-term proposition, and rejecting the notion that the Soviet Union would risk its own destruction by deliberately initiating a general war, he focused on building adequate American forces to contain communism and deter war until such time as the Soviet system collapsed from within under the weight of its own internal contradictions. As both sides developed new, more powerful weapons of mass destruction, Eisenhower recognized that the United States and its allies required only sufficient weapons to maintain a credible risk of nuclear retaliation rather than absolute superiority. On his watch, the United States developed the strategic triad of manned bombers, intercontinental ballistic missiles and submarine-launched ballistic missiles that would constitute the backbone of the American nuclear deterrent until the end of the Cold War, but the enthusiasm for new weapons generated a massive 'overkill' capacity (Rosenberg, 1983). Eisenhower also recognized the importance of maintaining free world solidarity against the Sino-Soviet bloc. To that end, he cultivated closer ties with the NATO allies, reluctantly acquiesced to the continued presence of American troops in Europe for the indefinite future, endorsed German rearmament, and supported further European economic cooperation and integration that promised to build a dynamic liberal-capitalist world economy. Eisenhower understood that the developing world, too, constituted important assets in the larger Cold War struggle, serving as sources of strategic materials, potential markets, military bases and manpower that could be used to contain regional conflicts. In Eisenhower's view, foreign military and economic aid programmes to promote capitalist economic development and cultivate friendly, pro-Western regimes in these areas represented wise long-term investments, although he never quite convinced Congress of this fact. In short, Eisenhower laid the foundation for the long-term strategy of containment that endured until the collapse of the Soviet Union.

Despite his commitment to winning the Cold War, Eisenhower was nevertheless willing to pursue negotiations with the Soviets towards limited agreements that would ease international tensions and reduce the likelihood of war by miscalculation. In the short term, he was largely unsuccessful. For all his eloquence about the dangers to humankind of an unregulated nuclear arms race, Eisenhower's early forays into arms control – such as Atoms for Peace and Open Skies – were too often exercises in psychological warfare and propaganda rather than realistic arms control proposals. Later, when world opinion recoiled from the dangers of atmospheric nuclear testing, Eisenhower took the important step of unilaterally suspending American tests and decoupling negotiations for a nuclear test ban from general disarmament discussions, but he ultimately failed to forge consensus within his administration for the test ban treaty that he apparently wanted and that, for a while, seemed to be within reach. The misguided final U-2 flight over the Soviet Union, the collapse of the Paris Summit and the impasse in the Geneva test ban negotiations momentarily destroyed any prospect for *détente* and a breakthrough in arms control. Eisenhower was bitterly disappointed at his personal failure, but it derived from his own inveterate anti-communism, mistrust of the Soviets and failure to follow through on his inclination to stem the arms race. Eisenhower's successors, however, would build on his strategy of simultaneously pursuing deterrence and *détente* by means of summitry and limited arms control initiatives.

Eisenhower left a far more controversial legacy for American relations with the developing world. While occasionally displaying a remarkable degree of prescience about the anti-colonial and nationalist aspirations of Third World peoples, Eisenhower and Dulles too often viewed such regions through Cold War-tinted lenses. Recognizing that overt armed intervention to protect perceived American interests might be counter-productive, especially in the Western Hemisphere, where the United States had pledged itself to non-intervention, Eisenhower readily turned to covert action by the CIA. The successful coup in Iran disposed of an independent-minded nationalist and opened the door for American oil companies, but it also sowed the seeds for future trouble by aligning the United States with an increasingly repressive ruler and fostering over-confidence in the efficacy of covert operations. The Iranian coup led logically to the overthrow of another nationalist reformer, Jacobo Arbenz, in Guatemala, and plans for what would become the ill-fated Bay of Pigs invasion of Cuba in 1961. Although Kennedy bore primary responsibility for the Cuban fiasco, the Eisenhower administration handed the incoming president a poisoned chalice. With invasion plans already well developed and an anti-Castro force in training, it is difficult to see how Kennedy could have called off the operation and disposed of the various elements without suffering immense political damage at home and conveying a message of weakness abroad. While Eisenhower privately scoffed that Kennedy's handling of the anti-Castro invasion, particularly his refusal to authorize supporting air strikes, was a 'profile in timidity and indecision', Eisenhower had initiated the covert war against Fidel Castro and bore a great deal of responsibility for the disaster (Ferrell, 1981: 390). Similarly, Eisenhower bequeathed to his successors an increasingly difficult situation in Indochina, where Ngo Dinh Diem's anti-communist regime encountered mounting internal opposition and external pressure. Having committed American resources and prestige to a non-communist, independent South Vietnam, subsequent administrations found themselves 'trapped' by Eisenhower's initial success. While Eisenhower might justifiably claim credit for having avoided overt

American military intervention in Indochina in the 1950s, in his post-presidential years he encouraged Lyndon B. Johnson to pursue military victory in Vietnam. Thus, in American relations with the Third World, the Eisenhower administration's conflation of nationalism with communism and expansion of covert capabilities and interventions undermined its stated commitment to democratic values and economic development and created the context for future difficulties.

Eisenhower's leadership has generally received higher marks for his handling of various crises and avoidance of war. He refused to be diverted from an armistice in Korea by Syngman Rhee's release of Communist prisoners in 1953, resisted pressures from the French and his own military advisers to intervene militarily in Vietnam in 1954, avoided war with mainland China over the offshore islands in 1955 and 1958, and remained firm in the face of Khrushchev's threats to West Berlin in 1959. In each of these instances, crises that might have resulted in war were averted. A close examination of the historical record, however, demonstrates that in some cases Eisenhower's leadership was by no means as effective as he might have believed, that his choices were often hamstrung by the decisions and actions of allies, and that contingency and luck sometimes facilitated an unexpected easing of the situation. Nevertheless, by delaying making final decisions or taking irrevocable measures, Eisenhower occasionally helped to defuse the sense of crisis and let cooler heads prevail. Sometimes, the cause of world peace was best served by restraint and inaction.

In the final analysis, of course, there is no denying the fact that Eisenhower presided over seven-and-a-half years of peace and relative prosperity. It would be more than a generation before another American president could make such a modest claim.

DOCUMENTS

President Eisenhower explains his 'middle-way' philosophy.

Frankly I think that the critical problem of our time is to find and stay on the path that marks the way of logic between conflicting arguments advanced by extremists on both sides of almost every economic, political and international problem that arises. ...

Coming down to our own day, we have those individuals who believe that the Federal government should enter into every phase and facet of our individual lives, controlling agriculture, industry and education, as well as the development of every natural resource in our country. These people, knowingly or unknowingly, are trying to put us on the path towards socialism. At the other extreme we have the people – and I know quite a number of them – who want to eliminate everything that the Federal government has ever done that, in one way or another, represents what is generally classified as social advance. For example, all of the regulatory commissions established in Washington are anathema to these people. They want to abolish them completely. They believe that there should be no trade union laws and the government should do nothing even to encourage pension plans and other forms of social security in our industry.

When I refer to the Middle Way, I merely mean the middle way as it represents a practical working basis between extremists, both of whose doctrines I flatly reject. It seems to me that no great intelligence is required in order to discern the practical necessity of establishing some kind of security for individuals in a specialized and highly industrialized age. At one time such security was provided by the existence of free land and a great mass of untouched and valuable natural resource throughout our country. These are no longer to be had for the asking; we have had experiences of millions of people – devoted, fine Americans, who have walked the streets unable to find work or any kind of sustenance for themselves and their families.

On the other hand, for us to push further and further into the socialistic experiment is to deny the validity of all those convictions we have held as to the cumulative power of free citizens, exercising their own initiative, inventiveness and desires to provide better living for themselves and their children. ...

The generality that I advance is merely this: Excluding the field of moral values, anything that affects or is proposed for masses of humans is wrong if the position it seeks is at either end of possible argument.

Eisenhower, letter to Bradford Grethen Chynoweth, 13 July 1954, in Louis P. Galambos et al. (eds) (1996), *The Papers of Dwight David Eisenhower*, vol. 15: *The Presidency: The Middle Way* (Baltimore, MD: Johns Hopkins University Press), pp. 1185–6.

DOCUMENT 2   THE HIDDEN HAND VERSUS McCARTHYISM

President Eisenhower outlines his indirect strategy for handling Senator Joseph R. McCarthy, 21 July 1953.

I was interested in a statement of yours in which you express your satisfaction that 'at last you are ready to crack down on McCarthy'. Now I have no doubt that you are correct in the later statement in the same paragraph where you say, 'I have always known that you feel about him much as I do'. At the same time, I must say that I am not quite certain as to the meaning of your first expression. Again referring to the special significance or, let us say, the popular standing of the Presidency, it is quite clear that whenever the President takes part in a newspaper trial of some individual of whom he disapproves, one thing is automatically accomplished. This is an increase in the headline value of the individual attacked.

I think that the average honorable individual cannot understand to what lengths certain politicians would go for publicity. They have learned a simple truth in American life. This is that the most vicious kind of attack from one element always creates a very great popularity, amounting to almost hero worship, in an opposite fringe of society. Because of this, as you well know, Huey Long [US Senator from Louisiana, 1931–35] had his idolaters. Every attack on him increased their number (an expression of the under-dog complex) and enhanced the fervor of his avowed supporters.

When you have a situation like this, you have an ideal one for the newspapers, the television and the radio, to exploit, to exaggerate and to perpetuate. In such a situation I disagree completely with the 'crack down' theory. I believe in the positive approach. I believe that we should earnestly support the practice of American principles in trials and investigations – we should teach and preach decency and justice. We should support – even militantly support – people whom we know to be unjustly attacked, whether they are public servants or private citizens. In this case, of course, it is necessary to be certain of facts if the defense is to be a personal one. Of course, the indirect defense accomplished through condemnation of unfair methods is always applicable.

Persistence in these unspectacular but sound methods will, in my opinion, produce results that may not be headlines, but they will be permanent because they will earn the respect of fair-minded citizens – which means the vast bulk of our population. To give way in anger or irritation to an outburst intended to excoriate some individual, his motives and his methods, could do far more to destroy the position and authority of the attacker than it would do to damage the attacked.

Eisenhower, letter to Swede Hazlett, 21 July 1953, in Robert Griffith (ed.) (1984), *Ike's Letters to a Friend, 1941–1958* (Lawrence, KS: University Press of Kansas), pp. 110–11.

DOCUMENT 3   **THE *BROWN* DECISION**

The United States Supreme Court rejects racially-segregated public educational facilities in the cases known as Brown vs Board of Education of Topeka, Kansas, *17 May 1954.*

In each of the cases, minors of the Negro race, through their legal representatives, seek the aid of the courts in obtaining admission to the public schools of their community on a nonsegregated basis. In each instance, they had been denied admission to schools attended by white children under laws requiring or permitting segregation according to race. This segregation was alleged to deprive the plaintiffs of the equal protection of the laws under the Fourteenth Amendment. ...

The plaintiffs contend that segregated public schools are not 'equal' and cannot be made 'equal' and that hence they are deprived of the equal protection of the laws. ...

In approaching this problem, we cannot turn the clock back to 1868 when the Amendment was adopted, or even to 1896 when *Plessy* v. *Ferguson* was written. We must consider public education in the light of its full development and its present place in American life throughout the Nation. Only in this way can it be determined if segregation in public schools deprives these plaintiffs of the equal protection of the laws.

Today, education is perhaps the most important function of state and local governments. Compulsory school attendance laws and the great expenditures for education both demonstrate our recognition of the importance of education to our democratic society. It is required in the performance of our most basic public responsibilities, even service in the armed forces. It is the very foundation of good citizenship. Today it is a principal instrument in awakening the child to cultural values, in preparing him for later professional training and in helping him to adjust normally to his environment. In these days, it is doubtful that any child may reasonably be expected to succeed in life if he is denied the opportunity of an education. Such an opportunity, where the state has undertaken to provide it, is a right which must be made available to all on equal terms.

We come then to the question presented: Does segregation of children in public schools solely on the basis of race, even though the physical facilities and other 'tangible' factors may be equal, deprive the children of the minority group of equal educational opportunities? We believe that it does. ...

To separate them from others of similar age and qualifications solely because of their race generates a feeling of inferiority as to their status in the community that may affect their hearts and minds in a way unlikely ever to be undone. ... Any language in *Plessy* v. *Ferguson* contrary to this finding is rejected.

We conclude that in the field of public education the doctrine of 'separate but equal' has no place. Separate educational facilities are inherently unequal. Therefore, we hold that the plaintiffs and others similarly situated for whom the actions have been brought are, by reason of the segregation complained of, deprived of the equal protection of the laws guaranteed by the Fourteenth Amendment.

US Supreme Court (1954), *Reports*, vol. 347 (Washington, DC: Government Printing Office), pp. 487–8, 492–5.

DOCUMENT 4   THE SOUTHERN MANIFESTO

White southern congressmen vow to defy school desegregation in the 'Southern Manifesto', 12 March 1956.

The unwarranted decision of the Supreme Court in the public school cases is now bearing the fruit always produced when men substitute naked power to established law. ...

We regard the decision of the Supreme Court in the school cases as a clear abuse of judicial power. It climaxes a trend in the federal judiciary undertaking to legislate, in derogation of the authority of Congress, and to encroach upon the reserved rights of the States and the people.

The original Constitution does not mention education. Neither does the Fourteenth Amendment nor any other Amendment. The debates preceding the submission of the Fourteenth Amendment clearly show that there was no intent that it should affect the systems of education maintained by the United States.

The very Congress which proposed the amendment subsequently provided for segregated schools in the District of Columbia. ...

In the case of *Plessy v. Ferguson* in 1896 the Supreme Court expressly declared that under the Fourteenth Amendment no person was denied any of his rights if the states provided separate but equal public facilities. This decision has been followed in many other cases. ...

Though there has been no constitutional amendment or Act of Congress changing this established legal principle almost a century old, the Supreme Court of the United States, with no legal basis for such action, undertook to exercise their naked judicial power and substituted their personal political and social ideas for the established law of the land.

This unwarranted exercise of power by the Court, contrary to the Constitution, is creating chaos and confusion in the States principally affected. It is destroying the amicable relations between the white and Negro races that have been created through 90 years of patient effort by the good people of both races. It has planted hatred and suspicion where there has been heretofore friendship and understanding.

Without regard to the consent of the governed, outside agitators are threatening immediate and revolutionary changes in our public school systems. If done, this is certain to destroy the system of public education in some of the States. ...

We pledge ourselves to use all lawful means to bring about a reversal of this decision which is contrary to the Constitution and to prevent the use of force in its implementation.

The Southern Manifesto, 12 March 1956, in *Congressional Record* (1956), 84th Congress,
2nd Session, pp. 4459–60.

DOCUMENT 5   **THE NEW LOOK**

The Eisenhower administration's basic national security policy is codified in NSC–162/2, 30 October 1953.

3.   a. The authority of the Soviet regime does not appear to have been impaired by the events since Stalin's death, or to be likely to be appreciably weakened during the next few years. The transfer of power may cause some uncertainty in Soviet and satellite tactics for some time, but will probably not impair the basic economic and military strength of the Soviet bloc. The Soviet rulers can be expected to continue to base their policy on the conviction of irreconcilable hostility between the bloc and the non-communist world. This conviction is the compound product of Marxist belief in their historically determined conflict with, and inevitable triumph over, 'world capitalism' led by the United States, of fear for the security of the regime and the USSR, especially in the face of a hostile coalition, of distrust of U.S. aims and intentions, and of long-established reliance on techniques of conspiracy and subversion. Accordingly, the basic Soviet objectives continue to be consolidation and expansion of their own sphere of power and the eventual domination of the non-communist world. ...

5.   b. The detachment of any major European satellite from the Soviet bloc does not now appear feasible except by Soviet acquiescence or by war. ...

c. The Chinese Communist regime is firmly in control and is unlikely to be shaken in the foreseeable future by domestic forces or rival regimes, short of the occurrence of a major war. ...

6.   a. The USSR does not seem likely deliberately to launch a general war against the United States during the period covered by current estimates (through mid-1955). The uncertain prospects for Soviet victory in a general war, the change in leadership, satellite unrest, and the U.S. capability to retaliate massively, make such a course improbable. ...

9.   In the face of the Soviet threat, the security of the United Sates requires:
a. Development and maintenance of:

(1) A strong military posture, with emphasis on the capability of inflicting massive retaliatory damage by offensive striking power;

(2) U.S. and allied forces in readiness to move rapidly initially to counter aggression by Soviet bloc forces and to hold vital areas and lines of communication; and

(3) A mobilization base, and its protection against crippling damage, adequate to insure victory in the event of general war.

b. Maintenance of a sound, strong and growing economy, capable of providing through the operation of free institutions, the strength described above over the long pull and of rapidly and effectively changing to full mobilization.

c. Maintenance of morale and free institutions and the willingness of the U.S. people to support the measures necessary for national security. ...

11.   Within the free world, only the United States can provide and maintain, for a period of years to come, the atomic capability to counterbalance Soviet atomic power. Thus, sufficient atomic weapons and effective means of delivery are indispensable for U.S. security. Moreover, in the face of Soviet atomic power, defense of the continental United States becomes vital to effective security: to protect our striking force, our mobilization base, and our people. Such atomic capability is also a major contribution to the security of our allies, as well as of this country.

12.   The United Sates cannot, however, meet its defense needs, even at exorbitant cost, without the support of allies.

a. The effective use of U.S. strategic air power against the USSR will require overseas bases on foreign territory for some years to come. ...

b. The United States needs to have aligned on its side in the world struggle, in peace and in war, the armed forces and economic resources and materials of the major highly-industrialized non-communist states. Progressive loss to the Soviet bloc of these states would so isolate the United States and alter the world balance as to endanger the capacity of the United States to win in the event of general war or to maintain an adequate defense without undermining its fundamental institutions. ...

15.   b. The major deterrent to aggression against Western Europe is the manifest determination of the United States to use its atomic capability and massive retaliatory striking power if the area is attacked. However, the presence of U.S. forces in Western Europe makes a contribution other than military to the strength and cohesion of the free world coalition. ...

19.   The United States must maintain a sound economy based on free private enterprise as a basis both for high defense productivity and for the maintenance of its living standards and free institutions. Not only the world position of the United States, but the security of the whole free world, is

dependent on the avoidance of recession and on the long-term expansion of the U.S. economy. Threats to its stability or growth, therefore, constitute a danger to the security of the United Sates and of the coalition which it leads. Expenditures for national security, in fact all federal, state and local governmental expenditures, must be carefully scrutinized with a view to measuring their impact on the national economy. ...

21.   Excessive government spending leads to inflationary deficits or to repressive taxation, or to both. Persistent inflation is a barrier to long-term growth because it undermines confidence in the currency, reduces savings, and makes restrictive economic controls necessary. Repressive taxation weakens the incentives for efficiency, effort, and investment on which economic growth depends. ...

34.   In the face of these threats, the United States must develop and maintain, at the lowest feasible cost, requisite military and nonmilitary strength to deter and, if necessary, to counter Soviet military aggression against the United States or other areas vital to its security.

35.   In the interest of its own security, the United States must have the support of allies.

a. The military striking power necessary to retaliate depends for the foreseeable future on having bases in allied countries. Furthermore, the ground forces required to counter local aggressions must be supplied largely by our allies.

b. The loss of major allies by subversion, divisive tactics, or the growth of neutralist attitudes, would seriously affect the security of the United States.

36.   United States policies must, therefore, be designed to retain the cooperation of our allies, to seek to win the friendship and cooperation of the presently uncommitted areas of the world, and thereby to strengthen the cohesion of the free world.

NSC–162/2, 30 October 1953, in US Department of State (1984), *Foreign Relations of the United States, 1952–1954*, vol. 2: *National Security Affairs* (Washington, DC: Government Printing Office), pp. 579–80, 582–3, 585, 588, 591–2.

DOCUMENT 6   MASSIVE RETALIATION

Secretary of State John Foster Dulles explains the concept of 'massive retaliation' to the Council on Foreign Relations, 12 January 1954.

The Soviet Communists are planning for what they call 'an entire historical era', and we should do the same. They seek, through many types of maneuvers, gradually to divide and weaken the free nations by overextending them in efforts which, as Lenin put it, are 'beyond their strength, so that they come to practical bankruptcy'. Then, said Stalin, will be 'the moment for the decisive blow'. ...

We need allies and collective security. Our purpose is to make these relations more effective, less costly. This can be done by placing more reliance on deterrent power and less dependence on local defensive power. ...

We want, for ourselves and other free nations, a maximum deterrent at a bearable cost.

Local defense will always be important. But there is no local defense which alone will contain the mighty landpower of the Communist world. Local defenses must be reinforced by the further deterrent of massive retaliatory power. A potential aggressor must know that he cannot always prescribe battle conditions that suit him. ...

The way to deter aggression is for the free community to be willing and able to respond vigorously at places and with means of its own choosing. ...

But before military planning could be changed, the President and his advisers ... had to take some basic policy decisions. This has been done. The basic decision was to depend primarily upon a great capacity to retaliate, instantly, by means and at places of our choosing. Now the Department of Defense and the Joint Chiefs of Staff can shape our military establishment to fit what is *our* policy, instead of having to try to be ready to meet the enemy's many choices. That permits a selection of military means instead of a multiplication of means. As a result, it is now possible to get, and share, more basic security at less cost.

John Foster Dulles, speech before the Council on Foreign Relations, 12 January 1954, in US Department of State, *Bulletin*, vol. 30 (25 January 1954), pp. 107–8.

DOCUMENT 7   **THE DOMINO THEORY**

President Eisenhower outlines the 'domino theory' in Indochina to reporters, 7 April 1954.

Robert Richards, Copley Press: Mr. President, would you mind commenting on the strategic importance of Indochina to the free world? I think there has been, across the country, some lack of understanding on just what it means to us.

The President: You have, of course, both the specific and the general when you talk about such things.

First of all, you have the specific value of a locality in its production the world needs.

Then you have the possibility that many human beings may pass under a dictatorship that is inimical to the free world.

Finally, you have broader considerations that might follow what you would call the 'falling domino' principle. You have a row of dominoes set up, you knock over the first one, and what will happen to the last one is the certainty that it will go over very quickly. So you could have a beginning of a disintegration that would have the most profound influences.

Now, with respect to the first one, two of the items from this particular area that the world uses are tin and tungsten. They are very important. There are others, of course, the rubber plantations and so on.

Then with respect to more people passing under domination, Asia, after all, has already lost some 450 million of its peoples to the Communist dictatorship, and we simply can't afford greater losses.

But when we come to the possible sequence of events, the loss of Indochina, of Burma, of Thailand, of the Peninsula, and Indonesia following, now you begin to talk about areas that not only multiply the disadvantages that you would suffer through loss of materials, sources of materials, but now you are talking really about millions and millions of people.

Finally, the geographical position achieved thereby does many things. It turns the so-called island defensive chain of Japan, Formosa, of the Philippines and to the southward; it moves in to threaten Australia and New Zealand.

It takes away, in its economic aspects, that region that Japan must have as a trading area or Japan, in turn, will have only one place in the world to go – that is, towards the Communists in order to live.

So, the possible consequences of the loss are just incalculable to the free world.

President Eisenhower's press conference, 7 April 1954, in US President (1960), *Public Papers of the Presidents of the United States: Dwight D. Eisenhower, 1954* (Washington, DC: Government Printing Office), pp. 382–4.

DOCUMENT 8   **QUEMOY AND MATSU**

President Eisenhower explains the importance of the offshore islands to British Prime Minister Winston Churchill, who had earlier cautioned that the British could not support a war over the islands and urged Eisenhower to pull Chiang's forces back to Taiwan, 18 February 1955.

I greatly appreciate the message from you and [Foreign Secretary] Anthony [Eden]. I have studied it long and carefully, as has [Secretary of State John] Foster [Dulles]. Quite naturally, it distresses us whenever we find ourselves in even partial disagreement with the conclusions that you two may reach on any important subject. ...

There are two important points that must be considered at every step of any analysis of this exceedingly difficult situation. The first is that this country does not have decisive power in respect of the offshore islands. We believe that Chiang would even choose to stand alone and die if we should attempt now to coerce him into the abandonment of those islands. Possibly we may convince him in the future of the wisdom of this course, but to attempt to do more at this time would bring us to the second major point, which is: We must not lose Chiang's army and we must maintain its strength, efficiency and morale. Only a few months back we had both Chiang and a strong, well-equipped French Army to support the free world's position in Southeast Asia. The French are gone – making it clearer than ever that we cannot afford the loss of Chiang unless all of us are to get completely out of that corner of the globe. This is unthinkable to us – I feel it must be to you.

In order to make an express or tacit cease-fire likely, we have, with difficulties perhaps greater than you realize, done, through our diplomacy, many things.

1. We rounded out the far Pacific security chain by a Treaty with the Nationalists which, however, only covered specifically Formosa and the Pescadores, thus making it clear to Chiang and to all the world that we were not prepared to defend the coastal positions as Treaty territory.

2. We obtained from Chiang his agreement that he would not conduct any offensive operations against the mainland either from Formosa or from his coastal positions, except in agreement with us. ...

3. Furthermore, we obtained an agreement from the Nationalists closely limiting their right to take away from Formosa military elements, material or human, to which we had contributed if this would weaken the defense of Formosa itself.

4. We made possible the voluntary evacuation of the Tachens and two other islands.

5. Finally, we secured the acquiescence of the Chinese Nationalists to the United Nations proceedings for a cease-fire. ...

However, what we have done has apparently been interpreted by the Chinese Communists merely as a sign of weakness. They have intensified their threats against Formosa and their expression of determination to take it by force. Also, they continue to hold, in durance vile, our airmen who were captured by them in the Korean War and who should have been freed by the Korean Armistice.

There comes a point where constantly giving in only encourages further belligerency. I think we must be careful not to pass that point in our dealings with Communist China. In such a case, further retreat becomes worse than a Munich because at Munich there were at least promises on the part of the aggressor to cease expansion and to keep the peace. In this case the Chinese Communists have promised nothing and have not contributed one iota towards peace in the Formosa area. Indeed, they treat the suggestion of peace there as an insult. ...

All of the non-Communist nations of the Western Pacific – particularly Korea, Japan, the Philippines, and, of course, Formosa itself, are watching nervously to see what we do next. I fear that, if we appear strong and coercive only towards our friends, and should attempt to compel Chiang to make further retreats, the conclusion of these Asian peoples will be that they had better plan to make the best terms they can with the Communists.
...

It would surely not be popular in this country if we became involved in possible hostilities on account of Hong Kong or Malaya, which our people look upon as 'colonies' – which to us is a naughty word. Nevertheless, I do not doubt that, if the issue were ever framed in this way, we would be at your side.

We are doing everything possible to work this situation out in a way which, on the one hand, will avoid the risk of war, and, on the other hand, preserve the non-Communist position in the Western pacific, a position which, by the way, is vital to Australia and New Zealand. However, if the Chinese Communists are determined to have a war to gain Formosa, then there will be trouble.

Eisenhower, letter to Winston Churchill, 18 February 1955, in Louis P. Galambos et al. (eds)
(1996), *The Papers of Dwight David Eisenhower*, vol. 16: *The Presidency: The Middle Way*
(Baltimore, MD: Johns Hopkins University Press), pp. 1574–8.

DOCUMENT 9   **THE CHANCE FOR PEACE**

President Eisenhower details the costs of the Cold War and pressures the new Soviet leadership to pursue the 'Chance for Peace' after Josef Stalin's death, 16 April 1953.

What can the world, or any nation in it, hope for if no turning is found on this dread road?

The worst to be feared and the best to be expected can be simply stated.

The *worst* is atomic war.

The *best* would be this: a life of perpetual fear and tension; a burden of arms draining the wealth and the labor of all peoples; a wasting of strength that defies the American system or the Soviet system or any system to achieve true abundance and happiness for the peoples of this earth.

Every gun that is made, every warship launched, every rocket fired signifies, in the final sense, a theft from those who hunger and are not fed, those who are cold and are not clothed.

This world in arms is not spending money alone.

It is spending the sweat of its laborers, the genius of its scientists, the hopes of its children.

The cost of one modern heavy bomber is this: a modern brick school in more than 30 cities.

It is two electric power plants, each serving a town of 60,000 population.

It is two fine, fully equipped hospitals.

It is some 50 miles of concrete highway.

We pay for a single fighter plane with a half million bushels of wheat.

We pay for a single destroyer with new homes that could have housed more than 8,000 people. ...

This is not a way of life at all, in any true sense. Under the cloud of threatening war, it is humanity hanging from a cross of iron. ...

Now a new leadership has assumed power in the Soviet Union. Its links to the past, however strong, cannot bind it completely. Its future is, in great part, its own to make. ...

So the new Soviet leadership now has a precious opportunity to awaken, with the rest of the world, to the point of peril reached and to help turn the tide of history. ...

We welcome every honest act of peace.

We care nothing for mere rhetoric.

We are only for sincerity of peaceful purpose attested by deeds. The opportunities for such deeds are many. The performance of a great number of them waits upon no complex protocol but upon the simple will to do them. Even a few such clear and specific acts, such as the Soviet Union's signature upon an Austrian treaty or its release of thousands of prisoners still held from World War II, would be impressive signs of sincere intent. They would carry a power of persuasion not to be matched by any amount of oratory. ...

Is the new leadership of the Soviet Union prepared to use its decisive influence in the Communist world, including control of the flow of arms, to bring not merely an expedient truce in Korea but genuine peace in Asia?

Is it prepared to allow other nations, including those of Eastern Europe, the free choice of their own forms of government? Is it prepared to act in concert with others upon serious disarmament proposals to be made firmly effective by stringent U.N. control and inspection?

If not, where then is the concrete evidence of the Soviet Union's concern for peace?

The test is clear.

Eisenhower, speech before the American Society of Newspaper Editors, 16 April 1953, in US President (1959), *Public Papers of the Presidents of the United States: Dwight D. Eisenhower, 1953* (Washington, DC: Government Printing Office), pp. 182–4, 187.

DOCUMENT 10   **THE SUEZ CRISIS**

Eisenhower's National Security Council discusses the appropriate response to Anglo-French military intervention in Egypt and the allies' veto of a UN Security Council cease-fire resolution, 1 November 1956.

Secretary Dulles warned with emphasis that if we were not now prepared to assert our leadership in this cause, leadership would certainly be seized by the Soviet Union. But asserting our leadership would involve us in some very basic problems. For many years now the United States has been walking a tightrope between the effort to maintain our old and valued relations with our British and French allies on the one hand, and on the other trying to assure ourselves of the friendship of the newly independent countries who have escaped from colonialism. It seemed ... that in view of the overwhelming Asian and African pressure upon us, we could not walk this tightrope much longer. Unless we now assert and maintain this leadership, all of these newly independent countries will turn from us to the USSR. We will be looked upon as forever tied to British and French colonialist policies. ...

Summing up, Secretary Dulles stated that basically we had almost reached the point of deciding today whether we think the future lies with a policy of reasserting by force colonial control over the less developed nations, or whether we will oppose such a course of action by every appropriate means. ... It is nothing less than tragic that at this very time, when we are at the point of winning an immense and long-hoped-for victory over Soviet colonialism in Eastern Europe, we should be forced to choose between following in the footsteps of Anglo-French colonialism in Asia and Africa, or splitting our course away from their course. ...

Secretary Dulles turned to President Eisenhower and warned that if he did not provide leadership at this point, the UN would be calling for a blockade likewise of Britain and France. It would not do for the United States to confine itself merely to calling for a cease-fire, with the Israeli forces running all over Egypt. ...

Turning to [Dulles], the President said that the thing for him to do was to go now and see what he could draft up in the way of the mildest things we could do in an effort to block the introduction of a really mean and arbitrary resolution in the UN General Assembly. ... After [Dulles] had left the Cabinet Room, the President ... said that of course no one in the whole world really expected us to break off our long alliance with Great Britain and France. We must not permit ourselves to be blinded by the thought that anything we are going to do will result in our fighting with Great Britain and France. Such a course of action was unthinkable, and no one can possibly believe that we will do it. ... The President brought the meeting to a close by stating that we must go now and see what we can do about this business. His idea was to do what was decent and right, but not to condemn more furiously than we had to. Secretary Dulles was dead right in his view that if we did not do something to indicate some vigor in the way of asserting our leadership, the Soviets would take over the leadership from us. He had told Anthony Eden a week ago that if the British did what they are now doing and the Russians got into the Middle East, the fat would really be in the fire.

Memorandum of discussion at the 302nd meeting of the National Security Council,
1 November 1956, 9 am, in US Department of State (1990), *Foreign Relations of the United States, 1955–1957*, vol. 16: *Suez Crisis, July 26–December 31, 1956* (Washington, DC: Government Printing Office), pp. 906–7, 912, 915.

DOCUMENT 11   LITTLE ROCK

President Eisenhower explains his decision to send troops into Little Rock, Arkansas, during the school desegregation crisis, 26 September 1957.

It is important that the reasons for my action be understood by all our citizens.

As you know, the Supreme Court of the United States has decided that separate public educational facilities for the races are inherently unequal and therefore compulsory school segregation laws are unconstitutional.

Our personal opinions about the decision have no bearing on the matter of enforcement; the responsibility and authority of the Supreme Court to interpret the Constitution are very clear. Local Federal Courts were instructed by the Supreme Court to issue such orders and decrees as might be necessary to achieve admission to public schools without regard to race – and with all deliberate speed. ...

Certain misguided persons, many of them imported into Little Rock by agitators, have insisted upon defying the law and have sought to bring it to disrepute. The orders of the Court have thus been frustrated.

The very basis of our individual rights and freedoms rests upon the certainty that the President and the Executive Branch of the Government will support and insure the carrying out of the decisions of the Federal Courts, even, when necessary, with all the means at the President's command.

Unless the President did so, anarchy would result. ...

Now, let me make it very clear that Federal troops are not being used to relieve local and state authorities of their primary duty to preserve the peace and order of the community. Nor are the troops there for the purpose of taking over the responsibility of the School Board and the other responsible local officials in running Central High School. The running of our school system and the maintenance of peace and order in each of our States are strictly local affairs and the Federal Government does not interfere except in a very few special cases and when requested by one of the several States. In the present case the troops are there, pursuant to law, solely for the purpose of preventing interference with the orders of the Court. ...

In the South, as elsewhere, citizens are keenly aware of the tremendous disservice that has been done to the people of Arkansas in the eyes of the world.

At a time when we face grave situations abroad because of the hatred that Communism bears towards a system of government based on human rights, it would be difficult to exaggerate the harm that is being done to the prestige and influence, and indeed to the safety, of our nation and the world.

Our enemies are gloating over this incident and using it everywhere to misrepresent our whole nation. We are portrayed as a violator of those standards of conduct which the peoples of the world united to proclaim in the Charter of the United Nations. There they affirmed 'faith in fundamental human rights' and 'in the dignity and worth of the human person' and they did so 'without distinction as to race, sex, language, or religion'.

And so, with deep confidence, I call upon the citizens of the State of Arkansas to assist in bringing to an immediate end all interference with the law and its processes. If resistance to the Federal Court orders ceases at once, the further presence of Federal troops will be unnecessary and the City of Little Rock will return to its normal habits of peace and order and a blot upon the fair name and high honor of our nation in the world will be removed.

Eisenhower, radio and television address to the American people on the situation in Little Rock, Arkansas, 24 September 1957, in US President (1960), *Public Papers of the Presidents of the United States: Dwight D. Eisenhower, 1957* (Washington, DC: Government Printing Office), pp. 690, 692–4.

DOCUMENT 12   **THE SPACE RACE**

The Eisenhower administration's space policy takes psychological factors into consideration, laying the groundwork for a 'space race' with the Soviet Union, 26 January 1960.

2. Outer space presents a new and imposing challenge. Although the full potentialities and significance of outer space remain largely to be explored, it is already clear that there are important scientific, civil, military, and political implications for the national security, including the psychological

impact of outer space activities which is of broad significance to national prestige.

3. Outer space generally has been viewed as an area of intense competition which has been characterized to date by comparison of Soviet and U.S. activities. The successes of the Soviet Union in placing the first satellite in orbit, in launching the first space probe to reach escape velocity, in achieving the first 'hard' landing on the moon and in obtaining the first pictures of the back side of the moon have resulted in substantial and enduring gains in Soviet prestige. ... In addition, the Soviets have benefited from their ability to conceal any failures from public scrutiny.

4. From the political and psychological standpoint the most significant factor of Soviet space accomplishments is that they produced new credibility for Soviet statements and claims. Where once the Soviet Union was not generally believed, even its boldest propaganda claims are now apt to be accepted at face value, not only abroad but in the United States. ...

6. Significant advances have been made in restoring U.S. prestige overseas, and in increasing awareness of the scope and magnitude of the U.S. outer space effort. Although most opinion still considers the U.S. as probably leading in general scientific and technical accomplishments, the USSR is viewed in most quarters as leading in space science and technology. There is evidence that a considerable portion of the world leadership and the world public expects the United States to 'catch up' with the Soviet Union, and further expects this to be demonstrated by U.S. ability to equal Soviet space payloads and to match or surpass Soviet accomplishments. Failure to satisfy such expectations may give rise to the belief that the United States is 'second best', thus transferring to the Soviets additional increments of prestige and credibility now enjoyed by the United States. ...

Objectives

31. Carry out energetically a program for the exploration and use of outer space by the U.S., based upon sound scientific and technological progress, designed: (a) to achieve that enhancement of scientific knowledge, military strength, economic capabilities, and political position which may be derived through the advantageous application of space technology and through appropriate international cooperation in related matters, and (b) to obtain the advantages which come from successful achievements in space.

POLICY GUIDANCE

Priority, Scope and Level of Effort

32. While relating the resources and effort to be expended on outer space activities to other programs to ensure that the anticipated gains from such

activities are properly related to possible gains from other programs which may be competitive for manpower, facilities, funds or other resources, commit and effectively apply adequate resources with a priority sufficient to enable the U.S. as soon as reasonably practicable to achieve the objectives stated in paragraph 31. ...

Psychological Exploitation

36. To minimize the psychological advantages which the USSR has acquired as a result of space accomplishments, select from among those current or projected U.S. space activities of intrinsic military, scientific or technological value, one or more projects which offer promise of obtaining a demonstrably effective advantage over the Soviets and, so far as is consistent with solid achievements in the overall space program, stress these projects in present and future programming. ...

38. Develop information programs that will exploit fully U.S. outer space activities on a continuing basis; especially develop programs to counter overseas the psychological impact of Soviet outer space activities and to present U.S. outer space progress in the most favorable light.

National Aeronautics and Space Council, 'U.S. Policy on Outer Space', 26 January 1960, in J. M. Logsdon (ed.) (1996), *Exploring the Unknown: Selected Documents in the History of the U.S. Civilian Space Program*, vol. 1 (Washington, DC: NASA History Office), pp. 362–3, 367–8.

DOCUMENT 13   **THE MISSILE GAP**

Senator John F. Kennedy positions himself for the 1960 presidential race by assailing the Eisenhower administration's defence policies and urging increased military spending to close the 'missile gap', 29 February 1960.

Winston Churchill said: 'We arm – to parley'. We prepare for war – in order to deter war. We depend on the strength of armaments, to enable us to bargain for disarmament. ... We compare our military strength with the Soviets, not to determine whether we should use it, but to determine whether we can persuade them that to use theirs would be futile and disastrous, and to determine whether we can back up our own pledges in Berlin, Formosa, and around the world.

In short, peace, not politics, is at the heart of the current debate – peace, not war, is the objective of our military policy. But peace would have no meaning if the time ever came when the deterrent ratio shifted so heavily in favor of the Soviet Union that they could destroy most of our retaliatory capacity in a single blow. ...

Those who uphold the administration defense budget are right on one count: We cannot be certain that the Soviets will have, during the term of the next administration, the tremendous lead in missile striking power which they give every evidence of building – and we cannot be certain that they will use that lead to threaten or launch an attack upon the United States. Consequently those of us who call for a higher defense budget are taking a chance on spending money unnecessarily. But those who oppose these expenditures are taking a chance on our very survival as a nation. ...

But I am convinced that every American who can be fully informed as to the facts today would agree to an additional investment in our national security now rather than risk his survival, and his children's survival, in the years ahead – in particular, an investment effort designed, first, to make possible an emergency stopgap air alert program, to deter an attack before the missile gap is closed; second, to step up our ultimate missile program that will close the gap when completed: Polaris, Minuteman and long-range air-to-ground missiles – meanwhile stepping up our production of Atlas missiles to cover the current gap as best we can; and third, to rebuild and modernize our Army and Marine Corps conventional forces, to prevent the brush-fire wars that our capacity for nuclear retaliation is unable to deter. ...

Whether the missile gap – that everyone agrees now exists – will become critical in 1961, 1962, 1963 – whether during the critical years of the gap the Russian lead will be 2 to 1, 3 to 1, or 5 to 1 – whether the gap can be brought to a close – by the availability in quantity of Polaris and Minuteman missiles – in 1964 or in 1965 or ever – on all these questions experts may sincerely differ. I do not challenge the accuracy of our intelligence reports – I do not charge anyone with intentionally misleading the public for purposes of deception. For whichever figures are accurate, the point is that we are facing a gap on which we are gambling with our survival – and this year's defense budget is our last real chance to do something about it. ...

I do not want to be told either that we cannot afford to do what is required, or that our people are unwilling to do it. In terms of this budget's proportion of our gross national product, we are not making nearly the defense effort today we were in 1953 – or one-fifth the effort we made during World War II when we knew it had to be done. The Russians, with a far poorer standard of living, and desperate shortages in some consumer goods and housing, are commanding a much greater proportional effort. ...

Unless immediate steps are taken, failure to maintain our relative power of retaliation may in the near future expose the United States to a nuclear missile attack. ...

Time is short. This situation should never have been permitted to arise. But if we move now, if we are willing to gamble with our money instead of our survival, we have, I am sure, the wit and resource to maintain the minimum conditions for our survival, for our alliances, and for the active pursuit of peace. ...

I repeat: We shall never be able to prove beyond all doubts that the efforts I have outlined are necessary for our security. We are taking a gamble with our money. But the alternative is to gamble with our lives.

Speech by Senator John F. Kennedy, 29 February 1960, in *Congressional Record* (1960), 86th Congress, 2nd Session, pp. 3801–4.

DOCUMENT 14   THE EISENHOWER DOCTRINE

A Joint Resolution of Congress authorizes President Eisenhower to contain communism in the Middle East, 7 March 1957.

Resolved by the Senate and House of Representatives of the United States of America in Congress assembled,

SEC 1. That the President be and hereby is authorized to cooperate and assist any nation or group of nations in the general area of the Middle East desiring such assistance in the development of economic strength dedicated to the maintenance of national independence.

SEC. 2. The President is authorized to undertake, in the general area of the Middle East, military assistance programs with any nation or group of nations of that area desiring such assistance. Furthermore, the United States regards as vital to the national interest and world peace the preservation of the independence and integrity of the nations of the Middle East. To this end, if the President determines the necessity thereof, the United States is prepared to use armed forces to assist any such nation or group of such nations requesting assistance against armed aggression by any country controlled by international communism: *Provided,* That such employment shall be consonant with the treaty obligations of the United States and with the Constitution of the United States. ...

House Joint Resolution 117, as amended, to Promote Peace and Stability in the Middle East, 7 March 1957, in US Department of State, *Bulletin,* vol. 36 (25 March 1957), p. 481.

DOCUMENT 15   CHINESE POLICY TOWARDS QUEMOY AND MATSU

Chinese Foreign Minister Zhou Enlai explains Chinese actions to the nervous Soviets during the second offshore islands crisis, 5 October 1958.

I talked to you on 30 September [about our policy towards Taiwan]. Originally, our plan had two steps: the first was to recover the offshore islands; the second to liberate Taiwan. Later, after we began shelling Quemoy (Jinmen), our bombardment played a role to mobilize the people of the world, especially the Chinese people. Thereafter, many countries launched and joined a new anti-American movement on a much larger scale than that after the Lebanon event. The situation already becomes clear. America knows that we do not want to fight a war against it. When it escorted Chiang Kai-shek's ships, we did not fire [on them]. We have no intention to liberate Taiwan immediately. We know that America does not want to fight a war against us over Quemoy either. It strictly restrained its air and naval forces from entering our territorial waters between three and twelve miles from our coast. Currently America works on how to persuade Chiang's troops to withdraw from Quemoy–Matsu to prevent its forces from being pinned down in this region.

As I said to you on 30 September, we realized that it was better to keep Chiang Kai-shek on Quemoy–Matsu. ... It is extremely beneficial [to us] that Chiang stays at Quemoy and Matsu, and America continues to intervene. It will educate the people of the world, especially the Chinese people. We will not let America go, when it wants to get away from Quemoy and Matsu. We demand that America withdraw its armed forces from Taiwan. Under this circumstance, if we need tension, we can shell Quemoy and Matsu; if we want relaxation, we can stop shelling. ... We can have shelling while negotiating, and we can stop shelling anytime we like. This is advantageous for us. So we are not going to recover these offshore islands in the near future. We will take them back together with the Pescadores (Penghu) and Taiwan later.

Thus, we decided to issue a 'Message to the Compatriots in Taiwan' in the name of our defense minister. [It indicates that] we will suspend our shelling for seven days from 1:00 p.m. on 6 October so as to allow Chiang's troops to transport their logistic supplies easily. Our suspension of bombardment, however, has a precondition that no American ships provide escort. Moreover, [it] suggests a direct negotiation with Chiang Kai-shek searching for peaceful solutions to the conflicts between both sides. Since our shelling is actually a punitive operation against Chiang's troops, we can slow it down as long as Chiang is willing to cooperate [with us]. If he is not, we will continue to punish him. Therefore, we will always be in a positive position. ...

Therefore, we cause a new dilemma for America. And it does not know how to cope with it. America is facing a very difficult situation right now. It originally planned to persuade Chiang's troops to withdraw [from Quemoy]. If it again suggests withdrawal, Chiang Kai-shek will say that America abandons him. If America stops persuading Chiang to withdraw, we will achieve our goal.

Memorandum of conversation between Chinese Foreign Minister Zhou Enlai and Soviet chargé d'affaires S. F. Antonov, 5 October 1958, in Cold War International History Project (1995–96), *Bulletin*, vol. 6–7, pp. 222–3.

DOCUMENT 16   KHRUSHCHEV AND THE BERLIN CRISIS

Nikita Khrushchev explains his thinking to Polish Premier Wladyslaw Gomulka on the eve of his ultimatum to the Western powers on Berlin, 10 November 1958.

Khrushchev: You know about our latest suggestions with regard to Berlin.

Gomulka: We know. We understand that they are aimed towards liquidating the western part of Berlin.

Khrushchev: It is not that simple. I am only announcing that matter. That is the beginning of the struggle. Our announcement in our presentations is only the beginning of the action. Undoubtedly it is an exacerbation of the situation. The GDR will aggravate the issue of transport, especially military, and they [the Western powers] will have to turn to them on matters of transport. Of course an exacerbation will result.

Gomulka: It is understood that in the longer term a situation cannot continue in which in the interior of one state, the GDR, stands another state – West Berlin. It would be different if the unification of Germany were a close prospect – and that was possible at the time of Potsdam, and it was considered a temporary status – until the unification of Germany. But currently the situation is different and such a prospect is lacking. Such a state of things cannot be maintained. There is not even a single state in the West that would support the unification of Germany. Even France and England do not wish that upon themselves.

Khrushchev: And France and England are afraid themselves of whether we might not give in on this issue. ...

My declaration today should be understood in such a fashion, that we are unilaterally ceasing to observe the agreement on Berlin's status, that we are discontinuing to fulfil the functions deriving from our participation in the Control Commission. Next, we will recall our military commander in West Berlin and our [military] mission. [East German Premier Otto] Grotewohl will ask the English and Americans to leave, along with their missions. Our military, however, will remain in the GDR on the basis of our participation in the Warsaw Treaty. Then the capitalist states will have to turn to the GDR on matters relating to Berlin, transit, and transport. They will have to turn to Grotewohl, and he is firm. And that's when the tension begins. Some form of blockade will result, but we have enough foodstuffs. We will also have to feed West Berlin. ...

War will not result from it. There will be tensions, of course, there will be a blockade. They might test to see our reaction. In any case we will have to show a great deal of cold blood in this matter. ...

According to the [1945] Potsdam agreement, the FRG [Federal Republic of Germany] should not join any alliance against the countries with which

Germany fought. But they joined NATO, which is clearly directed against us. That is clearly in conflict with the Potsdam agreement. West Berlin is there to be used as an attack base against us. They are turning to blackmail. Five years ago – that was different. Then, we did not have the hydrogen bomb; now, the balance of forces is different. Then, we could not reach the USA. The USA built its policies upon the bases surrounding us. Today, America has moved closer to us – our missiles can hit them directly.

> Memorandum of conversation between Khrushchev and Gomulka, 10 November 1958, in
> Cold War International History Project (1998), *Bulletin*, vol. 11, p. 202.

DOCUMENT 17   **THE COVERT WAR AGAINST CASTRO**

President Eisenhower approves covert actions to topple the government of Fidel Castro that would later culminate in the unsuccessful Bay of Pigs operation, 17 March 1960.

After Mr. Herter gave a brief comment concerning the use of the OAS [Organization of American States] in connection with the Cuban situation, Mr. Allen Dulles reported to the President an action plan ... for covert operations to effect a change in Cuba. The first step will be to form a moderate opposition group in exile. This will take about one month. Its slogan will be to 'restore the revolution' which Castro has betrayed. A medium wave radio station to carry out gray or black broadcasts into Cuba will be established, probably on Swan Island (south of Cuba, belonging to the United States) in two months. Concurrently a network of disaffected elements will be established within Cuba. ...

Mr. Allen Dulles said that preparations of a para-military force will begin outside of Cuba, the first stage being to get a cadre of leaders together for training. The formation of this force might take something like eight months.

The President said that he knows of no better plan for dealing with this situation. The great problem is leakage and breach of security. Everyone must be prepared to swear that he has not heard of it. He said we should limit American contacts with the groups involved to two or three people, getting Cubans to do most of what must be done. ...

The President told Mr. Dulles that he thought he should go ahead with the plans and the operations. He and other agencies involved should take account of all likely Cuban reactions and prepare the actions that we would take in response to these. ... The President said that he would like some groundwork laid with the OAS to let the Latin American countries know that if the Cubans were to start attacking our people in Cuba we would be obliged to take action. ...

The President said that at the next meeting he would want to know what is the sequence of events by which we see the situation developing – specifically what actions are we to take. He said our hand should not show in anything that is done. In the meantime, State should be working on what we can do in and out of the OAS. ... The President said that, as he saw it, Castro the Revolutionary had gained great prestige in Latin America. Castro the Politician running the government is now losing it rapidly. However, governments elsewhere cannot oppose him too strongly since they are shaky with respect to the potentials of action by the mobs within their own countries to whom Castro's brand of demagoguery appeals. Essentially the job is to get the OAS to support us.

Memorandum of a meeting with the President, White House, Washington, DC, 17 March 1960, in US Department of State (1991), *Foreign Relations of the United States, 1958–1960*, vol. 6: *Cuba* (Washington, DC: Government Printing Office), pp. 861–3.

DOCUMENT 18   THE MILITARY–INDUSTRIAL COMPLEX

President Eisenhower delivers a final warning about the dangers of the garrison state, 17 January 1961.

Throughout America's adventure in free government, our basic purposes have been to keep the peace; to foster progress in human achievement, and to enhance liberty, dignity and integrity among people and among nations. To strive for less would be unworthy of a free and religious people. ...

Progress towards these noble goals is persistently threatened by the conflict now engulfing the world. It commands our whole attention, absorbs our very beings. We face a hostile ideology – global in scope, atheistic in character, ruthless in purpose, and insidious in method. Unhappily, the danger it poses promises to be of indefinite duration. To meet it successfully, there is called for, not so much the emotional and transitory sacrifices of crisis, but rather those which enable us to carry forward steadily, surely, and without complaint the burdens of a prolonged and complex struggle – with liberty the stake. ...

A vital element in keeping the peace is our military establishment. Our arms must be mighty, ready for instant action, so that no potential aggressor may be tempted to risk his own destruction.

Our military organization today bears little relation to that known by any of my predecessors in peacetime, or indeed by the fighting men of World War II or Korea.

Until the latest of our world conflicts, the United States had no armaments industry. American makers of plowshares could, with time and as required, make swords as well. But now we can no longer risk emergency improvisation of national defense; we have been compelled to create a permanent armaments industry of vast proportions. Added to this, three and a half million men and women are directly engaged in the defense establishment. We annually spend on military security more than the net income of all United States corporations.

This conjunction of an immense military establishment and a large arms industry is new in the American experience. The total influence – economic, political, even spiritual – is felt in every city, every State house, every office of the Federal government. We recognize the imperative need for this development. Yet we must not fail to comprehend its grave implications. Our toil, resources and livelihood are all involved; so is the very structure of our society.

In the councils of government, we must guard against the acquisition of unwarranted influence, whether sought or unsought, by the military–industrial complex. The potential for the disastrous rise of misplaced power exists and will persist.

We must never let the weight of this combination endanger our liberties or democratic processes. We should take nothing for granted. Only an alert and knowledgeable citizenry can compel the proper meshing of the huge industrial and military machinery of defense with our peaceful methods and goals, so that security and liberty may prosper together.

Akin to, and largely responsible for, the sweeping changes in our industrial–military posture, has been the technological revolution during recent decades.

In this revolution, research has become central; it also becomes more formalized, complex, and costly. A steadily increasing share is conducted for, by or at the direction of, the Federal government.

Today, the solitary inventor, tinkering in his shop, has been over-shadowed by task forces of scientists in laboratories and testing fields. In the same fashion, the free university, historically the fountainhead of free ideas and scientific discovery, has experienced a revolution in the conduct of research. Partly because of the huge costs involved, a government contract becomes virtually a substitute for intellectual curiosity. For every old blackboard there are now hundreds of new electronic computers.

The prospect of domination of the nation's scholars by Federal employment, project allocations, and the power of money is ever present – and is gravely to be regarded.

Yet, in holding scientific research and discovery in respect, as we should, we must also be alert to the equal and opposite danger that public policy could itself become the captive of a scientific–technological elite.

It is the task of statesmanship to mold, to balance, and to integrate these and other forces, new and old, within the principles of our democratic system – ever aiming towards the supreme goals of our free society.

President Eisenhower's Farewell Radio and Television Address to the American People, 17 January 1961, in US President (1961), *Public Papers of the Presidents of the United States: Dwight D. Eisenhower, 1960–61* (Washington, DC: Government Printing Office), pp. 1035–40.

GLOSSARY

Atomic Energy Commission (AEC)   Federal agency established under the 1946 Atomic Energy Act, responsible for both promoting nuclear power development and producing and stockpiling nuclear weapons. The AEC hierarchy consistently opposed restrictions on nuclear tests.

Council of Economic Advisers (CEA)   The president's economic advisers, established by statute in the 1946 Employment Act. Eisenhower used the CEA as his economics research staff.

Federal Reserve   The central bank, governed by the Federal Reserve Board in Washington, DC. In the 1950s, the Federal Reserve generally followed a tight money policy to dampen inflationary pressures in the economy.

Formosa (Taiwan) Resolution   Congressional resolution, 29 January 1955, providing discretionary authority for the president to use US forces in defence of Taiwan and 'related areas'.

Fourteenth Amendment   Constitutional amendment that guaranteed 'equal protection of the laws' to all US citizens and became the basis for challenging the constitutionality of racially-segregated public education.

Gaither Report   November 1957 study by a group of distinguished civilian consultants to the NSC that warned of the rapidly growing Soviet economy and an array of military threats to the US deterrent forces necessitating immediate corrective measures. Eisenhower rejected the alarmist tone of the report and made only modest adjustments to his military programmes.

Joint Chiefs of Staff (JCS)   The president's principal military advisers, comprising the chiefs of staff of the Army, Air Force and Navy, and a chairman usually selected according to rotation among the services.

National Aeronautics and Space Administration (NASA)   Space agency established in 1958 responsible for civilian space science and exploration.

National Association for the Advancement of Colored People (NAACP)   The oldest civil rights organization, its Legal Defense Fund spearheaded the drive to eliminate racially-segregated public education.

National Security Council (NSC)   The president's principal civilian advisers on foreign and defence policy, established by the 1947 National Security Act. Eisenhower used the NSC to debate and define basic national security policy.

North Atlantic Treaty Organization (NATO)   Collective security system established in 1949 to contain the Soviet Union in Western Europe and considered by Eisenhower to be America's most important alliance. Eisenhower presided over the long-anticipated rearming of West Germany and its incorporation into NATO.

NSC–162/2 Eisenhower's 1953 statement of basic national security policy that codified the New Look. Eisenhower sought to harmonize defence and economic requirements by pursuing a long-term strategy of containment that emphasized collective security and strategic nuclear forces to deter general war.

Operation Solarium The Eisenhower administration's NSC exercise that staffed out alternative strategies of containment and built consensus among Eisenhower's advisers for his preferred New Look strategy.

Organization of American States (OAS) Established in 1948, the OAS became the principal forum for cooperation and collective security among the nations of the Western Hemisphere. The Eisenhower administration had limited success in mobilizing the OAS as an anti-communist bulwark.

President's Science Advisory Committee (PSAC) Eisenhower's part-time group of science advisers drawn from the nation's leading research institutions and corporations. The PSAC provided Eisenhower with a source of technical advice on a range of national security issues that was untainted by affiliation with other government agencies or the armed services.

South East Asia Treaty Organization (SEATO) Collective security system established by Dulles in 1954 to contain communism in Southeast Asia. The United States, Britain, France, Australia, New Zealand, Thailand, Pakistan and the Philippines agreed to consult in the event of a communist threat to the region.

Statism The centralization of power and authority in the national government, primarily the executive branch. Anti-statism had been a core value of American political ideology since the revolutionary era. By the 1950s, political leaders of all persuasions appealed to the anti-statist tradition in order to mobilize resistance to causes as diverse as African-American civil rights, federal aid to education, limitations on civil liberties, higher taxes and increased federal intervention in the economy.

Unilateralists Supporters of an independent, America-first foreign policy, primarily in the Republican Party, who wanted to minimize the US role in alliances and international organizations.

WHO'S WHO

Adenauer, Konrad (1876–1967) Chancellor of the Federal Republic of Germany, 1945–63, and Foreign Minister, 1951–55. Adenauer promoted European economic and political integration and aligned West Germany firmly with the West, even at the expense of postponing unification with Communist East Germany.

Anderson, Robert B. (1910–89) Secretary of the Treasury, 1957–61. Eisenhower's principal Cabinet ally in holding down spending and containing inflation during the second term. Anderson was Eisenhower's personal choice for the Republican presidential nomination in 1960.

Arbenz Guzmán, Jacobo (1913–71) President of Guatemala, 1951–54. Arbenz's land redistribution policies and tolerance of communists alienated the American-owned United Fruit Company and other landowners. A CIA-backed counter-revolution overthrew him in June 1954.

Benson, Ezra Taft (1899–1994) Secretary of Agriculture, 1953–61. Benson's efforts to reduce federal farm subsidies and restore free market forces in agriculture commanded Eisenhower's support but proved to be unpopular, even among Republicans, in the farm belt.

Brownell, Herbert, Jr (1904–96) Attorney General, 1953–57. The administration's foremost advocate of school desegregation and civil rights legislation, Brownell hoped to exploit divisions within the Democratic Party on the race issue.

Castillo Armas, Carlos (1914–57) President of Guatemala, 1954–57. A former Guatemalan army colonel who led the CIA-backed insurgent 'invasion' against President Arbenz in 1954. As president, he instigated a counter-revolution and purged suspected communists.

Castro, Fidel (1926–) Premier of Cuba, 1959–76. Castro led the popular uprising that toppled longtime dictator Fulgencio Batista in 1959, and alarmed the Eisenhower administration by pursuing a series of policies designed to break Cuba's traditional dependence on the United States.

Chamoun, Camille (1900–87) President of Lebanon, 1952–58. Chamoun was a Maronite Christian who invoked the Eisenhower Doctrine in 1958 to secure his regime against domestic Muslim opponents.

Chiang Kai-shek (1887–1975) Head of the Chinese Nationalists, 1928–49; President of Taiwan, 1949–75. Chiang insisted that his Nationalist regime in Taiwan remained the legitimate government of China and sought American aid to 'liberate' the mainland.

Churchill, Winston (1874–1965) British Prime Minister, 1951–55. Following Josef Stalin's death, Churchill pressed Eisenhower to pursue a limited *détente* with the Soviet Union and seek an early summit conference. He also secured Eisenhower's support to topple the nationalist Iranian Prime Minister Mohammed Mossadeq.

Dulles, Allen R. (1893–1969)   Director of Central Intelligence, 1953–61. Brother of John Foster Dulles, Allen Dulles emphasized the efficacy of CIA covert operations as an instrument of national security policy.

Dulles, John Foster (1888–1959)   Secretary of State, 1953–59. Eisenhower's closest foreign policy adviser until his fatal illness, Dulles's hard-line anti-communist public utterances belied a sophisticated understanding of international affairs. An advocate of collective security and nuclear brinkmanship, Dulles consistently resisted suggestions for summit talks and *détente* with the Soviet bloc.

Eden, Anthony (1897–1977)   British Foreign Secretary, 1951–55, and Prime Minister, 1955–57. Eden played an important role in the integration of West Germany into NATO. He later became obsessed with the threat of Egyptian President Nasser to British interests in the Middle East and badly misjudged the American position during the 1956 Suez crisis.

Eisenhower, Dr Milton (1899–1985)   President of Pennsylvania State University, 1950–56, and Johns Hopkins University, 1956–67. President Eisenhower's brother undertook several semi-official visits to Latin America and became an influential advocate of economic development aid to the region.

Faubus, Orval (1910–94)   Governor of Arkansas, 1955–67. Faubus's efforts to play racial politics with school desegregation led to the 1957 Little Rock crisis and Eisenhower's despatch of federal troops to the city.

Humphrey, George M. (1890–1970)   Secretary of the Treasury, 1953–57. Humphrey became a close personal friend of President Eisenhower and led the administration's drive for a balanced budget and tax cuts to aid business.

Johnson, Lyndon B. (1908–73)   Democratic Senator from Texas, 1949–61, and Senate Majority Leader, 1955–61. After the Soviet Sputnik, Johnson furthered his presidential aspirations by investigating alleged deficiencies in the nation's missile and space programmes and pushing through legislation to create NASA.

Kennedy, John F. (1917–63)   Democratic Senator from Massachusetts, 1953–60. Kennedy exploited the alleged 'missile gap' with the Soviet Union and sluggish economic growth in the late 1950s to promote his presidential candidacy in 1960.

Killian, James R., Jr (1904–88)   President of the Massachusetts Institute of Technology, 1949–59; Special Assistant to the President for Science and Technology, 1957–59. Eisenhower's first science adviser, he helped to establish a formal science advisory mechanism at the White House and became a leading proponent of a nuclear test ban agreement.

Knowland, William F. (1908–74)   Republican Senator from California, 1945–59; Majority Leader, 1953–55; and Minority Leader, 1955–59. A reliable supporter of Eisenhower's major domestic policies, Knowland nevertheless pressed for greater assistance to the Chinese Nationalists.

Lodge, Henry Cabot, Jr (1902–85)   Senator from Massachusetts, 1947–52; Ambassador to the United Nations, 1953–60. A moderate, internationalist Republican, Lodge courted Eisenhower as a presidential candidate and became his campaign manager in 1952. At the United Nations, Lodge became a principal spokesman for US foreign policy. He was Nixon's running mate in 1960.

McCarthy, Joseph R. (1908–57) Republican Senator from Wisconsin, 1947–57. McCarthy's headline-grabbing anti-communist crusade and smear tactics against his critics alienated Eisenhower but served Republican political purposes until 1953. When McCarthy attacked the Army, Eisenhower supported a quiet campaign to discredit him.

Macmillan, Harold (1894–1976) British Prime Minister, 1957–65. A wartime associate of President Eisenhower, Macmillan worked to rebuild the Anglo-American 'special relationship' after the Suez débâcle. He pushed for *détente* with the Soviet Union and, after securing American technical assistance for the British nuclear weapons programme, a nuclear test ban agreement.

Mao Zedong (1893–1976) Chairman of the Chinese Communist Party, 1949–76. Mao criticized the 'peaceful coexistence' policies of the post-Stalin Soviet leadership and competed with the Soviet Union for the allegiance of revolutionary socialist movements in the Third World. He adamantly opposed international recognition of Taiwan and used military pressure against the offshore islands to signal his displeasure with American policies.

Mossadeq, Mohammed (1889–1967) Prime Minister of Iran, 1951–53. Mossadeq's nationalist economic policies and courting of Soviet technical assistance led to his removal in an Anglo-American-inspired coup in August 1953.

Nasser, Gamal Abdel (1918–70) Premier of Egypt, 1954–56; President, 1956–70. Nasser's nationalization of the Suez Canal and pan-Arabism resulted in the unsuccessful Anglo-French–Israeli plot to overthrow him in 1956. The 1957 Eisenhower Doctrine was intended to contain Nasser's influence in the Middle East.

Nixon, Richard M. (1913–94) Republican Congressman, 1947–50; Senator from California, 1951–53; Vice-President of the United States, 1953–61. Nixon's outspoken anti-communism and partisanship made him a popular choice among Republicans for the vice-presidency in 1952, but Eisenhower never developed a close personal relationship with him. Eisenhower tried to manoeuvre Nixon out of the vice-presidency in 1956 and remained cool towards his presidential candidacy in 1960.

Oppenheimer, J. Robert (1904–67) Theoretical physicist who led the scientific effort in the World War II atomic bomb project. His coolness towards the hydrogen bomb and association with known communists raised suspicions about his loyalty among hard-line anti-communists and led to the removal of his security clearances.

Rockefeller, Nelson A. (1908–79) Chair of the President's Advisory Committee on Government Organization, 1953–55; Governor of New York, 1958–73. An adviser on psychological warfare, Rockefeller urged more rigorous prosecution of the Cold War. His critique of administration defence policies after Sputnik led Eisenhower to prefer Nixon in the contest for the Republican presidential nomination in 1960.

Russell, Richard B. (1897–1971) Democratic Senator from Georgia, 1932–71. One of the leading Southern Democrats who supported most of the administration's foreign and domestic policies, Russell strongly opposed civil rights legislation and condemned Eisenhower's use of federal troops in Little Rock, Arkansas.

Stevenson, Adlai (1900–65) Democratic Governor of Illinois, 1949–53. Unsuccessful Democratic presidential candidate in 1952 and 1956. Stevenson's eloquence and sophistication won plaudits from intellectuals and journalists but failed to command a popular majority in the two contests with Eisenhower.

Strauss, Lewis L. (1896–1974) Chair of the Atomic Energy Commission, 1953–58; Secretary of Commerce, 1958–59. An ardent Cold Warrior, Strauss consistently resisted any suspension of nuclear weapons tests. His outspoken support for private nuclear power development and role in ousting Oppenheimer from his advisory positions alienated powerful Democrats in Congress, who subsequently rejected his nomination as Secretary of Commerce.

Taft, Robert A. (1889–1953) Republican Senator from Ohio, 1939–53; Majority Leader, 1953. A conservative isolationist who had opposed NATO, Taft's decision to seek the 1952 Republican presidential nomination was a major reason that Eisenhower entered the Republican race.

Warren, Earl F. (1891–1974) Republican Governor of California, 1943–53; Chief Justice of the United States, 1953–69. He crafted the unanimous ruling in the *Brown* case that declared racially-segregated public schools unconstitutional.

Students of the Eisenhower administration now benefit from several important printed collections of primary source materials. The essential starting point is A. D. Chandler and L. P. Galambos (eds), *The Papers of Dwight David Eisenhower* (Baltimore, MD: Johns Hopkins University Press, 1970–), whose 17 volumes cover Eisenhower's career from the 1940s through to the end of his first term as president. These have recently been supplemented by D. D. Holt and J. L. Leyerzapf (eds), *Eisenhower: The Prewar Diaries and Letters, 1905–1941* (Baltimore, MD: Johns Hopkins University Press, 1998). Important insight into Eisenhower's views on a variety of contemporary topics is also provided by R. F. Ferrell (ed.), *The Eisenhower Diaries* (New York: Norton, 1981) and R. Griffith (ed.), *Ike's Letters to a Friend, 1941–1958* (Lawrence, KS: University Press of Kansas, 1984). Eisenhower's official statements are compiled in *Public Papers of the Presidents of the United States: Dwight D. Eisenhower*, 8 vols (Washington, DC: Government Printing Office, 1959–61). A convenient selection of documents can be found in R. L. Branyan and L. H. Larsen (eds), *The Eisenhower Administration: A Documentary History* (New York: Random House, 1971).

For the Eisenhower administration's role in international affairs, the official printed record, US Department of State, *Foreign Relations of the United States* (Washington, DC: Government Printing Office, 1984–), accompanied by microfiche supplements, is now practically complete for the period 1953–61. Eisenhower's relationship with British Prime Minister Winston Churchill can be followed through P. G. Boyle (ed.), *The Churchill–Eisenhower Correspondence, 1953–1955* (Chapel Hill, NC: University of North Carolina Press, 1990). Some important, recently-released documents from the former Communist bloc are available in the Cold War International History Project, *Bulletin*, available free of charge from the Woodrow Wilson International Center for Scholars in Washington, DC. Additional insight into Soviet and British policies can be gleaned from two useful memoirs. On the Soviet side, see N. S. Khrushchev, *Khrushchev Remembers* (Boston, MA: Little, Brown, 1970); *Khrushchev Remembers: The Last Testament* (Boston, MA: Little, Brown, 1974); and *Khrushchev Remembers: The Glasnost Tapes* (Boston, MA: Little, Brown, 1990). For a British perspective, see Harold Macmillan, *Tides of Fortune, 1945–1955* (London: Macmillan, 1969); *Riding the Storm, 1956–1959* (London: Macmillan, 1971); and *Pointing the Way, 1959–1961* (London: Macmillan, 1972), which also include selected extracts from official correspondence and Macmillan's diaries.

Eisenhower provides his own account of his eight years in office in two volumes of memoirs: *Mandate for Change, 1953–1956* (Garden City, NY: Doubleday, 1963); and *Waging Peace, 1956–1961* (Garden City, NY: Doubleday, 1965). He relates his pre-presidential years in *At Ease: Stories I Tell to Friends* (Garden City, NY: Doubleday, 1967). His brother and son have also produced memoirs of their service in the Eisenhower administration. See M. S. Eisenhower, *The President is Calling* (Garden City, NY: Doubleday, 1974) and J. S. D. Eisenhower, *Strictly Personal* (Garden City, NY: Doubleday, 1974). The vice president's recollections are in R. M. Nixon, *Six Crises* (Garden City, NY: Doubleday, 1962) and *RN: The Memoirs of Richard Nixon* (New York: Grosset and Dunlap, 1978).

Several other members of the Eisenhower administration kept diaries or wrote memoirs. Among the most useful are S. Adams, *Firsthand Report: The Story of the Eisenhower Administration* (New York: Harper and Row, 1961), by the man who served as Eisenhower's chief of staff until 1958; E. J. Hughes, *The Ordeal of Power: A Political Memoir of the Eisenhower Years* (New York: Atheneum, 1963), a rather critical view by a former speech-writer; H. C. Lodge, *As It Was: An Inside View of Politics and Power in the '50s and '60s* (New York: Norton, 1976), by Eisenhower's campaign manager and ambassador to the United Nations; and E. Z. Benson, *Cross Fire: The Eight Years with Eisenhower* (Garden City, NY: Doubleday, 1962), by the controversial secretary of agriculture. For insight into the administration's economic views, see N. R. Howard (ed.), *The Basic Papers of George M. Humphrey* (Cleveland, OH: Western Reserve Historical Society, 1965). Important recent additions to the literature include R. H. Ferrell (ed.), *The Diary of James C. Hagerty: Eisenhower in Mid-Course, 1954–1955* (Bloomington, IN: Indiana University Press, 1983); H. Brownell and J. P. Burke, *Advising Ike: The Memoirs of Attorney General Herbert Brownell* (Lawrence, KS: University Press of Kansas, 1993); and K. W. Thompson (ed.), *The Eisenhower Presidency: Eleven Intimate Perspectives of Dwight D. Eisenhower* (Lanham, MD: University Press of America, 1984), a collection of oral histories from administration insiders. Two accounts by Eisenhower's science advisers are essential sources for the post-Sputnik period. See G. B. Kistiakowsky, *A Scientist at the White House: The Private Diary of President Eisenhower's Special Assistant for Science and Technology* (Cambridge, MA: Harvard University Press, 1976), and J. R. Killian, Jr, *Sputnik, Scientists, and Eisenhower: A Memoir of the First Special Assistant to the President for Science and Technology* (Cambridge, MA: MIT Press, 1977).

Good introductions to the burgeoning secondary literature on Eisenhower and the phenomenon of 'Eisenhower revisionism' include M. Kempton, 'The under-estimation of Dwight D. Eisenhower', *Esquire*, 68, 1967; V. P. DeSantis, 'Eisenhower revisionism', *Review of Politics*, 38, 1976; M. S. McAuliffe, 'Commentary: Eisenhower, the President', *Journal of American Hisory*, 68, 1981; A. Brinkley, 'A president for certain seasons', *Wilson Quarterly*, 14, 1990; R. F. Burk, 'Eisenhower revisionism revisited: reflections on Eisenhower scholarship', *Historian*, 50, 1988; and J. Broadwater, 'President Eisenhower and the historians: is the general in retreat?', *Canadian Review of American Studies*, 22, 1991. Also useful is R. H. Immerman, 'Confessions of an Eisenhower revisionist: an agonizing reappraisal', *Diplomatic History*, 14, 1990.

There are several fine overviews of the Eisenhower presidency. The most comprehensive by far is S. Ambrose, *Eisenhower*, vol. 2: *The President* (New York: Simon and Schuster, 1984), but C. J. Pach, Jr and E. Richardson, *The Presidency of Dwight D. Eisenhower*, revised edition (Lawrence, KS: University Press of Kansas, 1991) provides an insightful critique. An essential essay on Eisenhower's political philosophy is R. Griffith, 'Dwight D. Eisenhower and the corporate commonwealth', *American Historical Review*, 87, 1982. Generally favourable interpretations of the Eisenhower administration are found in H. S. Parmet, *Eisenhower and the American Crusades* (New York: Macmillan, 1972) and R. A. Lee, *Dwight D. Eisenhower: Soldier and Statesman* (Chicago, IL: Nelson-Hall, 1981). Somewhat more critical is P. Lyon, *Eisenhower: Portrait of the Hero* (Boston, MA: Little, Brown, 1974), while P. Brandon, *Ike: His Life and Times* (New York: Harper and Row, 1986) is one of the few recent works that harkens back to the earliest, negative interpretations of Eisenhower's presidency.

For comprehensive analyses of Eisenhower's foreign policies, see the early revisionist works by R. A. Divine, *Eisenhower and the Cold War* (New York: Oxford University Press, 1981), and B. W. Cook, *The Declassified Eisenhower* (New York: Penguin, 1984), and the relevant portions of three works by J. L. Gaddis, *Strategies of Containment: A Critical Appraisal of Postwar American National Security Policy* (New York: Oxford University Press, 1982), *The Long Peace: Inquiries into the History of the Cold War* (New York: Oxford University Press, 1987) and *We Now Know: Rethinking Cold War History* (New York: Oxford University Press, 1997). Also useful are the essays in D. Mayers and R. A. Melanson (eds), *Reevaluating Eisenhower: American Foreign Policy in the 1950s* (Chicago, IL: University of Illinois Press, 1987). Two important and largely sympathetic recent reassessments of John Foster Dulles's diplomacy are the collection of essays in R. H. Immerman (ed.), *John Foster Dulles and the Diplomacy of the Cold War* (Princeton, NJ: Princeton University Press, 1990) and R. H. Immerman, *John Foster Dulles: Piety, Pragmatism, and Power in U.S. Foreign Policy* (Wilmington, DE: Scholarly Resources, 1999).

Eisenhower's New Look national security policy has been the subject of several recent works. The best overviews are R. Bowie and R. H. Immerman, *Waging Peace: How Eisenhower Shaped an Enduring Cold War Strategy* (New York: Oxford University Press, 1998), which focuses primarily on Eisenhower's first term, and the more comprehensive and critical S. Dockrill, *Eisenhower's New Look National Security Policy, 1953–1961* (New York: St Martin's Press, 1996). Eisenhower's battles with Congress over military reorganization can be followed in G. Clarfield, *Security with Solvency: Dwight D. Eisenhower and the Shaping of the American Military Establishment* (Westport, CT: Praeger, 1999), while his efforts to hold the line in the aftermath of Sputnik are the subject of R. A. Aliano, *American Defense Policy from Eisenhower to Kennedy: The Politics of Changing Military Requirements, 1957–1961* (Athens, OH: Ohio University Press, 1975), R. A. Divine, *The Sputnik Challenge: Eisenhower's Response to the Soviet Satellite* (New York: Oxford University Press, 1993), and P. J. Roman, *Eisenhower and the Missile Gap* (Ithaca, NY: Cornell University Press, 1995). The implications of nuclear abundance for American foreign policy are discussed in C. Craig, *Destroying the Village: Eisenhower and Thermonuclear War* (New York: Columbia University Press, 1998), and A. Wenger, *Living with Peril: Eisenhower, Kennedy, and Nuclear Weapons* (Lanham, MD: Rowman and Littlefield, 1997).

The Eisenhower administration's policy towards ending the Korean War has been the subject of much discussion. The best overview of the war's international dimension is W. Steuck, *The Korean War: An International History* (Princeton, NJ: Princeton University Press, 1995), while the administration's peacemaking efforts are detailed in R. Foot, *A Substitute for Victory: The Politics of Peacemaking at the*

Korean Armistice Talks (Ithaca, NY: Cornell University Press, 1990). The debate over the Eisenhower administration's nuclear threat can be followed in E. C. Keefer, 'President Dwight D. Eisenhower and the end of the Korean War', *Diplomatic History*, 10, 1986, and R. Dingman, 'Atomic diplomacy during the Korean War', R. Foot, 'Nuclear coercion and the ending of the Korean conflict', and M. Trachtenberg, '"A wasting asset": American strategy and the shifting nuclear balance, 1949–1954', all in *International Security*, 13, 1988/89.

The origins of American involvement in Indochina are detailed in two important books: L. C. Gardner, *Approaching Vietnam: From World War II through Dien Bien Phu* (New York: Norton, 1988); and D. L. Anderson, *Trapped by Success: The Eisenhower Administration and Vietnam, 1953–1961* (New York: Columbia University Press, 1991). The Dien Bien Phu crisis is the focus of M. Billings-Yun, *Decision Against War: Eisenhower and Dien Bien Phu* (New York: Columbia University Press, 1988). A more critical rendering is G. C. Herring and R. H. Immerman, 'Eisenhower, Dulles, and Dien Bien Phu: the "day we didn't go to war" revisited', *Journal of American History*, 71, 1984. For American policy at the subsequent Geneva Conference, see the essay by G. C. Herring, '"A good stout effort": John Foster Dulles in the Indochina crisis, 1954–1955', in the collection edited by R. H. Immerman cited above.

The discussion of the Eisenhower administration's relations with the People's Republic of China and Taiwan has benefited from several recent studies employing Chinese language sources. G. H. Chang, *Friends and Enemies: The United States, China, and the Soviet Union, 1948–1972* (Stanford, CA: Stanford University Press, 1990) is a solid overview, but should be supplemented with Q. Zhai, *The Lion, the Dragon, and the Eagle: Chinese–British–American Relations, 1949–1958* (Kent, OH: Kent State University Press, 1994), S. G. Zhang, *Deterrence and Strategic Culture: Chinese–American Confrontations, 1949–1958* (Ithaca, NY: Cornell University Press, 1993), and T. J. Christensen, *Useful Adversaries: Grand Strategy, Domestic Mobilization, and Sino-American Conflict, 1947–1958* (Princeton, NJ: Princeton University Press, 1996). The most sophisticated discussion of the 1954–55 offshore islands crisis is G. H. Chang and H. Di, 'The absence of war in the U.S.–Chinese confrontation over Quemoy and Matsu in 1954–1955: contingency, luck, and deterrence', *American Historical Review*, 98, 1993, but see also H. W. Brands, 'Testing massive retaliation: credibility and crisis management in the Taiwan Strait', *International Security*, 12, 1988.

The literature on United States policy towards the Middle East in the 1950s still focuses heavily on the Suez crisis. K. Kyle, *Suez* (New York: St Martin's Press, 1991) is a comprehensive overview, while P. L. Hahn, *The United States, Great Britain, and Egypt, 1945–1956: Strategy and Diplomacy in the Early Cold War* (Chapel Hill, NC: University of North Carolina Press, 1991) emphasizes British and American strategic considerations. Eisenhower's hands-on diplomacy during the crisis is documented in D. B. Kunz, *The Economic Diplomacy of the Suez Crisis* (Chapel Hill, NC: University of North Carolina Press, 1991) and C. C. Kingseed, *Eisenhower and the Suez Crisis of 1956* (Baton Rouge, LA: Louisiana State University Press, 1995). S. Z. Freiberger, *Dawn Over Suez: The Rise of American Power in the Middle East, 1953–1957* (Chicago, IL: Ivan R. Dee, 1992), notes the negative ramifications of Eisenhower's policies for relations with the Arab world. Other important studies that go beyond the Suez episode are I. L. Gendzier, *Notes from the Minefield: United*

States Intervention in Lebanon and the Middle East, 1945–1958 (New York: Columbia University Press, 1996); D. W. Lesch, *Syria and the United States: Eisenhower's Cold War in the Middle East* (Boulder, CO: Westview Press, 1992); D. Little, 'Cold War and covert action: the United States and Syria, 1945–1958', *Middle East Journal*, 44, 1990, and 'His finest hour? Eisenhower, Lebanon, and the 1958 Middle East crisis', *Diplomatic History*, 20, 1996; N. Ashton, *Eisenhower, Macmillan, and the Problem of Nasser: Anglo-American Relations with Arab Nationalism* (New York, St Martin's Press, 1996); and I. Alteras, *Eisenhower and Israel: U.S.–Israeli Relations, 1953–1960* (Gainesville, FL: University of Florida Press, 1993). On Iran, see M. Gasiorowski, *U.S. Foreign Policy and the Shah: Building a Client State in Iran* (Ithaca, NY: Cornell University Press, 1991), and M. A. Heiss, *Empire and Nationhood: The United States, Great Britain, and Iranian Oil* (New York: Columbia University Press, 1997).

The starting point for any examination of the Eisenhower administration's policy towards Latin America is S. G. Rabe, *Eisenhower and Latin America: The Foreign Policy of Anticommunism* (Chapel Hill, NC: University of North Carolina Press, 1987). For the Guatemalan intervention, see R. H. Immerman, *The CIA in Guatemala: The Foreign Policy of Intervention* (Austin, TX: University of Texas Press, 1982), and P. Gleijeses, *Shattered Hope: The Guatemalan Revolution and the United States, 1944–1955* (Princeton, NJ: Princeton University Press, 1991). The administration's difficulties with Fidel Castro are detailed in R. E. Welch, Jr, *Response to Revolution: The United States and the Cuban Revolution, 1959–1961* (Chapel Hill, NC: University of North Carolina Press, 1985), and T. G. Paterson, *Contesting Castro: The United States and the Triumph of the Cuban Revolution* (New York: Oxford University Press, 1994).

Several good studies examine specific aspects of the administration's policies towards Europe. On Eisenhower's support for European integration, see P. Winand, *Eisenhower, Kennedy, and the United States of Europe* (New York: St Martin's Press, 1993). The German question is the subject of M. Trachtenberg, *A Constructed Peace: The Making of the European Settlement, 1945–1963* (Princeton, NJ: Princeton University Press, 1999). The demise of the European Defence Community is covered in K. Ruane, *The Rise and Fall of the European Defence Community: Anglo-American Relations and the Crisis of European Defence, 1950–55* (New York: St Martin's Press, 2000), and B. R. Duchin, 'The "agonizing reappraisal": Dulles, Eisenhower, and the European Defence Community', *Diplomatic History*, 16, 1992. For Eisenhower's summitry, see G. Bischof and S. Dockrill (eds), *Cold War Respite: The Geneva Summit of 1955* (Baton Rouge, LA: Louisiana State University Press, 2000); W. W. Rostow, *Open Skies: Eisenhower's Proposal of July 21, 1955* (Austin, TX: Texas University Press, 1982); and M. Beschloss, *Mayday: Eisenhower, Khrushchev, and the U-2 Affair* (New York: Harper and Row, 1986). Eisenhower's disarmament efforts are covered in R. A. Divine, *Blowing on the Wind: The Nuclear Test Ban Debate* (New York: Oxford University Press, 1978), and R. G. Hewlett and J. M. Holl, *Atoms for Peace and War, 1953–1961: Eisenhower and the Atomic Energy Commission* (Berkeley, CA: University of California Press, 1989). W. L. Hixson, *Parting the Curtain: Propaganda, Culture, and the Cold War, 1945–1961* (New York: St Martin's Press, 1996) examines Eisenhower's forays into cultural diplomacy towards the Soviet Union. An important overview of Soviet policy is V. M. Zubok and C. Pleshakov,

Inside the Kremlin's Cold War: From Stalin to Khrushchev (Cambridge, MA: Harvard University Press, 1996).

Although the literature on Eisenhower's domestic policies is rather more limited, there are several important studies. The best general discussions of Eisenhower's economic policies are I. W. Morgan, *Eisenhower versus 'the Spenders': The Eisenhower Administration, the Democrats, and the Budget, 1953–1960* (New York: St Martin's Press, 1990); J. W. Sloan, *Eisenhower and the Management of Prosperity* (Lawrence, KS: University Press of Kansas, 1991); and R. W. Saulnier, *Constructive Years: The US Economy under Eisenhower* (Lanham, MD: University Press of America, 1991), which is part memoir and part historical analysis. For more specialized works, see E. L. Schapsmeier and F. H. Schapsmeier, *Ezra Taft Benson and the Politics of Agriculture* (Danville, IL: Interstate, 1975) on agricultural policy; R. A. Lee, *Eisenhower and Landrum–Griffin: A Study in Labor–Management Politics* (Lexington, KY: University Press of Kentucky, 1990) on labour reform; M. H. Rose, *Interstate: Express Highway Politics, 1941–1956* (Lawrence, KS: Regents Press of Kansas, 1979); and E. Richardson, *Dams, Parks, and Politics: Resource Development and Preservation in the Truman–Eisenhower Era* (Lexington, KY: University Press of Kentucky, 1973).

On the politics of the 1950s generally, see two fine works by G. W. Reichard, *The Reaffirmation of Republicanism: Eisenhower and the Eighty-third Congress* (Knoxville, TN: University of Tennessee Press, 1973), and *Politics as Usual: The Age of Truman and Eisenhower* (Arlington Heights, IL: Harlan Davidson, 1988). Several biographical studies of prominent congressional figures are also useful. See James T. Patterson, *Mr. Republican: A Biography of Robert A. Taft* (Boston, MA: Houghton Mifflin, 1972); J. Broadwater, *Adlai Stevenson and American Politics: The Odyssey of a Cold War Liberal* (New York: Twayne, 1994); R. Dallek, *Lone Star Rising: Lyndon Johnson and His Times, 1908–1960* (New York: Oxford University Press, 1991); and G. B. Montgomery and J. W. Johnson, *One Step from the White House: The Rise and Fall of Senator William F. Knowland* (Berkeley, CA: University of California Press, 1998).

There is an extensive literature on McCarthyism. Good overviews are: R. M. Fried, *Nightmare in Red: The McCarthy Era in Perspective* (New York: Oxford University Press, 1990); R. Griffith, *The Politics of Fear: Joseph R. McCarthy and the Senate* (Lexington, KY: University Press of Kentucky, 1970); and D. C. Caute, *The Great Fear: The Anticommunist Purge under Truman and Eisenhower* (New York: Simon and Schuster, 1978). Eisenhower's involvement in the 'red scare' is detailed in J. Broadwater, *Eisenhower and the Anti-Communist Crusade* (Chapel Hill, NC: University of North Carolina Press, 1992). Dulles's purge of the State Department is the subject of G. May, *China Scapegoat: The Diplomatic Ordeal of John Carter Vincent* (Washington, DC: New Republic Books, 1979).

On the Eisenhower administration's involvement in the African-American struggle for civil rights, R. F. Burk, *The Eisenhower Administration and Black Civil Rights* (Knoxville, TN: University of Tennessee Press, 1984) is the best overview. Eisenhower's role in the *Brown* case is examined in M. S. Mayer, 'With much deliberation and some speed: Eisenhower and the *Brown* decision', *Journal of Southern History*, 52, 1986. The Little Rock crisis is addressed in J. C. Duram, *A Moderate Among Extremists: Dwight D. Eisenhower and the School Desegregation Crisis* (Chicago, IL: Nelson-Hall, 1981) and E. Huckaby, *Crisis at Central High,*

Little Rock, 1957–58 (Baton Rouge, LA: Louisiana State University Press, 1980). The white backlash is examined in N. V. Bartley, *The Rise of Massive Resistance: Race and Politics in the South during the 1950s* (Baton Rouge, LA: Louisiana State University Press, 1969), and N. R. McMillen, *The Citizens' Council: Organized Resistance to the Second Reconstruction* (Urbana, IL: University of Illinois Press, 1971). Recently, more attention has been paid to the Cold War context of the civil rights movement and the Eisenhower administration's concern with the American image abroad. See M. J. Dudziak, *Cold War Civil Rights: Race and the Image of American Democracy* (Princeton, NJ: Princeton University Press, 2000).

REFERENCES

ABBREVIATIONS

CWIHP   Cold War International History Project
FRUS   US Department of State, *Foreign Relations of the United States*
PPP   *Public Papers of the Presidents of the United States:*
            Dwight D. Eisenhower
USDD   US Department of State, *Documents on Disarmament*

Place of publication is New York unless otherwise noted.

Adams, S. (1961) *Firsthand Report: The Story of the Eisenhower Administration.* Harper and Row.

Alexander, C. C. (1975) *Holding the Line: The Eisenhower Era, 1952–1961.* Bloomington, IN: Indiana University Press.

Ambrose, S. E. (1984) *Eisenhower*, vol. 2: *The President.* Simon and Schuster.

Ambrose, S. E. (1987) *Nixon: The Education of a Politician, 1913–1962.* Simon and Schuster.

Ambrose, S. E. and R. H. Immerman (1981) *Ike's Spies: Eisenhower and the Espionage Establishment.* Garden City, NY: Doubleday.

Bernstein, B. J. (1982) 'In the matter of J. Robert Oppenheimer', *Historical Studies in the Physical and Biological Sciences*, 12, pp. 195–252.

Bowie, R. R. and R. H. Immerman (1998) *Waging Peace: How Eisenhower Shaped an Enduring Cold War Strategy.* Oxford University Press.

Boyle, P. G. (ed.) (1990) *The Churchill–Eisenhower Correspondence, 1953–1955.* Chapel Hill, NC: University of North Carolina Press.

Branyan R. L. and L. H. Larsen (eds) (1971) *The Eisenhower Administration, 1953–1961: A Documentary History.* Random House.

Broadwater, J. (1991) 'President Eisenhower and the historians: is the general in retreat?', *Canadian Review of American Studies*, 22, pp. 47–60.

Brownell, H. and J. P. Burke (1993) *Advising Ike: The Memoirs of Attorney General Herbert Brownell.* Lawrence, KS: University Press of Kansas.

Burk, R. F. (1984) *The Eisenhower Administration and Black Civil Rights.* Knoxville, TN: University of Tennessee Press.

Burk, R. F. (1988) 'Eisenhower revisionism revisited: reflections on Eisenhower scholarship', *Historian*, 50, pp. 196–209.

Chandler, A. D., Jr, and L. Galambos (eds) (1970–) *The Papers of Dwight David Eisenhower*, 17 vols. Baltimore, MD: Johns Hopkins University Press.

Chang, G. H. and H. Di (1993) 'The absence of war in the U.S.–Chinese confrontation over Quemoy and Matsu in 1954–1955: contingency, luck, and deterrence', *American Historical Review*, 98, pp. 1500–24.

Cold War International History Project (CWIHP) (1993–) *Bulletin*, vols 1–11. Washington, DC: Woodrow Wilson International Center for Scholars.

Craig, C. (1998) *Destroying the Village: Eisenhower and Thermonuclear War.* Columbia University Press.

DeSantis, V. P. (1976) 'Eisenhower revisionism', *Review of Politics*, 38, pp. 190–207.

Divine, R. A. (1981) *Eisenhower and the Cold War.* Oxford University Press.

Dulles, J. F. (1952) 'A policy of boldness', *Life*, 32, pp. 146–60.

Dulles, J. F. (1954) 'The evolution of foreign policy', *Department of State Bulletin*, 30, pp. 107–10.

Duram, J. C. (1981) *A Moderate Among Extremists: Dwight D. Eisenhower and the School Desegregation Crisis.* Chicago, IL: Nelson-Hall.

Eisenhower, D. D. (1963) *Mandate for Change, 1953–1956.* Garden City, NY: Doubleday.

Eisenhower, D. D. (1965) *Waging Peace, 1956–1961.* Garden City, NY: Doubleday.

Eisenhower, J. S. D. (1974) *Strictly Personal.* Garden City, NY: Doubleday.

Ferrell, R. H. (ed.) (1981) *The Eisenhower Diaries.* W. W. Norton.

Ferrell, R. H. (ed.) (1983) *The Diary of James C. Hagerty: Eisenhower in Mid-Course, 1954–1955.* Bloomington, IN: Indiana University Press.

Fried, R. M. (1990) *Nightmare in Red: The McCarthy Era in Perspective.* Oxford University Press.

Gaddis, J. L. (1997) *We Now Know: Rethinking Cold War History.* Oxford University Press.

Greenstein, F. I. (1982) *The Hidden-Hand Presidency: Eisenhower as Leader.* Basic Books.

Griffith, R. (1970) *The Politics of Fear: Joseph R. McCarthy and the Senate.* Lexington, KY: University of Kentucky Press.

Griffith, R. (1982) 'Dwight D. Eisenhower and the corporate commonwealth', *American Historical Review*, 87, pp. 87–122.

Griffith, R. (ed.) (1984) *Ike's Letters to a Friend, 1941–1958.* Lawrence, KS: University Press of Kansas.

Herring, G. C. and R. H. Immerman (1984) 'Eisenhower, Dulles, and Dien Bien Phu: the "day we didn't go to war" revisited', *Journal of American History*, 71, pp. 343–63.

Howard, N. R. (ed.) (1965) *The Basic Papers of George M. Humphrey.* Cleveland, OH: Western Reserve Historical Society.

Hughes, E. J. (1963) *The Ordeal of Power: A Political Memoir of the Eisenhower Years.* Atheneum.

Immerman, R. H. (1982) *The CIA in Guatemala: The Foreign Policy of Intervention.* Austin, TX: University of Texas Press.

Immerman, R. H. (ed.) (1990) *John Foster Dulles and the Diplomacy of the Cold War.* Princeton, NJ: Princeton University Press.

Jurika, S., Jr (1980) *From Pearl Harbor to Vietnam: The Memoirs of Admiral Arthur W. Radford.* Stanford, CA: Hoover Institution Press.

Kempton, M. (1967) 'The underestimation of Dwight D. Eisenhower', *Esquire*, 68, pp. 108–9, 156.

Killian, J. R., Jr (1977) *Sputnik, Scientists, and Eisenhower: A Memoir of the First Special Assistant to the President for Science and Technology.* Cambridge, MA: MIT Press.

Kistiakowsky, G. B. (1976) *A Scientist at the White House: The Private Diary of President Eisenhower's Special Assistant for Science and Technology.* Cambridge, MA: Harvard University Press.

Larson, A. (1968) *Eisenhower: The President Nobody Knew.* Charles Scribner's Sons.

Lyon, P. (1974) *Eisenhower: Portrait of the Hero.* Boston, MA: Little, Brown.

McDougall, W. A. (1985) *The Heavens and the Earth: A Political History of the Space Age.* Basic Books.

Macmillan, H. (1972) *Pointing the Way, 1959–1961.* Harper and Row.

Mayer, M. S. (1986) 'With much deliberation and some speed: Eisenhower and the *Brown* decision', *Journal of Southern History*, 52, pp. 43–76.

Mayers, D. L. (1986) *Cracking the Monolith: U.S. Policy against the Sino-Soviet Alliance, 1945–1955.* Baton Rouge, LA: Louisiana State University Press.

Mayers, D. and R. A. Melanson (eds) (1987) *Reevaluating Eisenhower: American Foreign Policy in the 1950s.* Urbana, IL: University of Illinois Press.

Morgan, I. W. (1990) *Eisenhower versus 'the Spenders': The Eisenhower Administration, the Democrats, and the Budget, 1953–1960.* St Martin's Press.

Nixon, R. (1962) *Six Crises.* Garden City, NY: Doubleday.

Pach, C. J., Jr, and E. Richardson (1991) *The Presidency of Dwight D. Eisenhower*, revised edition. Lawrence, KS: University Press of Kansas.

Parmet, H. S. (1972) *Eisenhower and the American Crusades.* Macmillan.

Pickett, W. B. (2000) *Eisenhower Decides to Run: Presidential Politics and Cold War Strategy.* Chicago, IL: Ivan R. Dee.

Porter, K. H. and D. B. Johnson (eds) (1956) *National Party Platforms, 1840–1956.* Urbana, IL: University of Illinois Press.

Rabe, S. G. (1987) *Eisenhower and Latin America: The Foreign Policy of Anticommunism.* Chapel Hill, NC: University of North Carolina Press.

Roman, P. J. (1995) *Eisenhower and the Missile Gap.* Ithaca, NY: Cornell University Press.

Rosenberg, D. A. (1983) 'The origins of overkill: nuclear weapons and American strategy, 1945–1960,' *International Security*, 7, pp. 3–70.

Saulnier, R. W. (1991) *Constructive Years: The US Economy under Eisenhower.* Lanham, MD: University Press of America.

Schlesinger, A. M., Jr (1962) 'Our presidents: a rating by 75 historians', *New York Times Magazine*, 29 July, pp. 12, 40–1.

Shannon, W. V. (1958) 'Eisenhower as president: a critical appraisal of the record', *Commentary*, 26, pp. 390–8.

Shepley, J. (1956) 'How Dulles averted war', *Life*, 36, pp. 70–80.

Sitkoff, H. (1993) *The Struggle for Black Equality, 1954–1992.* Hill and Wang.

Smith, G. (1994) *The Last Years of the Monroe Doctrine, 1945–1993.* Hill and Wang.

Steuck, W. (1995) *The Korean War: An International History.* Princeton, NJ: Princeton University Press.

Trachtenberg, M. (1991) *History and Strategy.* Princeton, NJ: Princeton University Press.

Trachtenberg, M. (1999) *A Constructed Peace: The Making of the European Settlement, 1945–1963.* Princeton, NJ: Princeton University Press.

US Department of State (1960) *Documents on Disarmament, 1959–1960.* Washington, DC: Government Printing Office.

US Department of State (1977) *Foreign Relations of the United States, 1950*, vol. 1. Washington, DC: Government Printing Office.

US Department of State (1979–89) *Foreign Relations of the United States, 1952–1954*, 16 vols. Washington, DC: Government Printing Office.

US Department of State (1985–92) *Foreign Relations of the United States, 1955–1957*, 27 vols. Washington, DC: Government Printing Office.

US Department of State (1986–98) *Foreign Relations of the United States, 1958–1960*, 19 vols. Washington, DC: Government Printing Office.

US Department of State (1988–98) *Foreign Relations of the United States, 1961–1963*, 23 vols. Washington, DC: Government Printing Office.

US President (1959–61) *Public Papers of the Presidents of the United States: Dwight D. Eisenhower* (1953–61), 8 vols. Washington, DC: Government Printing Office.

Warren, Earl (1977) *The Memoirs of Earl Warren*. Garden City, NY: Doubleday.

Wills, G. (1969) *Nixon Agonistes: The Crisis of the Self-Made Man*. Boston, MA: Houghton Mifflin.

Zubok, V. M. and Pleshakov, C. (1996) *Inside the Kremlin's Cold War: From Stalin to Khrushchev*. Cambridge, MA: Harvard University Press.

INDEX

SEMINAR STUDIES IN HISTORY

General Editors: Clive Emsley & Gordon Martel

The series was founded by Patrick Richardson in 1966. Between 1980 and 1996 Roger Lockyer edited the series before handing over to Clive Emsley (Professor of History at the Open University) and Gordon Martel (Professor of International History at the University of Northern British Columbia, Canada and Senior Research Fellow at De Montfort University).

MEDIEVAL ENGLAND

The Pre-Reformation Church in England 1400–1530 (Second edition)
Christopher Harper-Bill   0 582 28989 0

Lancastrians and Yorkists: The Wars of the Roses
David R Cook   0 582 35384 X

Family and Kinship in England 1450–1800
Will Coster   0 582 35717 9

TUDOR ENGLAND

Henry VII (Third edition)
Roger Lockyer & Andrew Thrush   0 582 20912 9

Henry VIII (Second edition)
M D Palmer   0 582 35437 4

Tudor Rebellions (Fourth edition)
Anthony Fletcher & Diarmaid MacCulloch   0 582 28990 4

The Reign of Mary I (Second edition)
Robert Tittler   0 582 06107 5

Early Tudor Parliaments 1485–1558
Michael A R Graves   0 582 03497 3

The English Reformation 1530–1570
W J Sheils   0 582 35398 X

Elizabethan Parliaments 1559–1601 (Second edition)
Michael A R Graves   0 582 29196 8

England and Europe 1485–1603 (Second edition)
Susan Doran   0 582 28991 2

The Church of England 1570–1640
Andrew Foster   0 582 35574 5

STUART BRITAIN

Social Change and Continuity: England 1550–1750 (Second edition)
Barry Coward   0 582 29442 8

James I (Second edition)
S J Houston   0 582 20911 0

The English Civil War 1640–1649
Martyn Bennett   0 582 35392 0

Charles I, 1625–1640
Brian Quintrell   0 582 00354 7

The English Republic 1649–1660 (Second edition)
Toby Barnard   0 582 08003 7

Radical Puritans in England 1550–1660
R J Acheson   0 582 35515 X

The Restoration and the England of Charles II (Second edition)
John Miller   0 582 29223 9

The Glorious Revolution (Second edition)
John Miller   0 582 29222 0

EARLY MODERN EUROPE

The Renaissance (Second edition)
Alison Brown   0 582 30781 3

The Emperor Charles V
Martyn Rady   0 582 35475 7

French Renaissance Monarchy: Francis I and Henry II (Second edition)
Robert Knecht   0 582 28707 3

The Protestant Reformation in Europe
Andrew Johnston   0 582 07020 1

The French Wars of Religion 1559–1598 (Second edition)
Robert Knecht   0 582 28533 X

Phillip II
Geoffrey Woodward   0 582 07232 8

The Thirty Years' War
Peter Limm   0 582 35373 4

Louis XIV
Peter Campbell   0 582 01770 X

Spain in the Seventeenth Century
Graham Darby   0 582 07234 4

Peter the Great
William Marshall   0 582 00355 5

EUROPE 1789–1918

Britain and the French Revolution
Clive Emsley   0 582 36961 4

Revolution and Terror in France 1789–1795 (Second edition)
D G Wright   0 582 00379 2

Napoleon and Europe
D G Wright   0 582 35457 9

The Abolition of Serfdom in Russia, 1762–1907
David Moon   0 582 29486 X

Nineteenth-Century Russia: Opposition to Autocracy
Derek Offord   0 582 35767 5

The Constitutional Monarchy in France 1814–48
Pamela Pilbeam   0 582 31210 8

The 1848 Revolutions (Second edition)
Peter Jones   0 582 06106 7

The Italian Risorgimento
M Clark   0 582 00353 9

Bismarck & Germany 1862–1890 (Second edition)
D G Williamson   0 582 29321 9

Imperial Germany 1890–1918
Ian Porter, Ian Armour and Roger Lockyer   0 582 03496 5

The Dissolution of the Austro-Hungarian Empire 1867–1918 (Second edition)
John W Mason   0 582 29466 5

Second Empire and Commune: France 1848–1871 (Second edition)
William H C Smith   0 582 28705 7

France 1870–1914 (Second edition)
Robert Gildea   0 582 29221 2

The Scramble for Africa (Second edition)
M E Chamberlain   0 582 36881 2

Late Imperial Russia 1890–1917
John F Hutchinson   0 582 32721 0

The First World War
Stuart Robson   0 582 31556 5

Austria, Prussia and Germany, 1806–1871
John Breuilly   0 582 43739 3

EUROPE SINCE 1918

The Russian Revolution (Second edition)
Anthony Wood   0 582 35559 1

Lenin's Revolution: Russia, 1917–1921
David Marples   0 582 31917 X

Stalin and Stalinism (Second edition)
Martin McCauley   0 582 27658 6

The Weimar Republic (Second edition)
John Hiden   0 582 28706 5

The Inter-War Crisis 1919–1939
Richard Overy   0 582 35379 3

Fascism and the Right in Europe, 1919–1945
Martin Blinkhorn   0 582 07021 X

Spain's Civil War (Second edition)
Harry Browne   0 582 28988 2

The Third Reich (Third edition)
D G Williamson   0 582 20914 5

The Origins of the Second World War (Second edition)
R J Overy   0 582 29085 6

The Second World War in Europe
Paul MacKenzie   0 582 32692 3

The French at War, 1934–1944
Nicholas Atkin   0 582 36899 5

Anti-Semitism before the Holocaust
Albert S Lindemann   0 582 36964 9

The Holocaust: The Third Reich and the Jews
David Engel   0 582 32720 2

Germany from Defeat to Partition, 1945–1963
D G Williamson   0 582 29218 2

Britain and Europe since 1945
Alex May   0 582 30778 3

Eastern Europe 1945–1969: From Stalinism to Stagnation
Ben Fowkes   0 582 32693 1

Eastern Europe since 1970
Bülent Gökay   0 582 32858 6

The Khrushchev Era, 1953–1964
Martin McCauley   0 582 27776 0

NINETEENTH-CENTURY BRITAIN

Britain before the Reform Acts: Politics and Society 1815–1832
Eric J Evans   0 582 00265 6

Parliamentary Reform in Britain c. 1770–1918
Eric J Evans   0 582 29467 3

Democracy and Reform 1815–1885
D G Wright   0 582 31400 3

Poverty and Poor Law Reform in Nineteenth-Century Britain, 1834–1914:
From Chadwick to Booth
David Englander   0 582 31554 9

The Birth of Industrial Britain: Economic Change, 1750–1850
Kenneth Morgan   0 582 29833 4

Chartism (Third edition)
Edward Royle   0 582 29080 5

Peel and the Conservative Party 1830–1850
Paul Adelman   0 582 35557 5

Gladstone, Disraeli and later Victorian Politics (Third edition)
Paul Adelman   0 582 29322 7

Britain and Ireland: From Home Rule to Independence
Jeremy Smith   0 582 30193 9

TWENTIETH-CENTURY BRITAIN

The Rise of the Labour Party 1880–1945 (Third edition)
Paul Adelman   0 582 29210 7

The Conservative Party and British Politics 1902–1951
Stuart Ball   0 582 08002 9

The Decline of the Liberal Party 1910–1931 (Second edition)
Paul Adelman   0 582 27733 7

The British Women's Suffrage Campaign 1866–1928
Harold L Smith   0 582 29811 3

War & Society in Britain 1899–1948
Rex Pope   0 582 03531 7

The British Economy since 1914: A Study in Decline?
Rex Pope   0 582 30194 7

Unemployment in Britain between the Wars
Stephen Constantine   0 582 35232 0

The Attlee Governments 1945–1951
Kevin Jefferys   0 582 06105 9

The Conservative Governments 1951–1964
Andrew Boxer   0 582 20913 7

Britain under Thatcher
Anthony Seldon and Daniel Collings   0 582 31714 2

Britain and Empire, 1880–1945
Dane Kennedy   0 582 41493 8

INTERNATIONAL HISTORY

The Eastern Question 1774–1923 (Second edition)
A L Macfie   0 582 29195 X

India 1885–1947: The Unmaking of an Empire
Ian Copland   0 582 38173 8

The Origins of the First World War (Second edition)
Gordon Martel   0 582 28697 2

The United States and the First World War
Jennifer D Keene   0 582 35620 2

Anti-Semitism before the Holocaust
Albert S Lindemann   0 582 36964 9

The Origins of the Cold War, 1941–1949 (Second edition)
Martin McCauley   0 582 27659 4

Russia, America and the Cold War, 1949–1991
Martin McCauley   0 582 27936 4

The Arab–Israeli Conflict
Kirsten E Schulze   0 582 31646 4

The United Nations since 1945: Peacekeeping and the Cold War
Norrie MacQueen   0 582 35673 3

Decolonisation: The British Experience since 1945
Nicholas J White   0 582 29087 2

The Origins of the Vietnam War
Fredrik Logevall   0 582 31918 8

The Vietnam War
Mitchell Hall   0 582 32859 4

WORLD HISTORY

China in Transformation 1900–1949
Colin Mackerras   0 582 31209 4

Japan Faces the World, 1925–1952
Mary L Hanneman   0 582 36898 7

Japan in Transformation, 1952–2000
Jeff Kingston   0 582 41875 5

China since 1949
Linda Benson   0 582 35722 5

US HISTORY

American Abolitionists
Stanley Harrold   0 582 35738 1

The American Civil War, 1861–1865
Reid Mitchell   0 582 31973 0

America in the Progressive Era, 1890–1914
Lewis L Gould   0 582 35671 7

The United States and the First World War
Jennifer D Keene   0 582 35620 2

The Truman Years, 1945–1953
Mark S Byrnes   0 582 32904 3

The Korean War
Steven Hugh Lee   0 582 31988 9

The Origins of the Vietnam War
Fredrik Logevall   0 582 31918 8

The Vietnam War
Mitchell Hall   0 582 32859 4

Lightning Source UK Ltd.
Milton Keynes UK
UKOW06f1347080515

251154UK00001B/45/P